Unders
The Unity

by Zbigniew Czajkowski

With an Introduction by Richard Cohen
Author of By the Sword

Also available from SKA SwordPlay Books
http://www.swordplaybooks.com

Sergei Golubitsky
Fencing Is My Life

Aladar Kogler
One Touch at a Time (Second, Enlarged Edition)

István Lukovich,
Fencing: the modern international style
Electric Foil Fencing: advanced competitive training

Laszló Szabó
Fencing and the Master

Imre Vass
Epee Fencing: A complete system

Coming Spring 2006
Harry James
Strength Training for Fencers

ISBN 0-9659468-8-6
Published by SKA Swordplay Books
3939 Victory Boulevard
Staten Island, NY 10314

« Et c'est en quoi l'on voit de quelle considération nous autres nous devons être dans un État, et combien la science des armes l'emporte hautement sur toutes les autres sciences inutiles, comme la danse, la musique ...»

—Molière, *Le Bourgeois Gentilhomme*

"In this way it is evident with what consideration we should be regarded in the State, and how far the science of fencing excels all other useless sciences, such as dancing, music. . ."

--Molière, *The Citizen Turn'd Gentleman*

Analytical Table of Contents

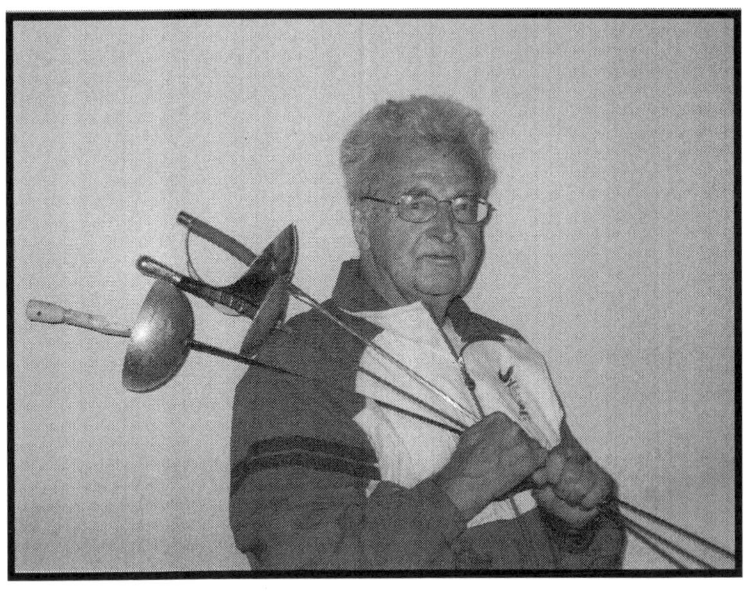

Fencing Master Zbigniew Czajkowski

Introduction

by Richard Cohen, Author of *By the Sword*

He sat there smoking a pipe. This wasn't quite what, in the summer of 1970, I expected to see a top coach from Eastern Europe doing, particularly as it was in a sports hall awaiting the arrival (tardy, as usual) of the British Olympic squad, whom he had agreed to help train during his four-week visit to Britain.

If I thought that the pipe-smoking suggested a calm, reflective nature, I was right; if an easy-going, undemanding amateur, I was entirely wrong. Zbigniew Czajkowski put us through our paces in a thorough and exhausting series of exercises, but what was worse was that he refused to allow us to get by on sweat and toil. We would be asked to think about what we were doing. We might practice, but never by rote. And woe betide the fencer who tried to impose his game on an opponent, content to win by force alone.

Later that year, I became editor of the British magazine of fencing, The Sword, and asked Professor Czajkowski to write about the state of the sport in my country. His opening paragraph was typical:

"I remember the time when a Hungarian fencing master was invited to our country to help with the development of our fencing. Sadly, some of us soon realized that he had come, not to help and teach, but to boast, to say how wonderful Hungarian fencing was, and to organize a clever publicity campaign to prove how wonderful he himself was. I should simply hate to give a similar impression. Still, you ask me for my views..."

Of course, he then went on, with cunning and considerable humor, to dissect the sad state of our sport, and make the most telling suggestions for improvement. He handed me the article, saying, "Please put what I have said in such a tactful way that what might be taken as criticism will be read as the highest compliment." The result of his piece was like the great Japanese court executioner, one of whose victims knew he was about to be beheaded, but had yet to feel a thing. "But you've not picked up your sword at all!" he said in wonder, yet almost complainingly. "Honorable Sir," the official replied, "Kindly nod head."

Professor Czajkowski was an excellent fencer in his day, not only the winner of numerous titles in his home country, at both foil and saber, but a member of the team that took the bronze medal at the 1953 world championships -- the first medal for Poland after the Second World War. It was that same year that he traveled with the rest of the squad to Moscow, summoned by their Soviet masters to parade their skills in full view of the Russian coaches, so they might produce championship teams themselves. At the end of the visit, a Polish – Russian match was held, at which the Russians, Czajkowski told me, cheated "like mad."

After a while, the cheating had become so blatant that the young Czajkowski took off his mask and looked at the Russian judges, grinning widely. One of the officials asked him what he was doing. He explained that it was his reaction to the constant dishonesty. The Russian glowered and simply said, "Smiling is not allowed."

This is a typical Czajkowski moment, the story funny but also making a point. He is not only extraordinarily gifted as a teacher and athlete, but he also has the precious gift of perspective -- more often than not, used to humorous effect. He is formidably clever, as his list of books and articles attest. He cares passionately about the sport, and art, of fencing. And, less obviously, he is a fighter – as shown by his exceptional bravery in World War II, and even by his teaching: he was the coach who introduced me to the idea of "competitive rage" -- the need to feel deeply, but to channel it towards victory.

He loves history, and literature, and travel -- rare enthusiasms in a professional sports coach --- but above all he strives for the highest standards in himself, and in his pupils. Even as early as 1963 the Polish Press dubbed him their "creator of successes," while Soviet fencers called him "the Father of the Polish School." That same sense of perspective means that still, in his ninth decade, Professor Czajkowski teaches fencing, and at the highest level. This book is the crystallization, and summation, of his remarkable career.

Only the pipe is missing.

—New York, 2004

About the Author

I. ZBIGNIEW CZAJKOWSKI—HIS COLORFUL, ADVENTUROUS AND SUCCESSFUL LIFE

by Maciej Łuczak

> *"Zbigniew Czajkowski is not only an excellent coach, pedagogue and man of learning, but above all, a most outstanding personality. He unites the links of generations of fencers, from the Olympic champion, Egon Franke, to European champion, Magdalena Jeziorowska. Also most interesting is his life story."*
>
> --Leszek Sobieraj

Zbigniew Czajkowski started fencing at the Cadet High School in Lvov under the tutelage of the very eminent fencing master, Jan Pieczyński. He finished school just before the outbreak of the war in 1939, with many awards.

In September, 1939, still a young boy, he fought against the Soviet army and Belorussian communist partisans in Polesie, in the eastern part of Poland. At the end of September, while trying to join the remains of the Polish detachments, Czajkowski was caught with four other young boys by communist partisans. They had wanted to hang him and had even prepared a rope.

He was saved by two Soviet officers who ordered him to go to Kobryn, where he was interrogated by a Soviet military commissar. After a short interview, the commissar told Czajkowski to go home. With great trouble, he managed to reach the city of Lvov, where his mother was (his father was in a prisoner of war camp in Starobielsk).

While waiting to cross the Romanian border in order to join the Polish forces in France, Czajkowski practiced fencing in Lvov (which was, at that time, under Soviet occupation).

In April, 1940, about 50 meters from the border river, he and his few colleagues were caught by Soviet guards. Czajkowski spent more than a year in Soviet prisons undergoing very unpleasant interrogations. Then, just before Germany invaded the Soviet Union, he was sent without trial to the infamous labor camp in Vorkuta, beyond the polar circle, where he had to work under very extreme conditions. In September, 1941, Czajkowski left the labor camp and, for many weeks on foot, on donkey, on camel, and on barge he managed to reach Uzbekistan in central Asia. There he worked for a few months on cotton and rice plantations.

On the fifth of February, 1942, his birthday, Czajkowski managed to reach the newly formed Polish forces in the USSR office. He begged the authorities to enlist him in the Polish Navy. Then, through Persia, India, and South Africa, he arrived in Great Britain and went to the Polish naval station in Plymouth. Here he embarked on the Polish destroyer, "Ślązak" (L26), and took part in convoys and battles, including the famous Dieppe raid, the invasion of Sicily, the battle of Salerno, the invasion of Italy, and many others. In 1942, his ship had the record of all the Allied Navies for the greatest number of German planes shot down, rescued sailors and airmen, and German prisoners of war taken aboard.

After the Normandy landing, where Czajkowski served on another Polish destroyer, "Błyskawica," he received leave from the Navy and began his medical studies at Edinburgh University. Here he resumed fencing and was very successful in many competitions. In Edinburgh, he fenced for the Edinburgh University fencing club and the Scottish Fencing Club, and he also founded the fencing section of the Polish Students Association in Great Britain, where he was an amateur coach.

In 1949, Czajkowski returned to Poland, finished his medical studies at the famous Jagiellonian University in Krakow and, of course, continued his fencing career. He won many medals at Polish championships, both in foil and sabre, and a bronze medal in the team sabre event at the 1953 World Championship in Brussels. The same year, while continuing to take part in competitions, he began his professional career, not in medicine, but in fencing, as a coach.

For many years, Czajkowski worked both in the club, GKS Piast Gliwice, and as the head and Olympic team coach for the Polish Fencing Union. He was, for many years, coach of the Polish National

Team and the University Games team. He introduced many new organizational and methodological changes in fencing training.

He has trained many outstanding fencers in all weapons—dozens of them. Just to give a few examples just from his own club: Egon Franke, Olympic champion in foil, Tokyo, 1964; Elżbieta Cymerman, nine times Polish champion in lady's foil, runner up at the University Games, Socialist countries champion; Jacek Bierkowski, silver medalist in sabre at the World Championships, Budapest, 1975; Bogdan Gonsior, World Champion in epee, 1963; Magdalena Jeziorowska, European champion in women's epee, 1996. As coach of the Polish National Team, he trained famous fencers outside his club, such as: R. Parulski, E. Ochyra, Z. Skrudlik, J. Różycki, and many others, including top women epeeists. As a matter of fact, he was a great champion for the introduction of women's epee. At the Academy of Physical Education in Katowice, he introduced training in women's epee and organized many competitions, including the Rector's Cup (a World Cup in women's epee).

Since 1980, he has been the director of the Fencing Department at the Academy of Physical Education in Katowice and, from 1980 to 2001, was head coach of the Students Fencing Club at the Academy. In 2002, working still as director of the Fencing Department at the Academy in Katowice, and responsible for the education of coaches in Poland, he returned as a fencing master to his old club, GKS Piast Gliwice.

Czajkowski's pupils have won many medals in Polish championships and have had very good results at international competitions in all weapons. In the last few years, he has educated more than a hundred certified fencing masters (some of whom came from abroad) and more than a hundred of his pupils have received the degree of Bachelor of Physical Education.

Czajkowski's chief interests in research has been technique, tactics, and the development of fencing; modern methods of teaching; psychology of sport; a coach's work, abilities, personality, and leadership style; sensory motor skills and abilities; various kinds of motor reactions in fencing; traits of personality and temperament, and their influence on fencing style; individualization of a fencers' training; psychological and tactical types of fencers; the principal of specificity of a fencer's training; and—with a deep interest—the history of fencing.

He has conducted dozens of various courses, conferences, and seminars in Poland and other countries, such as Great Britain,

Ireland, the United States, Russia, Uzbekistan, Holland, Belgium, Austria, the Czech Republic, Bulgaria, Yugoslavia, the Ukraine, etc. For his professional and honorary activities in fencing, he has received several, very high, State awards, awards from the Polish Olympic Committee and Polish Fencing Union, and many tokens of respect from foreign fencing federations—he is one of the few honorary members of the British Academy of Fencing.

Czajkowski has written more than 25 books and several hundred articles on fencing. Some of his more prominent books include (these are the English translations of the Polish titles) *New Fencing,* 1951, 1954; *Fencing with the Foil,* 1954; *Theory and Methodology of Modern Fencing,* 1968; *Fencing with the Epee,* 1977; *Tactics in Fencing,* 1982; *Teaching Sensory Motor Skills and Reactions,* 1982; *Motivation in Sport Activities,* 1982; *Tactics and Psychology in Fencing,* 1984; *Fencing—Foil,* 1987; *A Fencer's Training,* 1988; *Motivation in Sport Activities,* 1988; *Motivation in Sport,* 1989; *Teaching and Learning Technique,* 1991; *A Coach's Guide,* 1994; *Motor Skills in Sport Activities,* 1995; *The First Stage of Training,* 1995; *Psychology: the Coach's Ally,* 1997; *Theory, Practice and Methodology of Fencing* (written in English and Polish), 2001, *Teaching and Learning Technique,* Second, Enlarged Edition, 2004, and, of course, the current volume.

In spite of his advanced age, he remains very active and lively, continuing to give lectures, run practices, give lessons, and write books and articles. One of his favourite maxims is that of the famous 16th Century French surgeon, Ambroise Paré: "No effort is too big for a man who loves his art." Of course, Zbigniew Czajkowski also lives by his own saying: "The only people who get old are those who have the time and desire to do so."

II. ZBIGNIEW CZAJKOWSKI AND US FENCING

By Jason Sheridan

Zbigniew Czajkowski, firmly installed in fencing in Poland, keeps lively contact—competitions, training camps, exchanges of books and ideas, friendly relationships—with fencers all over the world.

He also has strong connections with the US. He knows, and is friendly with, many prominent figures of US fencing, including: Jack Keene, Richard Gradkowski, Dick Oles (Ryszard Olesinski), the famous Vinnie Bradford, Michael Marx, Jason Sheridan, Richard Cohen, and many others. He collaborated, for a long time, with Stanley Sieja, of Princeton University. Of course, Czajkowski knows the Polish coaches who work in the US—most of whom are his former students and pupils—Janusz Smoleński, Edward Korfanty, Janusz Bednarski, Wiesław "Wes" Głon, Dariusz Gilman, Anna Stokłosa, Adam Skarbonkiewicz, Leszek Stawicki, Robert Suchorski, Witold Rutkowski, and many others.

Czajkowski fenced against the US sabre team in Krakow in 1961. He became very friendly with US fencers and showed them the beauty of old Krakow and the very sad museum at the Auschwitz concentration camp.

Zbigniew Czajkowski has often been to the US for various competitions like the Martini Rossi tournament in New York and the Youth World Championship in South Bend.

Also, he has conducted many educational courses, workshops, and training camps: US Olympic Center, Colorado Springs (1990-1991); Princeton University; Salle Palasz, Johns Hopkins University; DC Fencers Club (1995-1996); Oregon Fencing Alliance; Rochester Fencing Center (1999); California Fencing Academy (2003); etc. Several US fencing coaches took part—and greatly enjoyed—the International Advanced Course for Fencing Coaches, conducted by Czajkowski at the Academy of Physical Education in Katowice in 2001.

He is an eager reader of, and contributor to, the USFCA magazine, *The Swordmaster,* and appraises it highly—which is very meaningful, considering that he reads and publishes his articles in many Polish and foreign fencing magazines.

III. ZBIGNIEW CZAJKOWSKI: AN APPRECIATION

by Michael D'Asaro

After his first month-long training course in Colorado Springs in 1990, this is what the late Master Mike D'Asaro wrote about Zbigniew Czajkowski:

Professor Czajkowski of Poland is a most flamboyant, colorful and scholarly master. He speaks a dozen languages, is a medical doctor and has advanced degrees in psychology, physiology and physical education. I am sure I have left out a bunch of other degrees he holds. He is the head of the Fencing Department of the Academy of Physical Education in Katowice, Poland. Professor Czajkowski has written many books and articles for the physical education professional and the scientific community. He was former Polish Olympic Team coach and has developed champions in all weapons [which doesn't happen often nowadays], most notably, Egon Franke, Tokyo Olympic foil champion. He is presently coach of his nation's women's epee team.

I first met Professor Czajkowski in 1961 in Warsaw at the sabre Match of Nations, where he was coaching the great Polish sabre team. He taught me many lessons and instilled in me many concepts, strategies, psychological considerations and training principles which served me for many years right up to the present. He is a walking encyclopedia of fencing knowledge. He knows the history of fencing in each country, knows every fencing school, development and theory that is known in fencing. He is quick to apply all of the current scientific knowledge of physiology, psychology and physical education in fencing. He also has a photographic memory. He is a fountain of information. His theory class at the college covered every possible aspect of fencing. His practical foil lessons were outstanding. Every single foil movement had a meaning and a fencing coach had to know exactly what he was doing and why he was doing it. The individual lessons were practical, fluid and with a particular purpose; they had continuity and the student knew what he was doing at all times. Professor Czajkowski was quick to demonstrate all of the fencing movements using the lunge and fleche during his lessons. Did I mention that he is in his seventies? He is in better condition than many at half his age.

Professor Czajkowski did not mince words with us. Where other coaches refer to our (American) fencing as "classical," he called it "antiquated." He said that we were still fencing with nineteenth-century styles and concepts. He thought that our teaching in this country had little connection with what actually takes place on the fencing strip. His lessons stressed perception, speed of reaction, decision making, observation, control of distance, the right choice of action, changing from offense to defense, changing the action, misleading the opponent, acceleration and many other decisions that a fencer has to make during the course of battle.

I'll never forget the remark he made to me in 1961, "In three to four months you could teach a monkey to make a parry four.... the important thing is how do you apply it, when do you use it and how do you use it—this is a true genius of the fencer, not whether he can execute the stroke, but when!"

Another important concept that he left us with was of a fencing master nowadays; it is not only what the master can do in the plastron, but how well he/she can organize and supervise fencing group and paired drills. It is very important that fencers take responsibility for their own development and that they learn to work together for their own improvement. The coach is there to assist and motivate the students.

Above: Master Czajkowski in his "Fencing Museum," surrounded by his collections and his trophies.

Below: Master Czajkowski with his student Jason Sheridan, who played a crucial role in preparing this book for publication *(Publisher's note).*

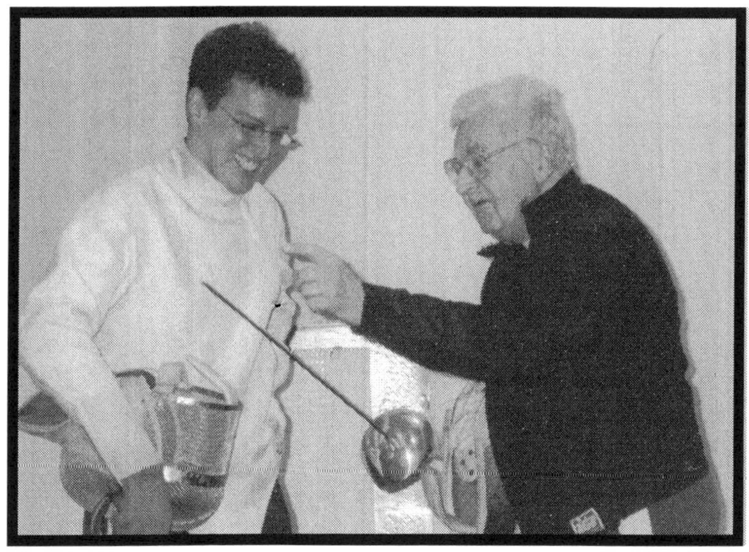

Author's Foreword

„Pańska szkoła jest dla ludzi inteligentnych."
("Your school is for intelligent people.")
--Janusz Smoleński

„Dobrym trenerem i wychowawcą może zostać tylko ten, kto zawodowi temu poświęci się bez reszty, kto posiada talent, umiejętność pracy nad sobą przez ciągłe wzbogacenie wiedzy i odrobinę natchnienia od Boga."

"Only he who sacrifices himself relentlessly to his coaching profession, who possesses talent and the ability to work on himself through constant enrichment of knowledge, and just a little bit of inspiration from God, may become a good coach and educator."
--Antoni Piechniczek

The well-known English master of arms, George Silver, in his famous *Paradoxes of Defence*, 1599, wrote that he possessed "ye ful p^{r}fection and knowledge of ye p^{r}fyt vse of all manner of weapons." He also stated that the exercising of weapons, among other things, expels "evil conceits." I have taken it to heart and am trying to be more modest, so I shall only state that I have been engaged in fencing activity—as a competitor, coach, organizer, official, researcher, and author—for nearly seventy years; I've managed to achieve some good results on the strip and have trained a large number of fencers, who have performed extremely well in Polish and international competitions, including high results in Olympic Games and World Championships. If some Readers doubt my modesty, I shall explain that I firmly believe that one cannot achieve anything very serious and important without a sense of humor.

Now I will be more serious. In my private "fencing museum and library," I have hundreds of fencing manuals—old and new—from many countries. I have studied them all with keen interest, and have learned a lot. What strikes me is the fact that the majority of even the most modern fencing textbooks are, in a way, very one-sided. They contain plenty of figures depicting the on-guard position, lunge, fleche, various parries, and detailed explanations of various positions and strokes. Of course these descriptions and drawings are very necessary and useful, but what surprises me is that very few authors discuss and describe in detail how to teach and apply these actions, what methods are used, or what the most important qualities of a fencing master are.

They often completely omit the most important principles of training and teaching motor skills. They do not devote enough attention to such important social and psychological aspects of sport activity, learning, training and competing, such as dimensions of personality; traits of temperament; the influence of motivation and arousal on our education and performance; various component parts of achievement motivation; various types of fencers, from the point of view of tactics and psychology; programming and planning training; stages of training; phases of teaching-learning motor skills.

Very often there is a lack of clear definitions and descriptions of a fencer's functional-motor fitness, comprised of energy fitness and coordination abilities. And—what is very, very surprising, taking into consideration its importance in fencing—most authors do not even mention the various kinds of sensory-motor responses—and yet it is obvious that all of a fencer's technical-tactical capabilities are based on various types of reaction. It is also obvious to me that one can actively and successfully work in a given branch of human activity—in our case, fencing—only if one knows a lot about it: you cannot be a good surgeon if you do not know, perfectly well, anatomy, physiology, pathology, etc.

So I try, in this book, to present fencing, to make it understood in its whole, many-sidedness, and complexity. As a British coach, Pat Pearson, aptly remarked, "Professor Czajkowski showed us that fencing is not so easy to comprehend as some people might superficially think." It is very true. Fencing is very complicated and is based on sensory-motor skills of a cognitive-motor type—meaning, that the motor activity of a fencer (his movements and actions) are strictly connected with perception, reaction, thinking, decision-taking, and, of course, with arousal, motivation, and emotions. I try very hard to present and explain this, in the present volume.

I would like to stress, once more, that I strongly believe in, and appreciate, the unity and interrelationship of theory and practice, of cognition and activity. I try to underline the great importance of theoretical knowledge. Without theoretical knowledge, one will commit many errors. For example: not knowing Yerkes-Dodson Laws, a coach will—by shouting words of wild encouragement, "orders," and tactical advice during a bout—lead to a competitor's too-high arousal and excitation, causing bad performance and defeat. (In very suspenseful situations of a bout, when, often, a victory or medal depends on one hit, and the fencer is highly motivated, nervous, and very excited, the coach should try to calm him down, and not excite him more). Or, not knowing the principles of teaching-learning motor skills, the coach will try to teach three new strokes in one lesson. Or, not knowing the principle of specificity of training, the coach will try to enhance a fencer's specific *(fencing)* endurance by… long-distance running—which is completely absurd.

Fully appreciating the immense value and importance of theoretical knowledge—and the necessity of a coach to constantly read, learn, and discuss various aspects of fencing, methodology of training, sports psychology, etc.—one should not forget that a coach's practical experience, pedagogical intuition, and common sense should also be valued and taken advantage of. As the 16th-century Parisian surgeon, Ambroise Paré, put it, "Mere knowledge without experience does not give the surgeon self-confidence."

The Reader will notice that there is quite a lot of repetition—the same themes are tackled in different chapters. I have done this on purpose—*"repetitio est mater studiorum"* (repetition is the mother of learning)—for I firmly believe that repeating certain statements, expressing certain opinions, giving various examples, and presenting a view, once more, in a different context, tremendously helps the Reader to deeply understand, broadly comprehend, and better remember different theories, practices, exercises, actions, attitudes, principles, methods, etc., and to notice various connections and interrelationships between them.

In this book, I try to abolish many myths and to demonstrate the many negative sides of "functional fixations"—although, like Einstein and Paderewski, I know how difficult it is (see Chapter

12: *Energy Abilities, Sensory-Motor Skills, and Competition Results in Different Stages of Training*).

I have studied, and greatly enjoy, the history of fencing, and try to preserve everything from the old schools that was good, sound, and may still be used and developed. But, I also reject the methods and actions which were good in the 19th Century, but are now obsolete.

I attach great importance to logical, coherent, clear, and up-to-date terminology. It never ceases to astonish me how many coaches in many countries try, clumsily, to present new ideas, new actions, and new tactical solutions, using terminology which was up-to-date 100 years ago. When I conducted a coaching course in Austria, I was astonished how the Austrian coaches were blindly attached to the theories, practices, terminology, and classification of fencing actions of Luigi Barbasetti. He was, of course, a very eminent master—his two books are most excellent and interesting—he advanced fencing very much and was a champion of the new Italian school in both sabre and foil, but since his days, fencing has developed and changed tremendously—rules and ways of presiding have changed, electrical scoring machines have been introduced, the rules and ways of conducting competitions have changed, and many new ideas, methods, actions and tactical capabilities have been introduced. For example, you cannot teach and explain such actions and capabilities as attack with unknown final or attack with change of intention during its execution, using 19th-century terminology, simply because such actions, at that time, were unknown or not taught.

Clarity of terminology and classification of fencing actions is particularly important in the United States where, for a very long time, there have been many coaches from many different countries and schools, who have created a certain chaos of various ideas, schools, and terminology.

I sincerely hope that, after reading the chapter *Fencing Actions – Terminology, Their Classification and Application in Competition*, the Reader will agree that the separation of the basic classification of fencing actions and the classification based on tactics, was very necessary for many reasons—if only in order to notice that one basic stroke may be applied with completely different tactical objectives (direct thrust may be used as an attack, riposte, counter-riposte, stop-hit, remise, etc.; or, for example, counter-time may be applied as a foreseen, second intention action; an unforeseen, change of intention action; or one possible final of an attack with unknown destination).

If any Reader expresses his surprise that, in this volume, there are no figures of the on-guard position, lunge, fleche, parries, various thrusts and cuts, nor of the parts of weapons and the dimensions of fencing strips, my answer is that they may be easily found in hundreds of other fencing books (including many of my own).

I should like to stress, with great emphasis, the importance of a coach's motivation and love of fencing (and this book is mainly for coaches). As the above-mentioned Ambroise Paré wrote, "He who becomes a surgeon for the sake of money will accomplish nothing." The same, of course, goes for a fencing master.

My pupils often call me the "angel of patience" (frankly, I called myself this much more often), but in preparing this book—typing, proof-reading, printing, sending innumerable e-mails—the real "angel of patience" turned out to be my student and pupil, and "honorary computer secretary," "Michael"—Fencing Master Jason Sheridan—who obtained his degree under me at the Academy of Physical Education in Katowice.

Finally, I would like to inform the Readers that I am now writing a new book, under the title *Fencing—Past and Present*, the first part of which will be devoted to the history of fencing, and the second part to a more comprehensive and detailed description of training, technique, tactics, psychomotor abilities, and a coach's work. I hope that it will soon be published in the United States.

Before finishing my foreword, I would like to add that—apart from fencing and other objects of interest—I am a great lover of Molière. I know well his life story, his plays, his views. I like very much his statement: *Je prend mon bien ou je le trouve* (I take my value where I find it). As a great author, he really took advantage of the simple Italian "commedia dell'arte;" he watched street life and observed people of various positions, poor and rich, he watched the behavior of important people and life in the court. I like very much his comedy "Citizen turn'd Gentleman," in which he presents a very colorful figure of a fencing master and describes in most interesting manner a fencing lesson of that period.

I am also trying to take my good where I can find it, and besides I strongly believe that we learn most while teaching others. So, with great pleasure and enthusiasm, I conduct many fencing courses, not only in Poland but in many other countries. Few months ago I conducted a fencing coaches' course in Montreal, Canada, in which fencing coaches from many countries of the Americas participated. One of the participants gave me a fencing manual published in—Honduras! Much to my surprise I found it most interesting, containing many valuable ideas, advice, rules and statements. One seems to me very actual and full of wisdom: *"Siempre que el individuo expresa una idea, solution o forma de condusta novedoza se expone a severas criticas por parte de los otros"* (Always, when somebody expresses a new idea, solution, or procedure, he exposes himself to sharp criticism from the others). My book contains many new ideas which sometimes differ greatly from generally accepted ones. I still hope, being a great optimist, I shall not be criticized. Anyway, as Walter Lippmann wittily and cleverly remarked: "When all think alike, no one thinks very much."

--Bytom, Poland, 2002

1. Characteristics of Fencing As a Sport

"The exercising of weapons putteth away many aches, griefs and diseases; it expelleth melancholic, cholericke and evil conceits; it keepeth a man in breath, perfect health and long lyfe."
--George Silver, 1599

"Fencing is as much a mind game as a physical test. Even though you face one another through the mesh in the mask, your confrontation with opponents is eyeball to eyeball, with all the mental pressure this entails."
--Terrence Kingston, 2001

The famous words of the Fencing Master in Moliere's *Citizen Turn'd Gentleman (Le Bourgeois Gentilhomme,* 1670) define the essence of fencing as giving hits without receiving them. Thus, fencing may be briefly defined as the art of wielding weapons with the intention of touching the opponent by cut or thrust, while avoiding being hit oneself.

In a real fight—fencing with sharp weapons in war, combat, or duel—the aim of the fight was to kill or wound the opponent in as short a time as possible.

Until very recently, the art of wielding cutting and thrusting weapons had still its place in army training: cavalry sabre, lance, and bayonet.

Since the beginning of the 20th Century, when we talk of fencing, we mean, nearly always, fencing as a sport. Contemporary fencing, in its athletic form, consists of a fight and preparation for competition between two opponents—equally armed with conventional weapons—according to established forms and rules. The aim of this sport combat is to score, on one's opponent, the maximum number of conventional hits, in a given time, while attempting to avoid being hit oneself or at least to receive as few hits as possible.

1. Characteristics of Fencing as a Sport

Apart from the modern sport of fencing, one can distinguish stage fencing and various national systems of fencing.

Stage fencing is the art of wielding various types of historical weapons, according to the style and tradition of the period depicted in the play, and also in accordance with the specific demands of the theatre. In stage fencing, various factors are concerned such as: knowledge of a variety of weapons; knowledge of the history of fencing; salutes, movements and manners of different periods; as well as the dexterity and general fitness of the actor. Apart from this, fencing is a well-tried and well-known method of achieving the physical fitness and grace of movement of an actor—used in schools of drama, ballet and film.

In several countries, old national forms of fencing are still known and cultivated, such as kendo in Japan and Parikaoba in Georgia.

The sport of fencing

- Shapes many valuable motor skills (motor habit patterns) and various kinds of motor responses (see Chapter 5).
- Develops various energy and coordination abilities.
- Strengthens and exercises muscles, ligaments and joints.
- Has a beneficial effect on the nervous and respiratory systems and on blood circulation.
- Improves the general health and functional and adaptive capacity of the organism.
- Improves perception, concentration, imagination, quick analytical thinking, orientation in space and time, and speed of reaction.

The practice of fencing does not require large sports grounds or expensive installations and is independent of the season of the year.

Fencing develops

- Lightning-speed orientation.
- The ability to concentrate during a bout.
- A certain craftiness in misleading the opponent.
- The ability to observe and reconnoitre the technique, reflexes and intentions of the opponent.

Furthermore, it improves such traits as

- Ambition
- Self-control
- Self-confidence and positive motivation (the right contents, direction and level of general motivation
- Motivation for success and task involvement in achievement motivation)

A fencing bout is a clash of two systems of tactics. Success in the "tactical battle" depends on: early and good reconnaissance of the opponent (his strong and weak points, style of fencing, favorite actions, and speed); forcing one's own intentions on the opponent; application of judicious tactics, often varying from bout to bout (see Chapter 3).

The sport of fencing develops unusual coordination of movements of the whole body (gross coordination) and hand and fingers (fine coordination), resulting, among other things, from the necessity of immediate action in an extremely short time—a fencer usually acts with a strong "deficit of time"—and depending on the development of the situation on the piste. Fencing also requires and develops the ability to keep one's balance while executing fast, varied, precise, and sometimes very complicated movements—it even sometimes demands strict coordination, and sometimes complete independence, of movement of the arms and legs. By cultivating fencing, one exercises all muscles, but, above all, the extensors.

1. Characteristics of Fencing as a Sport

Fencing bouts and exercises develop suppleness, flexibility, dexterity, nimbleness, and agility.

Fencing is, par excellence, a fast sport, in every sense of the word:

- Speed of perception
- Speed of reaction
- Speed of movement
- Fast change of action
- Fast change of rhythm, etc.

The speed of a fencer is much more complicated than the speed of a runner or a swimmer. Speed, especially speed in fencing, is a combination of energy ("physical") fitness abilities and coordination abilities. (Energy abilities are connected with the effort capacity of all organs, systems, and the organism as a whole, whereas coordination abilities are connected, above all, with the functional cooperation of the receptors, nervous system, and motor system [muscles].)

Fencing develops many coordination capabilities, which may be divided into three groups:

1. Motor *educability* (the ability to learn new strokes and to change "old" motor habit patterns).
2. Motor *control* (the ability to precisely direct one's movement).
3. Motor *adaptability* (the ability to execute and apply various fencing actions in a changeable manner, in very varied and often unpredicted situations).

In this respect, fencing (like other combat sports and games) differs considerably—both in its contents, methods of training, and performance—from sports with *closed* motor skills (like gymnastics, acrobatics, etc.).

As a special kind of motor adaptability, I distinguish lightning-like *speed of improvisation*, the essence of which is to apply, during a bout, a movement or set of movements—based on elementary skills—which have never been executed in such a form during practice.

In directing the weapon with the fingers, one acquires "sentiment de fer" and increases the sensitivity of tactile sense; apart from which fencing increases, to a high degree, kinesthetic sensitivity.

Major fencing competitions frequently last several days, during which a competitor may have many hours of bouting with interludes every day, particularly if he is taking part in more than one weapon (which recently happens rather rarely) and in both individual and team events—which is a most exacting and difficult test of stamina, psychological endurance, and specific fitness.

Let me say a word about endurance here. Many coaches identify the term endurance exclusively with the kind of endurance required in long-distance running. This is, of course, utterly wrong, because long distance running is connected with long, monotonous effort, rhythmic movements, lack of an opponent or a change of situation, aerobic processes, and slow-twitch muscle fibres. In fencing, on the other hand, the effort is very short and fast, entailing anaerobic processes, fast-twitch muscle fibres, facing an opponent, and constant change of situation, and the effort is not continuous (including the interludes between bouts and within the bouts, themselves).

Contrary to the opinions of many authors, I consider endurance to be a highly specific ability, so that there are *different kinds of endurance*: that of a watch-maker, a surgeon, a marathon runner, a figure skater, orchestra conductor, car driver, sprinter, soccer player, typist, film director, singer, pianist, a blacksmith, a ballet dancer, a fencer, etc. I define endurance as resistance to fatigue in a given specific variety of activity. Long-distance running, of course, does not develop fencing endurance. Fencing-specific endurance, in my opinion, means resistance to *perceptual fatigue* (closely watching the opponent; speed and accuracy of perception; a high level, and many other qualities, of attention; fast and appropriate reaction); *cognitive, or mental, fatigue* (trying to assess the opponent's tactics; fast analysis of the opponent's and one's own movements; choosing the right tactics; drawing immediate conclusions during and after the bout); *emotional fatigue* (state of anxiety; stressful situations; desire to win; trying to avoid failure; joy; despair; hope; lack of confidence; etc.); in addition to—for a trained fencer, *the least important*—"physical" fatigue.

Because of the great significance of precise, versatile and varied technique; experience; psychological factors (self-control, concentration, positive intrinsic motivation, motive of success, the appropriate level of arousal); and tactics; fencing is a sport which may be cultivated from early youth up to a ripe old age. Older competitors compensate for a certain loss of speed and endurance by better technique, experience, more mature tactical solutions and also by highly-developed fencing-specific motor responses (different varieties of reaction; see Chapter 5).

The development and perfection of a whole complex of physical and psychological traits and abilities—as well as the constant improvement of technical, technical-tactical, and tactical capabilities—are indispensable for a fencer.

In a modern, very mobile, fencing bout, specific energy fitness—strength and endurance, as well as specific speed—and specific coordination abilities are very necessary. Capability and skill in manipulating the weapon, and tactical capabilities, are extremely important and, in a certain sense, decisive.

But this is not enough—one also has to have very strong, well-exercised muscles of the arms and legs.

Strong and elastic legs are necessary for:

- Mastery of the fencing stance;
- Purposeful displacements on the fencing strip;
- Executing lunges, balestras, and fleches (very important here is the combination of strength and speed—power—especially in executing fast lunges and fleches).

Muscular strength of the arms and fingers (plus fine coordination) allows

- Long, continued and untiring holding and manipulation of the weapon,
- Brisk beats on the opponent's blade,

- Strong binds, and
- Parrying with the middle part of the blade—(since it is not always possible to parry with forte, especially in epee at a long distance.)

One cannot overestimate the significance of *speed* in fencing. Nowadays, one cannot imagine a great fencing champion who was not very fast. One must, however, bear in mind that *speed of assessment* of a situation, and speed of motor responses (to be more exact, the latent period of reaction)—combined with sense of timing (sense of surprise; see Chapter 4)—is far more important, although less visible, than speed of execution of movements (the executive, or effector, period of reaction).

To be able to achieve sudden changes of direction, varied rhythm of movement, and to attain a high turn of speed, a fencer must relax muscles and give suppleness and fluency to his movements while he is executing preparatory movements such as reconnoitering, maneuvering for the proper distance, trying to catch his opponent by surprise, etc. With fencers with rigid muscles who usually fence as if they were glued to the piste, intention of executing a blade movement is nearly always "signaled" by excessive amplitude and rigidity of movement which not only slows their own actions, but also acts as a warning signal for the opponent.

A beautiful, efficient and fast style of fencing depends on economic and relaxed movements, in which only the appropriate group of muscles contract with adequate intensity and rhythm, and with the proper cooperation (relaxation) of antagonistic muscles.

On the psychological side, motivation and—strictly connected with it—arousal are the most important basic attributes. One could say that proper training and success in competition are a consequence of *the right kind and level* of motivation, and the *intensity* of arousal. It requires the optimal contents, direction, and level of motivation, and the appropriate level of arousal to conscientiously and diligently repeat, again and again, exercises which are difficult and may be tedious. Only ambition and the appropriate level of a motive of success can enable a fencer to make the sustained and obstinate effort needed to improve his fencing capabilities, to overcome difficulties and obstacles, to keep up his desire to fight in spite of fatigue and the unfavorable conditions of a bout, and to reach the best possible results in tournaments.

As far as achievement motivation (a set of motives occurring in situations of fight, rivalry, external assessment) is concerned, many coaches think that a very high, nearly maniacal, motive of success ("victory at any cost") and very hard, tedious, murderous effort is best. My opinion, based on many, many years of practical experience and careful observation, is that the best and most effective—both for results in competitions and development of the pupil's personality—are the following component parts of achievement motivation:

- An optimum, appropriate level of *motivation* for success—desire to win, desire to compete, belief in one's success, but not "winning is the only thing;"
- *Task involvement*—the desire to improve one's knowledge, skills, abilities and capabilities;
- Feeling of independence, responsibility, and self-confidence;
- *Sport enjoyment*—getting pleasure out of training and competing, *love* of fencing (the emotional factor) and *interest* in fencing (the mental factor).

So far, in trying to characterize fencing as a sport, I have emphasized its general value and attraction, and the beneficial effects on the fencer himself. Let us consider now, more deeply perhaps, what makes fencing such a peculiarly attractive and valuable sport in comparison with other disciplines which, after all, are easier to cultivate, more "natural", easier to understand and appreciate, and which also give pleasure and are healthful and educational.

It seems to me that the specific charm of fencing and its high value in the whole family of various sports lies in the close combination of the following factors:

1. The sheer joy of a fast, mobile and versatile fight with a light weapon in the face of kaleidoscopic, unexpected changes of the tactical situation.

2. Exceptional and decisive significance of psychological traits and intellect in the fencing bout, including psychomotor abilities (psychological processes—like perception, reaction, decision making—strongly connected with motor activity).

3. The rich romantic and historical tradition of fencing which stirs the imaginations of both youths and adults.

4. The possibility of cultivating fencing from youth to well beyond middle age.

5. The exceptionally high social and educational value of fencing as an attractive form of preparation for life and work in the contemporary world; gross and fine motor abilities, a high level of perception, and various qualities of attention (a high level of concentration, range of attention, selectivity of attention, divisibility of attention, shifting of attention) are very practical and useful in modern life, professional work, artistic activity, while driving a car, using various apparatus, etc.—weight-lifting, running, and so on, develop mostly muscles and physical abilities and are not so useful in contemporary life and work.

The last point underlines the fact that physical culture—of which, sport is the most important form in the modern world—serves as preparation for life, productive activity, transport, communication, fighting, etc., and for fulfilling one's role in the society of a given epoch, nation, class and state.

Taking all this into consideration, fencing, *perhaps the oldest sport in the world*, is, paradoxically enough, the most modern of sports—that is, the most versatile and best adapted to the life and activity of the 21st Century.

There have been times in the history of mankind when sheer muscular strength and unusual physical endurance and toughness, played a colossal and dominant role in struggles against forces of nature, animals and other people, as well as in primitive productive activity.

Nowadays, however, with a high degree of development of productive forces; an outburst of development of technology at the service of human beings; with a colossal increase in forms and speed of transport and communication; with the steady increase of application of various machines, installations, apparatuses and precise steering mechanisms; with the extreme bustle and hurry of modern life; the following traits, abilities and attributes take on a decisive importance:

- Very fine coordination of movement without the use of brutal force;
- Delicate manipulation of fingers;
- High development of kinesthetic sense;
- The ability for long-sustained concentration of attention;
- The ability to divide and shift attention, spatial orientation and fast reaction in constant and rapid changes of situations;
- The ability to make instant decisions;
- The ability to make a rapid and purposeful change of decision while executing an action.

These skills and abilities are more and more necessary in modern industry, in research laboratories, while driving a car, flying, in military activity, etc., and these are the very traits which are shaped and developed while cultivating fencing.

The task of a good coach is to patiently perfect these qualities in his pupils so that they may transfer them from the narrow field of the fencing strip to their work, life and study. The considerable social and educational value of fencing and other sports is not a spontaneous quality, but has to be carefully fostered and influenced by the coach and affected by the attitude of fellow athletes.

It has to be realized that, without suitable pedagogical influence, certain attributes and attitudes shaped by sport, may exert a negative influence. For example: fencers, badly handled, may exhibit such unfortunate characteristics as aggressiveness, egocentrism, selfishness, quarrelsomeness, and lack of consideration for others. Hence it is necessary to interweave technical teaching and pedagogical influence during the process of training. Taking this into consideration, one must realize that the best styles of leadership in coaching—to enhance a rich development of a pupil's personality and allow him to play many social roles in life—are the cooperative and friendly styles (see Chapter 9).

While doing full justice to the social aspects of fencing and underlining its instrumental meaning, we must not forget its autonomous meaning—the fine glow of achievement, the feeling of physical fitness, longevity and strong muscles are not only important for productive work and its social consequences, but are *in themselves* of high value for the development and happiness of the individual.

The Polish writer Andrzej Tyszka, in his important essay on the humanistic values of sport, very rightly says, "A person, as an individual, has a right to health as such, and not only to health as an uninterrupted capacity for productive work—he has a right to joyful longevity in the fullness of strength as such, and not in order to avoid becoming an early pensioner, burdening the social budget. The value of a successful life is independent and can be found, among others, in sports—physical recreation and the enjoyment of watching and playing matches. Among the humanistic values of life, sport is not the only one, but not the last of independent values."

A good lesson and a fencing bout are pleasant experiences which allow one to shake off tiredness and impart a feeling of well-being, optimism and energy—probably because fencing absorbs so much thought, strength and concentration that it eliminates worries and every day troubles.

Some year ago, Dr Roger Tredgold, as expert a sabreur as a psychiatrist, pertinently summed up the good points of sabre fencing:

> "Life is full of frustrations today and many jobs lead to emotional tension which is better relieved in action than pent-up. No doubt many people express on the football or cricket field antagonism engendered against their

> superiors, or sometimes even against their wives. But the cricket-, tennis- or football is far less satisfying in this way than the body of one's opponent on the piste and, in my experience, far less easy to hit. And, of course, there can be no doubt that it is more blessed to give (if not to receive) a cut with a sabre than a touch with a foil. Which is why most sabreurs—even if tempestuous on the piste—are such very good-tempered equable people off it. . . ."

Carrying this argument a step further, one can realize that fencing, even more than other competitive sports, satisfies secret, imperfectly realised, subconscious desires such as: the need to dominate; the desire for recognition and approbation; the desire for achievement and success; avoidance of failure, frustration and disappointments; the feeling of belonging to a social group; the need for friendly empathy; the need for security, adventure and aggression.

Let us then briefly consider just what attracts youths and adults to fencing.

The motivation for cultivating fencing is unusually many-sided and variable. It varies according to the age, sex and the individual traits of an athlete, and undergoes changes together with the increase of skill and development of a fencer's career. Young people, particularly children, find their way to the salle mostly under the strong influence of emotional experiences connected with romance, heroism and fencing skill displayed by heroes of novels, films and theatre. Among teenagers and young adults, the desire for and joy of energetic motor activity, fighting, rivalry, and an outlet for gregarious instincts, come to the fore. Nearly all adult fencers when talking about the pleasure they get from the sport, underline enjoyments derived from the tactical aspect of a bout such as trying to foresee the opponent's move, trying to draw a given action from him, catching him by surprise, etc.

Some people are under the spell of the personality of great fencers, their successes and travels. They read with interest interviews with fencing stars, become enthusiastic about their successes, and ask for details and impressions connected with their stay in foreign countries (for example, the great Polish sabreurs Wojciech Zablocki and Jerzy Pawlowski published several memoirs describing, very colorfully, their adventures on the strip, their sightseeing, meetings with interesting people, etc.). The Olympic champion Gillian Sheen of Great Britain writes in her book that, thanks to her foil, she visited many foreign countries and towns and met many interesting people whom she would never have known had she not been an excellent foilist.

Another important motive for the cultivation of fencing is the possibility of raising oneself above average, developing one's personality, and emphasizing one's assets and value, as well as obtaining recognition and approbation. This motive was particularly important in socialist countries where there was considerable support from the government, political authorities, trade unions, press and society in general, and where both the authorities and the public were very interested in the results of an athlete's efforts.

But practically in every country, irrespective of system, regime or religion, a leading athlete will usually gain a high social position, become popular and be rewarded with honorary titles and state awards.

Recently, due to the constantly increasing prestige of the Olympic Games and World Championships, and the increasing significance of sport in modern society, this latter motive becomes more and more important. Considering the need for appreciation and recognition, inborn in everyone, this motive for trying to achieve good results in sport is particularly significant in people blessed (or perhaps cursed) with keen ambition.

Another indirect motive for cultivating fencing is the desire to keep trim, in good health, and physically fit. It is interesting to note that recently in the US, a lot of detailed and interesting research was conducted to choose new forms of exercises for fitness clubs and, "strangely enough," though it was not strange for me, it turned out that the most versatile, fitness-producing exercises were those derived from fencing, especially fencing footwork.

Generally speaking, however, the motives are more obvious and direct: pure pleasure in energetic movements, fame, fight, etc.

Some people are impressed by the grace and chivalry of fencing. A certain degree of snobbishness sometimes may play a part—a remnant of the times when swordsmanship was an attribute of the privileged classes. Still others are attracted by a fast, complicated game which, at the same time, is a confrontation of ideas, technique, tactics, quick reaction and motivation.

Dr Wiktoria Nawrocka, a well-known Polish sports psychologist, carried out, some years ago, extensive tests of leading Polish athletes from various disciplines of sport and found the following motivation for cultivating highly competitive sports:

1. Desire for success, proving one's value, fulfillment of ambitions to secure social recognition (51% of tested athletes);

2. Need for motor activity and the pleasant emotions connected with it (25%);

3. Need for rivalry and competition (18.7%);

4. Fascination with the specific character of a particular sport, and overcoming difficulties arising from cultivating this sport (16.4%);

5. Other motives, like reasons of health, aesthetic experiences, etc.

From her examinations and reflections it would appear that, as she puts it, "in cultivating competitive sport, the chief role is played by motivation of a sociological nature. It also is mainly responsible for the spontaneous and powerful development of sport in civilised society."

For children, the chief motivating factors for cultivating competitive sports are:

- Sheer pleasure of motor activity,
- Outbursts of energy,
- A high level of arousal, and
- A feeling of gaining competence.

A good coach should realize this and take advantage of it in the way he organizes and conducts exercises with children.

While dealing with children, the fencing master should also cleverly take advantage of children's fascination with swords and the charm of the historical past of fencing.

As the children grow—and when training adults—the important task of a good coach is to emphasize and develop the whole, rich scale of various socially positive motives for cultivating fencing while, at the same time, combating negative motivation.

With adults, he should point out the most valuable aspects of fencing as a sport:

1. Consideration of a fencing bout as a fast, versatile, game of skills, abilities, capabilities, conflict, motor responses, dexterity, dimensions of personality and traits of temperament, in which intellect, concentration and motivation play a decisive part;
2. The hygienic and educational value of fencing and its role in adaptation to life and work in modern society;
3. A pleasant and attractive way of developing one's personality.

A chapter characterizing fencing would be incomplete without the addition of an observation particularly pleasing to those of an aesthetic or dramatic turn of mind. Fencing—as performed by competitors of a high class, of rich and varied technique and constantly new and surprising tactical conceptions, fighting with complete concentration, ambition and motivation to win—takes on the attributes of an art; without losing its character of a sport, it can give the spectators an emotional experience as dramatic and breathtaking as any theatre or ballet. A fencing bout or the progress of a competition, with its intermingling of victory and defeat, creates tense and exciting situations, revealing to the spectator the feeling and emotions lived, at that moment, by the competitors—their triumphs and disappointments; ambition; courage, indecision or tactical cleverness. In a fencing bout, not only the physical, but the intellectual and emotional characteristics of the fencers are seen: their motivation, arousal, personality, and temperament. The graceful figure of a fencer performing, with lightness and verve, the most complicated manipulations of his weapon, is a sight full of aesthetic emotion.

Summing up, we may state that what George Silver wrote in his *Paradoxes of Defence*, more than five centuries ago (see the epigraph at the start of this chapter), is very true and up-to-date. A good modern coach will be even able to add, and put into practice, more assets of the sport of fencing.

2. Fencing Actions: Terminology, Classification, and Application

"Being able to give proper names to things is the first step toward wisdom."
--Confucius

"To look is not the same as to see, to see is not the same as to perceive. We perceive, really—on a higher, conceptual-functional level—only what we know, understand well and can give a name to."
--Zbigniew Czajkowski

INTRODUCTION

In order to understand fencing actions, and especially tactics and their application in a bout, as well as to conduct of fencing exercises rationally and effectively, it is necessary to fully understand the theory of training, to know and understand the classification of fencing actions and their application in the bout. This is especially important in countries where there are many foreign fencing coaches (for example, the United States) who use the terms of their own national schools—which vary in meaning from school to school and are also sometimes outdated and confusing. One cannot describe modern fencing—teaching, training and tactics—using only the 19th-century terminology of Luigi Barbasetti, great master as he was in his day: many contemporary concepts, practices, exercises and tactical skills were simply not known at that time. In this paper I am going to give my views on modern fencing and a modified classification of fencing actions—a basic classification of fencing actions and a classification based on tactical intentions. My ideas on the subject are based on nearly seventy years of the practice of fencing, my experience as both a competitor and coach, as a lecturer at the Fencing Department at the Academy of Physical Education in Katowice and innumerable courses, seminars and workshops for coaches conducted in Poland and many countries abroad.

Risking the accusation of having a lack of modesty, I shall quote David Tischler, the famous professor at the Moscow Institute of Physical Culture—and an excellent fencer and coach—"The terminology and classification of fencing actions introduced some years ago by Professor Zbigniew Czajkowski is very logical, comprehensive, takes into account the modern development of fencing and has great practical value."

In a bout, the fencer's thoughts and attention are concentrated on many elements, for example:

- Watching the opponent,
- General assessment of the opponent's style and strength,
- Reconnoitering his movements and intentions in various stages of the bout,
- Planning one's own actions,
- The concrete, detailed, practical tasks in order to score the next hit,
- Misleading the opponent about one's own intentions, etc.

These objects of the fencer's attention are only a few examples of the whole complexity of tactical tasks which occur in a bout in close interrelation with each other.

Observation of the opponent plays a vital role in tactics. It becomes more precise, comprehensive and penetrating when the fencer has learned to see, perceive and understand the opponent's movements, psychological state and intentions, very often gaining the information from barely discernible cues such as change of stance, certain delicate movements, preparatory actions and so on. It is particularly important to understand the opponent's intentions, guessing and foreseeing his tactics. To achieve this, it is indispensable to have a combination of tactical perception and the knowledge of fencing theory as well as the necessary level of self-control to see and think calmly in spite of emotional tension. Without a deep understanding of the tactical significance of various fencing actions, watching a fencing competition is very superficial, not very useful and may become even boring as the blade actions and movements of the two antagonists are rather incomprehensible.

A fencer who can foresee his opponent's intentions will not easily be taken by surprise and can better prepare his/her own plan of action. After the successful reconnaissance of the opponent, one may plan one's own actions, taking advantage of one's own strong-points and the opponent's weak points.

Before discussing the application of various fencing actions in a bout, it is necessary to introduce certain classifications of them. Here I am going to describe and discuss two systems of classifications of fencing actions:

I. The basic, fundamental, classification of fencing actions

II. Tactical classifications of fencing actions (from the point of view of tactics; the psychological base of choosing certain fencing strokes in a bout; fencer's intentions).

I. THE BASIC CLASSIFICATION OF FENCING ACTIONS

All fencing actions applied in a bout may be divided into two main categories:

A. Preparatory actions.

B. Actual actions (real or ultimate actions).

A. Preparatory Actions

Preparatory actions are the numerous and various fencing actions that are not intended to score a hit, directly or indirectly, but facilitate and prepare the successful application of actual (real) actions.

Preparatory actions serve the following purposes:

1. Assessment of the opponent and orientation in the psychological and factual situations in the bout.

2. Concealing one's own intentions.

3. Misleading the opponent and using tactical feints

4. Drawing certain actions from the opponent and trying to influence his movements.

5. Maneuvering, gaining the feel of play, gaining the initiative, preparing one's own attacks and other actions.

6. Hindering the opponent's concentration, assessment of distance, etc.

B. Actual Actions

Actual actions are ultimate, specific actions intended to ward off a hit or to score a hit, directly or indirectly (see below: discussion of first and second intention). From the point of view of the most elementary tactical application, the actual actions can be divided into: offensive actions, defensive actions and counter-offensive (offensive-defensive, counter-attacks).

Offensive actions comprise:

1. Attacks

2. Ripostes

3. Counter-ripostes

4. Counter-time

5. Renewed offensive actions (remise, reprise, redouble)

Counter-offensive actions comprise:

1. Point-in-line (arm straight and point threatening the opponent's target).

2. Counter-attacks, consisting of simple counterattacks (stop-hit, stop-hit with opposition, derobement, stop-hit with evasion) and compound counter-attacks: feint of stop-hit, deceive the parry; and feint of derobe, derobe (feint in time, *finta in tempo*).

Defensive actions comprise:

1. Parries

2. Evasions

3. Retreats (defense with distance)

(The basic classification of fencing actions is represented on Table 3 at the end of this chapter.)

If, at first, this classification system seems complicated, consider the terminology of the 16th Century rapier play which was even more complex and colourful as shown by the following quotation from Charles Kingsley's *Westward Ho*:

> Thy fincture, carricade, and sly passatos,
> Thy stramazone, and revolving stoccata,
> Wiping mandritta, closing embrocatta,
> And all the cant of the honorable fencing mystery...

The understanding of fencing actions and their application in fighting becomes simpler and better understood when one realizes that all fencing actions, even the most complicated ones, consist of four groups of component parts. They are:

1. On guard position and displacements (all variety of steps, lunge, fleche).

2. Basic hand positions. In the thrusting weapons, these are positions one through eight: four are in supination (sixth, fourth, eighth, seventh), and four in pronation (third, second, fifth, and first). In sabre, the main positions are one through five).

3. Change of weapon position (used as engagements, bindings, presses, beats and blade transfers and, of course, parries).

4. Fundamental, basic thrust and cuts.

We shall focus on the basic thrusts.

Table 2-A: Basic Arm/Hand Positions/Parries in Thrusting Weapons		
Area of Valid Target	*Hand in Supination*	*Hand in Pronation*
Outside High Line	Parry 6 (sixte)	Parry 3 (tierce)
Inside High Line	Parry 4 (quarte)	Parry 1 (prime)
Outside Low Line	Parry 8 (octave)	Parry 2 (seconde)
Inside Low Line	Parry 7 (septime)	Parry 5 (quinte)
Note: Additionally, one should mention the ninth position/ ninth parry (in the French School called high septime or *demi-cercle;* in the Italian school called *quinta* or *mezzo-cerchio*).		

The Basic Thrusts

The basic arm-hand positions in thrusting weapons (parries) are presented in Table 1. The basic thrusts can be executed as *direct thrusts* (without change of line) or as *indirect thrusts* (with change of line). Indirect thrusts may be accomplished by disengagement, counter-disengagement or cut-over (coupé). In sabre, thrusts can be used but, much more often, cuts are employed. The basic cuts of sabre include: cut to head, cut to cheek, cut to flank, cut to chest and various cuts to the arm.

The basic thrusts are simple movements (one movement, one "tempo").

Direct Thrusts

The direct thrust begins and ends in the same line, without any change of line in between. In other words, it is a straight extension of the arm conducting the weapon directly towards the target (which may be executed, of course, with different varieties of footwork). Depending on its purpose, the direct thrust is named as follows:

1. *Direct attack*: a direct thrust applied as an offensive action on one's own initiative.

2. *Direct riposte:* a direct thrust executed immediately after successfully parrying the opponent's attack.

3. *Direct counter-riposte:* A direct thrust executed directly after successfully parrying the opponent's riposte.

4. *Stop-hit:* A direct thrust executed into the opponent's attack (a variety of counter-attack).

5. *Remise:* A direct thrust applied as a continuation of the attack in the same line.

6. *Feint:* A direct thrust may also be used as a threat: feint of direct attack, feint of counter-attack, etc.

Indirect Thrusts

Disengagement and cut-over (coupé) are indirect thrusts which end in a new line. With disengagement, we avoid the opponent's blade near the guard and with cut-over we avoid the opponent's blade near its point with a cutting movement.

Counter-disengagement is an indirect thrust that ends in the same line. It is executed on the opponent's change of engagement or any circular movement (for example, a circular parry) and it ends in the same line from which it began, but constitutes an indirect thrust because it must first avoid the opponent's circular movement.

Simple and Complex Actions

Regarding the complexity of movements, all fencing actions may be divided into simple actions (one movement) and compound actions (more than one movement). Generally, we may state that simple actions consist of one movement of the weapon while compound actions comprise more than one movement of the weapon (for example, a compound attack or a thrust preceded by actions on the opponent's blade).

Note: Even though this classification is accepted by all fencing schools, it may sometimes be slightly misleading from the point of view of tactics, since it does not reflect the fencer's intentions and applies only to the number of movements and the simplicity or complexity of their execution.. For example, a simple action from a technical perspective (basic description of actions) may be the result of a rather complex tactical process, whereas a compound technical action may be a tactically straightforward solution (for example, a first intention compound attack).

Here it must be mentioned that in the French school, all actions on the blade (engagement, pressure, beats, bindings, transfers) are considered as preparatory actions—so called preparations of the attack. In my opinion, actions on the blade ought to be considered as preparatory only when they fulfill the purposes listed previously under Preparatory Actions (hindering the opponent's concentration, trying to assess how strongly or lightly the opponent holds the weapon, disturbing his attention, etc.). Actions on the blade ought to be considered an integral, introductory part of a compound attack when the beat, binding, pressure or transfer is followed smoothly and immediately by a thrust, cut or feint. In other words, when the action on the blade and the following part of the attack form one technical and tactical unit and are executed fluently, they should be classified as a compound action (for example, fourth-beat and disengagement in foil, sixth-binding and direct thrust with opposition in epee, fourth-beat and cut to head in sabre, etc.).

Offensive, Defensive, and Counter-offensive Actions

When discussing the application of actual actions in a bout, one should bear in mind that they may be executed either on one's own initiative (offensive actions) or as a response to the opponent's initiative (defensive and counter-offensive actions).

Offensive actions are executed on one's own initiative, except riposte. In a bout, the parry and subsequent riposte are composed of first a defensive action and then an immediate offensive action. Parry and riposte form one technical and tactical unit in which the parry is defensive and the riposte is offensive.

The Importance of Preparatory Actions

In a competition, the actual actions are easily seen and understood and are more spectacular and obvious in their technical execution than are the preparatory actions. For these reasons, the technique of actual actions is much more often discussed and noticed and more attention is paid to its technical development in the training process, particularly in the individual lesson. The preparatory actions are practised much less. Such an attitude is highly "unjust" to preparatory actions, since the success of actual actions depends to a large extent on the judicious use of preparation, as well as speed and accuracy of perception. The preparatory efforts of a fencer often take a lot of the time in a bout (especially so in epee), and they not only constitute the background of the bout, but also form an integral part of the tactics. To an onlooker who does not know fencing, preparatory actions, full of concentration, maneuvering on the strip, misleading the opponent, waiting for an opportunity to take the opponent by surprise, very often seem incomprehensible. This is why we often hear such comments from the lay public as: "Nothing is happening! Both fencers simply jump about for a bit, then suddenly throw themselves at each other, shout, then tear their masks off and look with triumph or anxiety at the referee."

Preparatory actions are an extremely important factor in deciding the struggle in the fencing bout, and the fencer must know, understand and practice these actions. Still, even nowadays, in the training of the vast majority of fencers, there exists a paradoxical situation in which exercises include only the more easily seen and understood actual actions to the detriment of the equally important preparatory actions.

In a modern fencer's training the fencing master should introduce special tactical exercises including learning and perfecting preparatory actions as well as shaping various technical-tactical and tactical skills.

Tactical Feints

One of the very important tasks of preparatory actions is to gain maximal information about one's opponent—his/her style of fencing, favorite strokes, strong and weak points, etc. While trying to obtain maximum information about the opponent, the fencer should take strong advantage of general (tactical) feints (as distinct from feints of thrusts or cuts used as a part of a real compound action that draw the opponent's parry in order to deceive it and score in the opening area of the target or to draw a counter-attack, to apply the appropriate variety of counter-time). Tactical or general feints are the stances, changes of position, movements and actions intended to supply information about the opponent, to mislead the opponent and to make it difficult for the adversary to understand or predict the fencer's actions.

Such tactical feints include not only movements of the weapon arm but actions on the blade, movements of the legs and trunk, false attacks, etc. Perhaps it would not be an exaggeration to say that the fencer's skill in tactics is displayed to a large degree by the ability to mislead an opponent, to recognize the opponent's intentions and to discern any attempts to be mislead.

Plans and tactical tasks in a bout ought to be changeable and adaptable to various tactical situations and in accordance with the nature of the opponent. The ways to mislead the opponent (real feints, feints of thrusts or cuts which are meant to elicit certain movements from the opponent) may be generally divided into two categories: first degree tactical feints (direct feints) and second degree tactical feints (indirect feints). The following examples will illustrate the point.

First Degree Tactical Feint (Direct Feint)

Foil— During preparation, Fencer A has led the opponent to believe that a compound attack composed of multiple cut-overs is his intention. At the beginning of Fencer A's actual attack, the opponent, sensing the opportunity, counter-attacks with a stop-hit. Fencer A, who has been expecting this response, parries the counter-attack and scores with a riposte, thus executing counter-time.

Sabre— Fencer A commences a compound attack and, apparently unwittingly, slightly exposes his forearm. Fencer B tries to hit the "carelessly" exposed forearm with a stop-cut. Fencer A, expecting to draw this movement, parries the stopcut and scores a hit with the riposte, thus executing a variety of counter time.

Second Degree Tactical Feint (Indirect Feint)

Foil— Fencer A jumps forwards with the point of the foil raised high with an "apparent" attempt to draw and parry Fencer B's stop-hit (simple counter-attack). Fencer B, sensing the "trap," executes a compound counter-attack (he wants to execute feint of stop-hit and deceive the parry: Italian *"finta in tempo"*). Just as Fencer B begins the execution of the compound counter-attack, Fencer A finishes his movement with a direct thrust which causes Fencer B to fail as the counter-time of Fencer A arrives on B's first movement (feint of counterattack).

Sabre— Fencer A, beginning his attack, uncovers his forearm in such an obvious and spectacular manner that the opponent cannot fail to notice purposefulness of the "mistake." Fencer B expecting a trap in the form of a parry by Fencer A (counter-time), attempts to apply a compound counter-attack (feint of stop-hit—deceive the parry: *"finta in tempo"*). As Fencer B executes a feint of stop-hit, with an intention to deceive the expected parry, Fencer A executes a stop-cut during Fencer B's first movement.

These are also examples of second intention actions, executed by counter-time.

II. CLASSIFICATION OF FENCING ACTIONS FROM THE POINT OF VIEW OF THEIR TACTICAL APPLICATION

The psychological basis (perception and ways of choosing the actions) of applying the actual actions in the bout lead to the division of these actions into three groups:

1. Foreseen actions.

2. Unforeseen actions.

3. Partly foreseen actions.

Foreseen Actions (preconceived or premeditated actions)

a. First intention actions (foreseen actions of first intention).

b. Second intention actions (foreseen actions of second intention).

These terms are generally well-known. Generally, foreseen actions are the actions executed according to a previously chosen plan/motor program (see Table 3). Additional explanations are given in the discussion of attacks.

Unforeseen Actions (spontaneous or unpremeditated actions)

These actions are automatic, mostly applied in the form of defensive or counteroffensive actions. They are executed as "reflex" motor responses to unexpected offensive actions from the opponent—typically in the form of parry or counter-attack "on the spur of the moment." They are responses to an opponent's action which was neither expected nor foreseen.

Partly Foreseen Actions (actions containing both foreseen and unforeseen parts)

a. Actions (typically attacks) with a known beginning but a choice of possible endings: the so called "open-eyes attacks."

b. Actions (mostly attacks) with a known beginning but a change of intention during the execution.

Note that in both types, the beginning is known and foreseen and the final part is unforeseen. The two above mentioned varieties of partly foreseen actions superficially are very similar and yet there is a striking difference between them. An "open-eyes" action begins with a foreseen and planned movement (feint or action on the blade) and proceeds *by plan* according to the opponent's reaction. Actions with a change of decision are conceived, initially programmed and put into execution as preconceived actions (either first or second intention) and then, under the influence of the opponent's *unexpected* movement, are changed mid-way.

(The classification of fencing action from the point of view of their tactical application in a bout is presented in Table 2-D, at the end of this chapter.)

Attacks

The most efficacious means of fighting are offensive actions—above all attacks. In all weapons, the majority of fencers score the largest amount of hits by attacks (although the proportion both of attempted and successful attacks varies among different fencers).

The simple attack, especially direct attack, is both efficacious and powerful, but quite difficult to bring off.

The necessary conditions for its successful applications are:

1. The right timing and taking the opponent by surprise ("à propos," "scelta di tempo"),

2. Correctness of execution,

3. Absence of unnecessary muscular tension,

4. Not betraying one's intentions,

5. Speed of execution, and

6. Acceleration.

In a bout, an important element is the struggle of both fencers to seize the right moment of opportunity for an attack (tempo, a propos, taking the opponent by surprise). The timing of the attack itself is equally important in compound attacks—the feint should take the opponent by surprise, "forcing" him to take a parry.

The advantage of an attack, as compared to other fencing actions, resides in the fact that the attacker is able to choose a moment and situation when he/she is fully ready, has the initiative and is highly concentrated. Conversely, the defender is very often taken by surprise at an inconvenient moment (i.e. while he/she is off balance, not fully concentrated, not expecting the opponent's attack, preparing his/her own attack, etc.). A second factor which enhances the advantage of an attack, especially in sabre fencing, is that an attacker is quite often able to change his/her movements (change of intention) while executing a foreseen offensive action. A fencer who is being attacked, especially when taken by surprise, has considerably less opportunity for controlling and changing his defensive responses.

The main difficulty of launching an attack—apart from the necessity of taking the opponent by surprise—is the necessity of getting close to the opponent, who may retreat, attack or counter-attack.

Classifying the Attacks

According to various criteria of classification, we may differentiate several varieties of attack. Knowing and understanding the classification of attacks and, indeed, all other actions, is very important in the classification of tactics, both in the process of training and in competitions. As I keep saying to my students, "To look is not the same as to see, and to see is not the same as to perceive. We really perceive—on a higher, conceptual-functional level—only what we know well, understand well, can explain and give a name to." As Confucius said many hundreds of years ago, the ability to giving a proper name to things is the first step toward wisdom.

The various classifications of attacks are presented in Table 2.

Table 2-B: The Various Classifications of Attacks		
1	False Attacks	Real Attacks
2	Simple Attacks	Compound Attacks
3	First Intention Attacks	Second Intention Attacks
4	Attacks with Known Final	Attacks with Unknown Final
5	Attacks without change of primary intention during execution	Attacks with change of primary intention during execution

These classifications of attacks are fairly self-explanatory. A short description below, however, will serve to clarify the details.

False Attacks

False attacks are attacks made with no intention of scoring a hit, but that serve some other purpose, such as reconnoitering or drawing the opponent's action. For example, Fencer A, by means of a false attack, draws a parry-riposte from Fencer B and then scores a hit with counter-riposte (the entire action is typical second intention). Or Fencer A, starting with false attack, draws a stop-hit from Fencer B and subsequently executes a counter-time action which scores a point (also a second intention action). Or Fencer A uses a false attack to draw a parry, observes the parry, and plans an attack to deceive it (reconnoitering).

Fencers with a phlegmatic temperament—with slow reaction and slow mobility of nervous processes—can compensate to a certain degree for their lack of speed by using second intention actions. In other words, they can use false attack to draw an expected movement from the opponent and score a hit with a previously programmed action which may be counter-riposte, counter-time, remise or redouble. By using second intention actions, the attacker may react earlier to the opponent's movements and execute his own foreseen final movement with more certainty and accuracy.

False attacks serve also the purpose of reconnoitering the opponent's attitudes, behavior, and reactions or of preparing a convenient distance and situation to launch a real attack.

Real Attacks

Real attacks are attacks made with the intention of scoring a point either directly or indirectly. A simple attack is an attack executed with one movement of the weapon arm (one "tempo"). A compound attack is executed with one or more feints or actions on the opponent's blade or feints following actions on the blade.

An attack which is intended to score without drawing and taking advantage of an opponent's riposte or counter attack is called a first intention attack. This class of attack may be simple or compound and may or may not include actions on the opponent's blade (i.e. beat, bind or press).

A second intention attack consists of a false attack which draws the opponent's parry-riposte, counter-attack or parry and delayed riposte and finishes with a foreseen counter-action by the original attacker. It may finish by parry—counter-riposte, counter-time, remise or redouble.

Parrying or counter-attacking the opponent's counter-attack is called counter-time. Counter-time, like many other fencing actions, may be applied "on the spur of the moment" as an "automatic" motor response (motor reaction) or may be executed as a premeditated (foreseen) action constituting one of the many varieties of second intention attacks. Attacks with a known final, regardless of their simplicity or complexity, are attacks which are conceived and executed according to the attacker's original program. On the other hand, attacks with an unknown final ("open-eyes") are executed with the first movement being foreseen (premeditated, pre-programmed) and the final movement depending on the opponent's response.

Attacks without change of intention are actions which are executed from the beginning to end, strictly according to the attacker's original program, even when the attacker incorrectly anticipated the opponent's response.

As I have mentioned before, attacks with a change of the original intention may seem to be, to the superficial observer, an "open-eyes" attack. However, this type of attack greatly differs from the open-eyes attack. In open-eyes attack, the fencer knows how the attack begins and finishes according to what his opponent does. In attacks with change of decision in execution, the fencer originally has a foreseen plan for the entire action and wants to execute it according to a preconceived motor program. He changes his action, however, when he sees his opponent does not react in the way he predicted. Attacks with a change of intention during their execution are originally conceived as foreseen—first or second intention—and are modified during their execution under the influence of the opponent's unanticipated movement.

Example 1: Sabreur A intends to score a hit with a first intention direct attack to the head (cut to head), taking advantage of speed and good timing. While actually executing the preconceived attack, Sabreur A notices that Sabreur B is taking a very fast quinte parry. The attacker changes intention in mid-attack and finishes the attack with a cut to flank, deceiving the opponent's parry.

Example 2: An epeeist wants to execute first intention compound attack by feinting in the low line, drawing the opponent's octave parry and finishing with a disengagement hit to the top of the forearm. Contrary to expectations, however, the opponent does not parry, but attempts a stop hit over the arm. The attacking epeeist quickly changes intention and scores a hit by using a variety of counter-time: executing a direct thrust with opposition in sixth line.

Example 3: Fencer A wants to execute a preconceived (foreseen) second intention attack by feinting, drawing Fencer B's stop-hit, then parrying and scoring with a riposte. Contrary to expectations, the opponent does not react to the feint. Noticing the lack of the expected reaction, Fencer A changes his/her intention and finishes with a real direct thrust.

The Importance of Defense to an Attacking Strategy

It is impossible to prepare an attack, particularly when fencing an experienced opponent, without the essential concentration of thought and attention necessary for fast and correct perception and fast and correct motor response. A fencer with a strong offensive drive who is preparing and concentrated on his attack, may suddenly be attacked by his opponent. Such an unexpected attack forces the attacked fencer to rapidly switch his/her thoughts and attention to avoid being hit. In order not to lose an active and offensive style of fencing, in which the fencer maintains control of the initiative and often uses offensive actions, the technique of defense—parries and counter-attacks—must be perfectly mastered in order to be certain of being effective at any moment in the bout. Only then can the fencer prepare his attacks and attack with courage and efficacy. Although it may sound paradoxical, the technical and psychological basis of an offensive style of fencing is confidence in defense. Confidence in defense allows the competitor to maneuver freely on the strip, to push the opponent to the end line of the piste and to prepare attacks comparatively calmly and with assurance. Such a style of fencing, active and offensive yet confident in defense, is characteristic of many great fencers. A fencer who has an excellent command of parries and counter-attacks may allow himself/herself to come almost dangerously close to the opponent to launch an attack at the appropriate moment.

Without the backing of sure parries, an offensive style of fencing leads to double hits, simultaneous attacks and primitive escapes when the fencer is taken by surprise.

Counter-Attacks and Counter-Time

A counter-attack is any defensive-offensive movement against an offensive action (typically against attacks but also against ripostes, etc.). Counter-attacks may be simple or compound.

Simple counter attacks:

a. Stop-hits.

b. Stop-hits with opposition (they used be called time-hits, coup de temps, colpa di tempo).

c. Stop hits with evasion.

d. Derobe (derobement), used against attacks which are proceeded by an attempted taking of the blade.

Compound counter-attacks (Italian, *finta in tempo*) comprise:

a. Feint of a stop hit—deceive the parry or taking of the blade.

b. Feint of derobe—derobe of the second action of the blade.

In my view, any action against a counter-attack should be called counter-time. (In French it is called *contretemps;* in Italian it is *contra tempo.*) Let me explain.

In the old Italian rapier play, "tempo contra tempo" meant a counter-attack against a counter-attack.

Example: In rapier play, the attacker begins a cut to head, the defender starts to execute a cut to flank as a stop-hit, and then the original attacker finishes with a thrust with opposition, thus executing tempo contra tempo. (In the old Italian rapier school, "tempo" meant counter-attack and taking the opponent by surprise.)

In the French school, however, counter-time is mainly a tactical concept and the essence of it consists of deliberately drawing the opponent's attack or counter-attack (second intention) in order to parry and riposte. So, the salient feature of the French conception of counter-time is, as I mentioned above, purely tactical: drawing the opponent's action—any action—and scoring with parry-riposte. Roger Crosnier, a very prominent French master, describes counter-time as: An action of drawing the opponent's stop-hit or time-hit, parrying it and riposting from it. The F.I.E,. rules state that counter-time is: Every action made by the attacker against a stop-hit made by his opponent.

To me, as stated before, *counter-time is every action against counter-attack,* irrespective of the intentions of the fencer executing the action (whether foreseen or unforeseen).

Counter-time may be executed as a parry followed by riposte, a stop-hit, a stop-hit with opposition (time hit), or a beat-thrust. Counter-time against a compound counter-attack may be applied by successive parries, successively taking the blade.

Counter-time may also be applied while riposting—this is especially prevalent in epee. For example, an epee fencer defends with parry six and then begins a riposte to the leg. The opponent attempts to remise on the epeeist's arm (counter-attack against riposte) and the attacker deflects the remise with a stop-hit in opposition in sixth line (counter-time).

Tactically speaking, counter-time, like many other actions, may be applied as:

a. A foreseen action,

b. An action with change of intention during its execution, or

c. One of the possible ways of finishing an attack with unknown destination. Below are some examples.

Foreseen Counter-Time (second intention action)

Example 1: An epee fencer deliberately draws a stop-hit, then parries it and scores with a riposte—or, by a rather slow taking of the opponent's blade, draws a derobe and scores with a hit by taking the blade for the second time and then thrusting in opposition.

Example 2: A sabreur starts an attack with a deliberately bent arm, thus drawing a stop-hit, then confidently parries it and ripostes.

Example 3: A sabreur feints a cut to flank with a step forward, drawing an expected compound counter-attack from opponent by feint to head, cut to flank. On the first movement of the opponent, the attacker either swiftly finishes his attack or, after his own fifth parry, parries seconde and scores with a riposte.

Unforeseen Counter-Time (change of intention during the execution of an action)

Example 1: An epeeist starts to execute a foreseen attack with a feint in the low line, tries to draw the opponent's octave parry, intending to deceive the parry and touch in the high line. His opponent, however, does not attempt to take the expected parry but, instead, executes a stop-hit to the forearm. The attacker changes his original intention and finishes his attack by hitting with opposition in sixth line.

Example 2: A foilist intends to apply a foreseen attack by quarte binding, direct thrust. The attacked fencer, contrary to the attacker's expectations, takes fourth parry. The attacker changes his intention and finishes the attack by disengagement, thrust.

Example 3: Sabreur A begins a foreseen attack, intending feint to head, cut to flank. Suddenly, he notices that Sabreur B is executing a stop-cut instead of the expected quinte parry, so he changes his intention and makes a beat four, cut to head.

Counter-Time as a Possible Ending of an "Open Eyes" Attack (Attack with Unknown Destination)

Example: An epeeist begins an open eyes attack, starting with a feint and a step forward and intending to finish according to what his opponent will do. If the opponent does not respond, the attacker finishes with a direct thrust. If the opponent tries to parry, the attacker will deceive the parry, scoring with a disengagement or counter-disengagement hit. If the opponent chooses to counter-attack, the attacker will parry-riposte or do any other action in counter-time.

Counter-time is usually used by an attacker but it may also be used, on any other offensive actions. For example, a fencer may execute riposte by counter-time or even counter-time by counter-time.

Examples:

a. Epeeist A attacks to the low line. Epeeist B parries opponent's attack by octave parry. Epeeist A immediately follows his attack by a redouble in the high line (stop-hit against a riposte). Epeeist B parries the redouble with a sixth parry and scores the hit with opposition (riposte by counter-time).

b. Epeeist A begins his attack and parries opponent's stop-hit. Epeeist B executes an immediate remise of his stop-hit which is parried again by the original attacker (counter-time in counter-time).

c. Sabreur A begins his attack with feint to head. Sabreur B executes a stop-cut to head, which is parried with quinte parry by Sabreur A (counter-time). Sabreur B immediately remises to forearm of his stop-cut, which is parried again by the original attacker (counter-time by counter-time).

Defense

Let us now briefly consider the defensive aspects of fencing. Defense consist of all actions that counter an opponent's offensive actions with the purpose of avoiding being hit. Very often and preferably, defense, at the same time, allows us to take advantage of the opponent's nearness and his failure to score a hit—in order to score with a riposte or counter-attack. Defensive and counter-offensive actions are a reply to the opponent's offensive actions. Consequently, the defender usually does not have the initiative and is frequently caught unprepared. Most often, with exception of the cases when the defender deliberately draws the attack, the situation, the timing and type of attack are chosen by the attacker.

On the other hand, the diversity of defenses (the multitude of defensive actions— different parries and combinations of parries as well as the many varieties of counter-attack and displacements of the body) which the attacking fencer may meet often paralyzes or lowers his/her courage and self-assurance and hinders his/her choice, speed and accuracy of attack.

The actions of defense are mostly unforeseen—we do not know when or how our opponent will attack. When an unexpected attack occurs, fencers generally react with a retreat, parry, evasion (defensive actions) or counter-attack (offensive-defensive action) applied as a learned and highly automated motor response (motor reaction).

Foreseen Defensive Actions

Sometimes, however, though not very often, the actions of defense (both defensive actions and offensive-defensive actions) are applied as foreseen actions when an attack is expected or even drawn from the opponent. Among the foreseen actions of defense, we may distinguish:

1. Actions of defense, foreseen in general.

2. Actions of defense, foreseen in detail.

Actions of defense foreseen in general occur when a fencer expects or deliberately draws the opponent's attack—without, however, knowing what kind of attack it will be. The appropriate form of defense—parry or counter-attack—is chosen on the basis of signals received by visual and tactile stimuli while the opponent's attack is in progress.

Actions of defense foreseen in detail occur when the fencer expects or deliberately draws a particular attack (foreseen variety) from the opponent. The defending fencer, then has an already "prepared" parry or counter-attack (the appropriate motor program taken from the long memory store), taking into account the type of attack expected from the opponent. To make it clear, here are a few examples of defense, foreseen in detail:

a. Epeeist A rushes forward, exposing his forearm. This, most likely, will provoke a direct attack to the forearm and Epeeist A can execute a sixth circular parry and score with a riposte with opposition.

b. Sabreur A, on his opponent's offensive, exploratory movements, escapes rather wildly, pretending to be scared and showing the opponent wild parries. This provokes the attacker to make a very energetic compound attack with many feints—which leads him/her to expose the forearm. Sabreur A, expecting this kind of attack, scores at the very beginning of the opponent's attack with a premeditated stop-hit to the forearm.

c. Foilist A makes an apparent faulty preparation by executing wild counter-sixth presses on the opponent's blade. This preparation is designed to draw the opponent's attack with a counter-disengagement, thrust, taking advantage of the "faulty and clumsy" preparation. Foilist A, who is expecting this attack, executes a parry four and scores a riposte.

Incidentally, the above are also good examples of a simple reaction (simple sensory motor response) applied in a bout, i.e., a fencer expects, or even provokes, a given movement and responds with an already known, premeditated, prepared stroke (known stimulus—known response); the motor program of the action is prepared before the actual stimulus arrives in the pre-program part (preparatory part) of the motor reaction.

It is worth noting that unforeseen actions of defense and generally foreseen actions of defense are examples of choice reaction (choice sensory motor response). A choice reaction occurs when a fencer chooses the appropriate response to the stimulus only after the appearance of the stimulus—opponent's movement—in the latent period of motor reaction. In other words, whenever there is an action (attack) from the opponent, the defending fencer must recognize the stimulus (the variety of action) and make the correct choice of response.

The use of a foreseen action of defense gives a fencer several advantages:

- It ensures a state of high concentration, perception and preparedness.

- It shortens the reaction time—the defensive movement may be started sufficiently early.

- It facilitates the correct technical—and fast—execution of the defensive (parry, retreat, evasion) or counter offensive (counter-attack) action—there is no deterioration of technique, which very often occurs when a fencer is taken by surprise.

- It provides more of an opportunity and time to change a defensive response should the opponent change his/her offensive movement.

- The defender may prepare the motor program of the action (parry or counter-attack) even before the appearance of the stimulus (the opponent's attack).

Unforeseen Defensive Actions

Unforeseen actions of defense are carried out "on the spur of the moment" or "instinctively," almost without the fencer realizing it. He often realizes what he did only at the end or after the action, or when he has committed an error in choosing, timing or executing a movement. The attention of the fencer is focused, not on how to execute the defensive stroke but, rather, on choosing the right response—on the appropriately chosen stroke. Unforeseen actions of defense are, as we have mentioned, choice or differential reactions to a surprise movement by the opponent. This type of defense (unforeseen) depends, to a high degree on the quality of acquired sensory-motor skills (fencing strokes) and specific motor reactions.

Well-learned and highly automated actions of defense—particularly parries—are very important for the efficacy of the fencer's actions, in order to insure that his/her conscious mind may be free from fear of the opponent's unexpected attack and able to create the best conditions (psychological state, optimistic mood, self control, feeling of confidence) for active, bold, creative and effective conduct of the bout, as well as the confidence in preparing his/her own attack. It is worthwhile to stress, once again, that the best psychological and technical basis of an active, courageous, mobile and offensive style of fencing is confidence in one's unforeseen actions of defense, especially strong parries. The best defense is a parry followed by an instantaneous, fast riposte or a counterattack combined with a complete avoidance of the hit. The other forms of defense, retreat or evasion, although allowing us to avoid being hit, are less valuable because we have less chance of hitting the opponent.

Some fencers prefer to base their style of fencing and tactics on foreseen, premeditated actions in which careful observation, accurate and fast perception, rational thinking, planning and often simple reaction play an important part. Others prefer to rely on their own improvisation, on what may be called "the feeling of surprise", these types of fencers rely on compound and other varieties of sensory-motor reaction on intuitive and operative thinking, great mobility of the nervous processes, a high level of specific technical-tactical abilities and very high motor coordination. They rely on choice reaction, deferential reaction, intuitive reaction, anticipation of moving object reaction, and changing of intention while executing a foreseen action. Many great fencers rely on both foreseen and unforeseen actions and on offensive, defensive and counteroffensive actions.

FINAL REMARKS

At the end of this article on fencing terminology, fencing actions and their application in fighting, allow me to remind you once more that knowledge of proper terminology, understanding the importance of sensory-motor skills, special technical-tactical and tactical abilities combined with many aspects of attention enhance the fencer's ability to quickly and correctly perceive tactical situations and solutions in a bout and to understand the course of training. In other words, repeating what Confucius said, being able to assign the proper names to things is the first step toward wisdom.

The importance of speech, verbal communication, and exact up-to-date terminology is, unfortunately, very often neglected by many coaches and fencers, which leads to low efficacy of the training process and poor tactics in competition. If you are not convinced by this article and Professor David Tischler's words (see above), consider what the already mentioned great Chinese sage and philosopher, Confucius (551-479 BC) said,

> "If names are not correct, language is not in accordance with the truth of things. If language is not in accord with the truth of things, affairs cannot be carried on to success. Therefore, a superior man considers it necessary that the names he uses may be spoken appropriately. What the superior man requires is that in his words there is nothing incorrect."

I sincerely hope that every fencer and coach will take these words to heart and be a superior man or woman.

(The basic classification of fencing actions and classification based on tactics are presented inTables 2-C and 2-D).

Table 2-C
Basic Classification of Fencing Actions

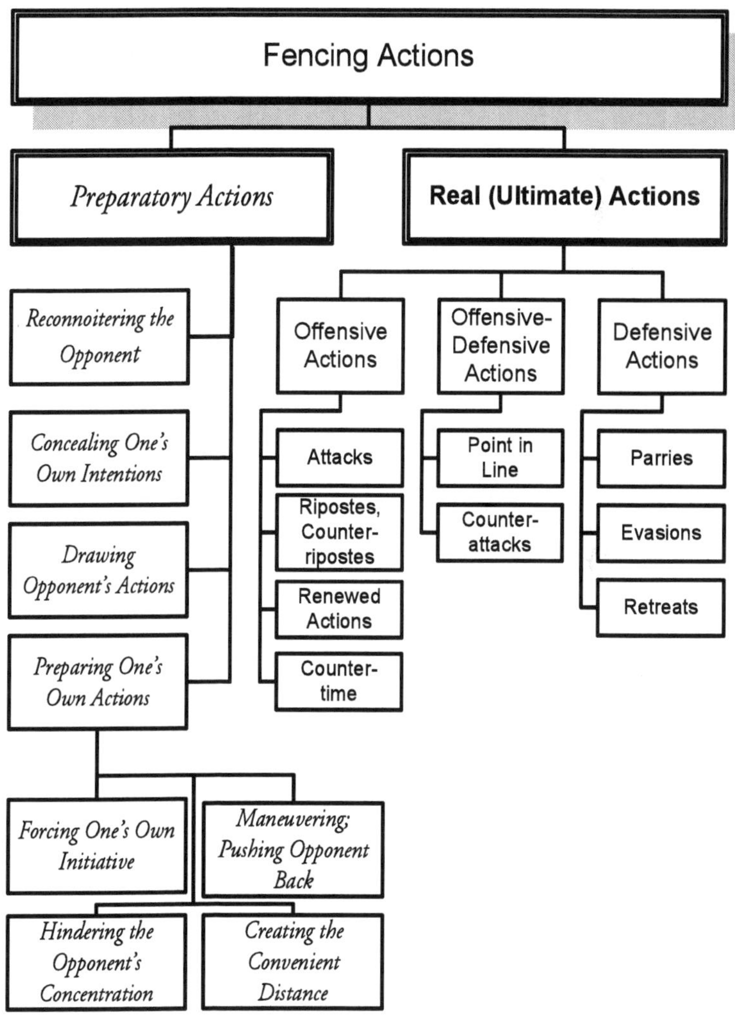

Table 2-D

Classification of Fencing Actions from the Point of View of Their Practical Application in a Bout

Foreseen Actions			Unforeseen Actions	Partly Foreseen Actions		
	First Intention	Second Intention	Unknown	Open Eyes (Unknown final)	Change of Decision While Executing the Action	
In Head (Primary Intention)			?			
In Reality (Actual Performance)						

Foreseen

Unforeseen

3. Some Remarks on Tactics in Fencing

"The tactical preparation of a fencer is the main part in his development as a competitor. That is the most difficult part of his training but also the most practical one."

--V. Arkadiev

GENERAL REMARKS ON TACTICS

"Once a fencer has learned the mechanisms of basic fencing movements, the activity loses its primary, total physical requirements and becomes more of a mental exercise. Concentration, self-control, and a quick decision command muscles and reflexes for successful scoring."

--Michel Alaux

Every young fencer experiences a great deal of difficulty when it comes to his first free bout with an opponent. His fencing master has taught him certain movements and also indicated when and how to use them in a bout. However, when on his own in a bout, facing an active opponent, he still does not know which movements he can use and when.

After many encounters, both in training and competition, with real opponents, he learns, step by step, to apply his fencing actions in a bout. Slowly, he develops the ability to evaluate his opponent and to choose the most appropriate action in a given tactical situation.

The selection of the right stroke is probably the most basic tactical ability of a fencer. This is connected closely with timing, "feeling of surprise," and acuity of perception.

Fencing tactics are described, briefly, as using all fencing actions, both preparatory and ultimate ones, in such a way as to avoid being hit, score hits against one's opponent and thus ensure victory.

Tactics may be defined in a simplified manner as *applying technique in a bout.*

We could say, a little more precisely, that tactics are a fencer's application of all his technical and tactical knowledge, motor qualities, and psychological preparedness for the purpose of winning a bout or achieving the best score, taking into consideration the strengths, technique, fencing style and tactics of his opponent.

Tactics are closely connected with technique and other factors of training, as I have described in other articles and books. The significance of timing—"feeling of surprise"—is described in Chapter 4. In the following chapter, I would only like to emphasize the most important features of tactics.

Technique

Technical versatility is the base of richness of tactics and enables the fencer to surprise his opponent, not only by speed and choice of time, but also by variety of action. It is obvious that if a fencer has a rich technical repertoire, then his tactical "plays" and solutions will be more effective and more surprising for the opponent.

Various ideas and practical solutions require mastery of an extensive technical base. In gymnastics, figure skating, diving and similar sports, which are based on closed motor skills, (internal motor habit patterns), it is most important to reproduce, with as much precision as possible, the prescribed form of a movement that is conventionally accepted as full of grace and beauty. In these sports, technique is the most important goal—a purpose in itself. In fencing, technique, which is based on open motor skills (external motor habit patterns), is not a purpose in itself, but should serve as a base for the psychological and tactical preparation of a fencer.

It is well known from practical experience—even if not everybody wants to admit it—that excellent technique, in the narrow sense of the word, does not guarantee success in competition. Technique, important though it undoubtedly is, must be combined in a bout with physical and psychological abilities and tactical capabilities.

It is obvious that a fencer should not think about how to execute a stroke during a bout, but must concentrate on watching his opponent and on preparing his tactics. This is why fencing must be highly automated and flexible—a high level of an open motor habit pattern. The level of technical competence certainly influences the style and tactical repertoire used by a fencer. He may choose and perfect his technical actions while creating his own style of fencing tactics.

If we say that the role of technique is to enhance tactics, and that tactics depend on technique, then we have to emphasize that *the real basis of tactics and tactical abilities is technique.* We mean technique, however, in the wider sense of the word: not limited only to a structure of movement—which some conservative fencing masters believe to the present day—but as a modern, elastic and universal knowledge, combined with a whole gamut of special, technical, and other qualities.

The following technical—and other—qualities of a fencer help in the development of his tactics:

- A high degree of automatization of movements and their relaxed, economical, and purposeful execution.

- The ability, when executing a movement, to take into consideration time, space and the whole tactical situation (open motor skills, adapted to changeable situations).

- Speed of movement, its correct rhythm, and the capacity to accelerate or change the direction of the movement.

- Speed of simple and (various kinds of) compound reactions.

- High coordination, dexterity, and swiftness of movements; the ability to apply and execute the same stroke in a fast and variable manner, depending on conditions.

- The ability to control muscular contraction and relaxation at the appropriate times.

- The ability to fluidly build up compound actions, based on simple basic strokes.

- Fencing-specific endurance in all its aspects: combating muscular, sensory, mental and emotional tiredness.

- The ability to reproduce, in actual movements, the mental picture of an action.

- High quality of neurophysiological processes, connected with the execution and application of fencing actions in a bout: selective perception, precision and speed of perception, qualities of attention (high concentration, a large range of attention, divisibility of attention, etc.), operative thinking and memory, etc.

The most important factors in tactics are:

- The ability to assess, in a fraction of a second, the situation on the strip (speed and accuracy of perception on a higher conceptual functional level).

- The ability to perform an action unforeseen by the opponent and take him by surprise. The best tactical application of a new stroke creates a situation in which the opponent has difficulty anticipating the timing, speed, and real intention of the fencer.

In trying to hit while avoiding being hit, one has to forestall one's opponent. In foil and sabre, a fencer tries to get priority in the eyes of the director—which nowadays leads to the abuse of conventional rules. In epee, one has to be literally faster than one's opponent. The necessity to score hits "in good time" means, not only the speed of movement, but also, and most of all, more selective, precise and quicker transformation of information. To win, a fencer has to think quicker and to see more than his opponent. In competition, slow movements are not so dangerous as slowness of seeing, thinking, and taking decisions,

It is very important for a fencer to be able to come close to his opponent in a bout, in a situation most inconvenient for the opponent. Generally, the purpose of many preparatory movements on the piste is to get within the opponent's "critical" distance, at the same time keeping the initiative and the possibility of ending the action—when the opponent has a lapse of concentration, is off-balance, is preparing an attack, or is surprised by a sudden change of rhythm or distance.

It is also very important to predict the opponent's movement and intention without revealing one's own intention.

A fencer's tactical mastery depends a lot on his repertoire and the quality of his preparatory actions, giving him more effective use of the ultimate, "real," actions with which he scores a hit.

After watching many important international events in fencing for many, many years, I have come to the conclusion that the principal tactical characteristics of top fencers are as follows:

1. The most frequently used successful actions are relatively uncomplicated (simple attacks, attacks with one feint, attacks preceded by action on the blade, parry-riposte, simple counter-attacks—in other words, short "phrases d'armes").

A first intention simple attack is very effective, although difficult to carry out. The success of such an attack depends on timing, speed, precision, and acceleration. However, simplicity of style and movements should not be confused with an excessively one-sided or poor technical repertoire. Simplicity and crudeness are definitely not the same.

In training, however, one should use, not only simple, but also complicated movements because, used from time to time, they are very effective and they are a first-class means of developing many technical fencing abilities (continuity of action, precision of movement, feeling of rhythm and cadence, motor coordination, etc.).

2. Great fencers are noted, not only for the simplicity, but for the variety of their actions. Variety of actions and tactics is characterized by:

    - A relatively large amount of strokes used (rich technique),

    - Alternating actions—offensive, defensive, counter-offensive; simple and compound actions, etc.,

    - Various ways of executing the same strokes depending on the situation,

- Clever use of preparatory actions,
- Alternative use of premeditated (foreseen), unpremeditated (unforeseen), and partly anticipated (partly foreseen) actions,
- Various solutions to the same tactical situation, both in offensive and in defensive actions.

Variety of tactical movements—both preparatory and ultimate—confuses the opponent. He does not know what sort of action to expect in certain situations. That makes him less sure of himself and increases his difficulty in planning his own actions. It is worth emphasizing this because some fencing masters and fencers maintain that, for efficient participation in competition, it is enough to master a few very well-trained strokes. Such limited training leads to a one-sided fencer who cannot cope with the great variety of styles of various opponents.

A wide variety of fencing actions and tactical ideas, successfully employed by a fencer in a bout, by no means excludes the use of one's own favorite actions. Fencers should, however, both in training and in competition, try not to rely too heavily on their favorite strokes, thus avoiding the danger of losing the "element of surprise" and of "ossification" of their repertoire. Overuse of favorite actions in training bouts may lead to them becoming "reflex-compulsory" actions: the fencer using them in the most inappropriate situations.

3. Top-class fencers are marked by their own highly characteristic style of fencing and the practical application of their doctrines. Looking at the technique and style of great fencers, one can recognize the influence of particular fencing schools and particular fencing masters. But apart from these, it is the fencer's individuality which has the greatest influence upon his style and tactics: height, traits of temperament, agility, power of concentration, and various other traits of personality.

In training, we want to teach and perfect a number of basic positions, movements, and fencing actions. We want the pupil to master the correct and most typical sensory-motor skills (motor habit patterns) of fencing technique. We teach them the typical basic strokes, not to make everybody fence in exactly the same way, but in order to make them able to find and elaborate their own individual style of fencing according to their character, temperament, body structure, and entire personality.

A fencing master should resist the temptation of imposing the same technique and style on all his pupils; on the contrary, he should undertake the difficult task of helping each fencer to find his own style.

Various fencers may like various fencing styles and tactics. In international competitions, there are successful fencers who represent totally different schools and styles. One should, however, warn those wishing to blindly imitate great champions, for the technique and tactics useful for one fencer could be completely useless for others.

Type of nervous system and traits of temperament are very important factors in building up a fencer's own style of fencing and his tactics. It is known, for example, that only a fencer with a strong, lively, and balanced temperament and with great mobility of neuro-physiological processes can base his style and tactics on lightning-speed improvisation, using unforeseen actions based on compound—mostly choice—reaction. On the other hand, a phlegmatic fencer who is not so fast, and whose nervous processes have a certain amount of inertia, must base his style and tactics on careful observation and premeditated actions, taking advantage of simple reaction, and using mostly second intention actions.

VARIOUS TYPES OF PREPARATORY ACTIONS

> *"Success depends to a great extent on the fencer's ability to deal with the opponent's game: to evaluate his strong points as well as take advantage of his weaknesses."*
>
> --Michel Alaux

As we remarked in the previous chapter, all fencing actions, from the point of view of tactics, can be divided into actual actions and preparatory actions.

Actual actions are ultimate, specific actions intended to ward off a hit or to score a hit, directly (first intention) or indirectly (second intention).

Preparatory actions are numerous and varied fencing actions, not intended to score a hit directly or indirectly, but facilitating and preparing the successful application of actual actions.

Preparatory actions are very often neglected in training and yet they play an important part in competition. Preparatory actions in a bout serve the following tactical purposes:

- General assessment of the situation in a bout;
- Misleading the opponent;
- Drawing certain actions from the opponent and subtly directing the opponent's game;
- Maneuvering, gaining the field of play and preparing one's own attacks;
- Hindering the opponent's concentration and his assessment of distance, etc.

Obvious lack of appreciation of preparatory actions in modern sabre is one of the symptoms of its degeneration. Sabreurs, nowadays, do not seem to remember an apt remark of the old master, Vincentio Saviolo, "Some set upon their enemies with rage and fury after the fashion of Rammes, and for the most part come to misfortune."[1]

Preparatory actions play an important part in foil and, above all, in epee, which has recently become the most spectacular, versatile, technical, and "honest" weapon.

Generally speaking, however, a fencer's tactical mastery depends heavily on his repertoire and the cleverness of his preparatory actions. As a matter of fact, some of the greatest fencers use only a very limited number of real actions, but prepare their application with great variety and ingenuity.

It is important for a fencer to be able to change a preparation into a "real" action, as well as to be able to deceive the opponent by a long, slow preparation followed by an accelerated real action—for example: a slow, preparatory lunge and a very fast renewal of the attack by fleche.

Preparatory actions often contain several tactical goals. For example, a false attack serves the purpose of reconnoitering the opponent's reaction, revealing his intention, misleading him about our own intentions, and getting good distance for a fast real attack.

Let us now briefly describe some types of preparatory actions.

Reconnaissance/Exploratory Moves

The aims of reconnaissance and preparatory actions are very varied as are their forms.

The general aim of reconnaissance is the assessment of the opponent's strengths and style of fencing and orientation in the tactical situation during the course of a bout. This entails evaluation of the opponent's tactical type, his technical possibilities, his intentions and psychological state.

Among the more detailed aims of reconnaissance, by means of exploratory movements, is an attempt to answer the following questions:

- In which situation does the opponent attack most often?
- Which are his favorite strokes?
- Taken by surprise, does he generally parry or use counter-attacks?

- How does he react to various movements such as a jump forward, sudden attack, beat on the blade, etc.?

- What are the external signs of his concentration or lack of concentration?

- Does he change his posture prior to an attack?

- Does he unwittingly betray his intention or is he trying to mislead his real intention, etc.?

Reconnaissance of the opponent's defense is carried out by the initial movements of various attacks or complete false attacks with a slightly shorter reach. Sometimes, in order to assess the opponent's defensive system, technique and speed, it is necessary to engage in an exchange of parry and riposte. This, of course, is dangerous, but gives us good information.

Evaluation of the opponent's reaction to various attacks, feints, actions on the blade, and other actions, is carried out by means of cautious, isolated execution of these strokes, accompanied by steps forward or a half lunge. A general impression of the opponent's technique, style, and speed is not gained only in the actual bout, but also by careful observation of his warm-up exercises, pre-competition lessons with his fencing master, and, above all, by watching him fence with other opponents.

The importance of reconnaissance to the fencer cannot be exaggerated. This is why lessons should not be limited to practicing and perfecting ultimate actions, but should also comprise exploratory and other preparatory movements. In applying a fencing stroke, it is not only the actual execution of the stroke which counts, but also the perception and anticipation of the opponent's movements.

Counteracting the opponent's reconnaissance consists essentially of two kinds of closely connected preparatory actions:

- Concealing one's own intentions,

- Misleading the opponent.

Concealing One's Own Intentions

This is the more passive form of counteraction against the opponent's reconnaissance. The essence of it consists of the ability to not betray unwillingly—by unnecessary gestures and movements—one's own intention or state of mind. The successful hiding of one's own intention is possible only when a fencer, in the course of his training—both in lessons and competition—has learned to discriminate finely between real and false actions. This ability is based on compound differential reaction, allowing him to discriminate between very similar stimuli.

Misleading the Opponent

This may be described as an active form of counteracting the opponent's reconnaissance. On recognizing the opponent's exploratory movement, the fencer "shows" a certain line of action while, when the real attack comes, he uses a completely different stroke.

The active and passive forms of counteracting the opponent's reconnaissance lead to a very subtle and crafty psychological struggle—the greater part of it often taking place in the heads of both fencers. Charles de Beaumont summed up this point excellently when he said, "Fencing is a game of subtlety, and bluff can be met with counter-bluff."[2]

A fencer who is making a reconnaissance has to be very careful and consider whether the opponent's reaction to his exploratory movements is really an unwitting betrayal of his intentions or an attempt to purposefully mislead him. After he decides whether the opponent betrayed himself unwittingly, it is not the end of his troubles: now he has to decide whether the opponent has noticed his mistake or not. In accordance with each of these possibilities the fencer's action must, of course, be different.

Directing the Opponent's Game

A good fencer not only takes advantage of his opponent's mistakes and of certain tactical situations arising during the progress of the bout, but tries actively to create such a tactical situation as is convenient for his own plan—warding off an attack to score with a riposte or to launch an attack in a situation favorable to him. By the use of certain moves, he draws the opponent's movements and actions, influences his tactics and even his psychological mood. In other words, he tries to control the opponent's game.

This ability allows a fencer to foresee and even provoke his opponent's movements in order to nullify his efforts by means of already prepared actions.

The most typical and extreme example of drawing the opponent's action is the second intention, false attack with the object of drawing the opponent's counter-attack or parry-riposte. A counter-attack or parry riposte, so provoked, is more easily dealt with (second intention counter-time and second intention parry-riposte are, of course, "real," ultimate actions, not preparatory; see the previous chapter.

Thus, by certain false attacks, feints, changes of position, maneuvering on the strip and actions on the blade, one may draw concrete, foreseen actions from the opponent. An experienced fencer, however, not only provokes certain actions but tries to influence his opponent's psychology and tactics. For example, when fencing against an opponent who has a strong defense, one may assume the role of a very panicky fencer, very much afraid of the opponent's attacks. This may induce the opponent to make a rather wild and badly chosen attack, which is easy to parry. A forward movement with an expression of concentration, as if one is going to attack at any moment, may draw out the opponent's attack which is easy to parry and counteract in such circumstances.

Maneuvering

Maneuvering on the strip may serve a series of practical purposes. One of them may be to push the opponent into a less convenient position near the end of the strip. One gains distance by steps forward, short lunges, and short advance-lunges, accompanied by feints. Maneuvering also plays an important part in defense—for example, parrying with a step back. Another important purpose served by maneuvering is to find the appropriate distance from which to commence one's own attack. The struggle for "one's own distance" is complicated, very often accompanied by various movements of the blade and consists of steps forwards and back—of various lengths and rhythm, sometimes creeping towards the opponent, sometimes executing lively jumps, etc.

Hindering the Opponent's Game

Hindering the opponent's game means hindering the opponent's concentration, assessment of distance, and application of attack. By various movements and maneuvers, a fencer tries to lower the opponent's state of concentration, to induce a false sense of security, to make it difficult for him to assess distance and to launch his attacks. A fencer who is about to attack has an advantage when his opponent's concentration and watchfulness is lulled. This may be attained by drawing the opponent into a rather slow and phlegmatic interchange of footwork or slow, rhythmic movements of the blade.

The ability to control the rhythm of one's own movement and, by using that rhythm, to influence the opponent's psychology and state of concentration, is the quality possessed by great champions.

There are other, more active, ways of distracting the opponent's attention, which also make it difficult for him to assess the distance and to find the right moment for launching an attack.

Among such preparatory actions one may quote:

- Constant jumps forward and backwards,
- Combined use of jumps, movements of the blade and actions of the blade,
- Very strong, perhaps even brutal, beats on the blade which irritate certain opponents, upset their concentration and lower their precision,
- Holding the weapon in line against an opponent who favors compound attacks,
- Absence of blade and constant movement of the weapon against an opponent who likes engagement and attacks preceded by actions on the blade,
- Sudden closing of the distance against an opponent who likes attacks from long distance, etc.

Other, less subtle, ways of distracting the opponent's attention and hampering the initiation of his attacks belong rather to "gamesmanship" than to swordsmanship and this is why we shall not deal with them now.

The description of a few chosen preparatory actions has been, of necessity, brief and sketchy, but I hope that it still stresses their tactical significance and the necessity for studying and practicing them.

I think that it is appropriate to end this chapter on tactics by quoting the words of the famous French master—who, for some years, worked in the USA—Michel Alaux: "For most fencers, fencing is a unique combination of quick thinking and elegant movements."[3]

References

1 Saviolo V. *His Practise in Two Books, the First Entreating on the Rapier and Dagger, his Second on Honour and Honorable Quarrels.* London, 1595.

2 de Beaumont, G.L. *Fencing – ancient art and modern sport.* Nicholas Key: London 1960.

3 Alaux, M. *Fencing.* Charles Scribner's Sons: New York 1975.

4. The Value of Timing in Tactics

"The sense of tempo is the most essential of the speed abilities. It is one of the most valuable assets, and virtually nothing can compensate the lack of it. But a sense of tempo can compensate for inadequate physical speed to a considerable extent"

--István Lukovich

INTRODUCTION

"The most important indication of fencing talent is the ability of lightning-speed assessment of a situation; either someone possesses this ability or does not."

--Vera Kuznietsova

The following could be considered among the most important aims of a tactical fight and one the most salient aspects of fencing:

1. Very generally, one may say that the main purpose of a fencing action is to forestall, or be ahead, of the opponent. In epee, this is literal. One has to forestall the opponent in time—a hit, to be valid, has to be a fraction of a second earlier. In sabre and foil, forestalling takes a more subtle form. A sabreur or foilist, when counter-attacking, must either close the line of the opponent's attack or be ahead by a period of fencing time. In offensive actions, he fights to be ahead in gaining the right of way: he must be first to initiate the attack (not only in his own, but, above all, in the referee's opinion). The conception of forestalling, or keeping ahead of the opponent, is expressed, not only by the mere speed of movement, but also, and perhaps above all, by the

necessity for more selective and acute perception, and by the necessity for faster transformation of information (to understand, at once, what one sees, feels, and hears). To put the idea colloquially, the fencer has to be a thought ahead of his opponent.

2. A factor of immense tactical importance is surprise—the ability to act in a way unpredicted by the opponent. The more skillful the fencer is in exploiting the element of surprise, the less his opponent will be able to anticipate the time, speed, type, and intention of the action employed.

3. A very important feature and aim of tactical combat is the ability to gain the appropriate distance in a situation most inconvenient for the opponent. It is not sufficient to maneuver into lunge distance, for example, if the opponent is concentrated and waiting for an attack. It is far more valuable to gain the distance when the opponent is temporarily off balance, not concentrated, or expecting something quite different. Generally speaking, one may state that practically all fencing actions, and the footwork accompanying them, aim, in a way, at gaining "nearness" while preserving combat initiative.

4. Of equal importance in tactics is recognition and understanding of the opponent's actions and intentions—at the same time, misleading him by concealing one's own (confusion of display).

5. In their application, tactics are connected with technique and other factors of training and fights. This point will be discussed below.

6. The main tasks of tactical fencing activities are: a) to avoid being hit, b) to prepare an action and c) to score a hit. These tasks are given here in a logical sequence, but in practice they are intermingled.

Purposeful and efficient application of technical-tactical and tactical capabilities on the strip depends upon the specific energy and coordination abilities, technical skill and degree of psychological preparedness.

The ability to conduct a bout and use proper tactics is closely connected with the fencer's psychological state, his power of concentration, and self control. Undue nervousness, over-excitation, lack of confidence, overestimation of the opponent's strength, apathy, insufficient warm-up, prevalence of inhibitory processes—all these factors may hamper the fencer in conducting a tactical bout, realizing the tactical solutions, and displaying his technical abilities. Conversely, self-control, adequate level of arousal, consciousness of his own experience and of his technical and tactical capabilities, positively influence the psychological state of the fencer, increasing his calm, assurance, dexterity and courage in action.

SENSE OF SURPRISE (SCELTA DI TEMPO, L' INTRODUCTION, L'A PROPOS)

> *"L'à propos est la faculté qui nous pemet de choisir le moment le plus favorable a l'execution d'une action d'escrime."*
>
> *"The sense of surprise is the ability which allows us to choose the moment most favorable for the execution of a fencing action."*
>
> --Paul Pattesti and Louis Prost

In tactics, a very important role is played by the sense of surprise—often called choice of time *(scelta di tempo, l'à propos).* Every fencer—even one who has just begun to do loose play—has been told, and realizes from experience, how important it is to choose the right time for attacking his opponent. Of course, we realize that the expression "choice of time" or "timing" is inadequate. There is also a question of distance, tactical situation, and taking the opponent by surprise—all of which make a very complicated phenomenon nearly as difficult to describe as the conception of time or space.

It was noticed long ago that certain situations are more conducive to scoring a hit. This has been called, in English, "timing" or "choice of time," in Italian, *"scelta di tempo,"* in French, *"l'á propos."* The expression used by Polish fencers, *"zaskoczenie"* (literal translation: "surprise") or *"wyczucie zaskoczenia"* ("sense of surprise"), better depicts the situation than any expression which only considers the element of time.

The expression "tempo" (literally, "time" in Italian) originates from 16th Century Italian rapier play. When a fencer made a preliminary movement to cut to head, and his opponent executed a very fast cut to flank, they called it "tempo" (we call it stop-hit). If somebody attempted to execute a stop-hit—"tempo"—and his opponent counteracted it with a stop-hit in opposition, it was called "tempo contra tempo"—the origin of contemporary counter-time, understood as an action against a counter-attack. In later years, the expression "tempo" lost its meaning as "stop-hit," and began to be used to describe a sense of surprise (and the stop-hit in opposition was called *"colpo di tempo"*—time-hit). Since then, the expression, "to attack in good tempo," has come to mean to attack, taking one's opponent by surprise. It is not a very fortunate description as everything we do occurs in time, and the success of an attack depends on assessing the situation with lightning-like speed and surprising the opponent by immediate action.

Most fencing textbooks, while stressing the element of "choice of time," delicately side-step the difficult problem of defining, describing, and discussing it.

The well-known fencing masters, Paul Battesti and Louis Prost, simply call it the ability to choose the moment most favorable for the execution of a fencing action.[1]

Kazimierz Laskowski, the director of the military school of fencing in Warsaw before the war, stated that "tempo, or surprise, is the moment of taking unawares an opponent who, in that particular situation, is hit most easily by an unexpected action."[2]

Janos Kevey gave his conception of timing as follows: "by the expression "tempo," we mean the moment which is the most favorable for the beginning and execution of a fencing action... in such a moment the opponent is helpless and not capable of making a defensive movement."[3]

The Hungarian author of a well-known textbook on sabre fencing, Zoltan Ozoray Schenker, wrote that "a fencer must catch the moment when his opponent is totally or partially incapable of action" and "such favorable moments occur when the opponent executes badly thought-out or purposeless blade movements or footwork, when his attention is distracted and his readiness for action is diminished. Such moments occur also when the opponent is, for example, preoccupied with planning the bout, or is distressed by its unsuccessful course."[4]

Raoul Cléry stated, "L'à propos... c'est l'art de profiler des inattentions ou des fautes adverses á l'instant précis ou elles se produisent." ("The sense of timing is the art of taking advantage of the opponent's inattention or mistakes at the precise moment when they occur.")[5]

Professor Leon Bertrand, in his *Cut and Thrust,* describes timing in slightly more detail, and in combination with other elements. He advises that, in the construction of attacks, the fencer should employ three essentials:

> "What the Italians call *'scelta di tempo'*—choice of time, judgment of distance and speed. They are three further lodes in the main stratum. The first is by far the most important of the three. Assuming the possession of the highest technique, the sabreur stands or falls by the presence or lack of this vital sense. Choice of time means the selection of the psychological moment to launch the offensive, it means executing the movement when your opponent is unprepared or least expects it. That is choice of time in its broadest significance. The final definition of 'scelta di tempo' is the seizing of the precise fraction of a second to move at the slightest sign of mental irresolution on the part of your rival. He may be keyed up to the highest pitch of concentration yet that fractional measure of time must come when, by some movement or thought, that concentration wavers. This lapse must be reflected by some sign, infinitesimal perhaps, but it is your 'cue', your signal, and on this golden opportunity you must act immediately. If we could imagine a highly sensitive machine registering a graph of your adversary's mental concentration, we should visualise an undulating line and we should attack with every downward turn of the pen, with the recording of each depression."[6]

Generally it is accepted that when a fencer catches his opponent by surprise, when the opponent is off balance and not fully concentrated, that fencer has chosen the right "tempo." Everybody knows that it is extremely difficult to sustain the highest concentration of attention for a very long time, and, invariably, lapses of attention occur in a bout: a fencer, concentrating on his own attack, may forget about his defense; a competitor, maneuvering on the strip, may expose himself dangerously to his opponent's action; a fencer, executing blade movements, may open certain lines of his target—such and similar situations may be taken advantage of for surprise action. The ability to recognize and instantly take advantage of such situations is usually inborn, but it may be further developed by special exercises, and constitutes the "sixth sense" of a fencer.

When describing the clever seizing of an opportunity to score a hit, and in the majority of definitions (see above), the expressions "moment" and "time" are commonly used. Even the names given to the "sixth sense" of a fencer by various fencing schools are closely connected with the conception of time. And yet it is very obvious that this is not a question of mere time. The opportune application of an action in a bout, taking the opponent unawares, is closely connected with many factors of the tactical situation, such as distance, the movements of the two fencers, the opponent's state of attention, etc.

"Timing" or a fencer's "sense of surprise" may be, perhaps, a little more exactly described as perceiving, based on lightning-speed assessment of the situation, the opportunity to score a hit (convenient distance, careless movements by the opponent, signs of the opponent's inattention or that he is preparing to launch an attack, etc.) and taking immediate advantage of it.

A fencer may take advantage of potentially suitable situations or he may, himself, create situations suitable to his purpose by the use of carefully chosen and executed preparatory actions.

My suggested definition above, like all attempts at simple definitions of complicated phenomena, is inadequate. In order to better understand *"scelta di tempo"*—so complex and difficult to define and yet so important in fencing—we have to discuss it more fully, on the base of personal experience as competitor and coach, observation of many tournaments, reflections, and literature.

The right *choice of time,* using the expression in the accepted English (since I know no better expression in English), means, in a very broad sense: to surprise, to attack the opponent unaware, to make a surprise action, to take by surprise, etc.

Professor Tadeusz Kotarbinski, one of the creators of praxeology, in his general theory of conflict, when discussing surprise, states, "We may assume that taking the opponent unaware derives its technical value from anticipation and from misleading the opponent or, at least, from taking advantage of the opponent's mistakes or lack of knowledge" (this last part meaning lack of information or inadequate appreciation of the situation).[7]

Let us now analyze this element in a fencing bout. Since a tactical intention (task, resolution, solution) has chances of success only when it is executed in the right time (Greek, *"kairos;"* French, *"l'à propos;"* Russian, "moment") and is adequate to a given situation, it is obvious that it is very important

1. To be able to seize the opportunity to launch an attack or any other action.

2. To display psychological resistance in view of the opponent's sudden attack.

Every manifestation of "sense of surprise" ("timing," "sense of tempo"), understood as an opportunity to score a hit, has two aspects:

1. A situation—a complex of conditions—that gives possibilities of receiving a hit (being caught unawares, being taken by surprise, being attacked when one least expects it). This might be called "negative timing" or "negative surprise."

2. A situation favorable to scoring a hit (catching the opponent by surprise, catching the opponent unawares). This might be called "positive timing" or "positive surprise."

Neither positive nor negative timing occurs separately. In a fight they occur as two aspects of the same situation, comprising both external and psychological factors. What is "positive" for one fencer is "negative" for his opponent, and vice versa.

Full and successful application of the right timing ("positive surprise"; taking the opponent unawares)—i.e., scoring a hit—may happen only with the occurrence of an adequate complex of various factors such as attention, distance, speed, accurate and fast perception, quick decision, appropriate choice of action and it efficacious execution, etc.

The sense for "fencing surprise" is inborn but, under the influence of training, it improves in that:

1. The ability to recognize and take advantage of appropriate situations increases with practice and experience,

2. Resistance to the opponent's surprise actions is also increased.

"Negative surprise" often leads to a temporary loss of technique, both in standard of execution and repertoire of strokes. A high degree of fencing skill, good automatization and variety of sensory-motor skills (motor habit patterns), and ease of application of technique, are fundamental factors in increasing a fencer's psychological and technical resistance to "negative surprise." By developing, in the course of training, technical prowess, technical-tactical capabilities, specific fitness and coordination, accuracy of perception, speed of reaction and movements, one, at the same time, shapes "sense of fencing surprise"—choice of time.

In an attempt to penetrate more deeply into the phenomenon of "timing" let us try to classify it.

A competitor who "picks up" the initiative and begins a movement may create a situation in which he falls into "negative time" and receives a hit or, to the contrary, the same fencer who initiates the development of a certain tactical situation may create for himself the advantage of "positive time," and so score a hit.

Among the manifestations of "fencing surprise" are situations in which:

1. A competitor, usually when defending himself, takes advantage of a situation which has arisen, mostly on the opponent's initiative;

2. The situation giving rise to the "fencing surprise" is created by the fencer (mostly attacker), who imposes his movements and initiative.

We can further differentiate the ways in which a competitor perceives and assesses the tactical situation as: a) visual, b) tactile, c) kinesthetic, or d) auditory. In assessing a situation, not only is one receptor, but several, are involved to varying degrees (e.g., not only touch, but touch and sight and kinaesthetic sense; not only sight, but sight and hearing). For example,

- In the execution of parry-riposte, a very important role is played by tactile sensation, but under the control of sight;

- When timing the beginning of an attack to the movement of the opponent's feet, not only sight, but hearing the rhythm of steps plays a large part.

Usually, however, one sense plays a dominant role in the perception of a particular situation.

Luigi Barbasetti—the famous Italian master at the turn of the 20th Century who produced hundreds of fencing masters and greatly influenced European fencing—differentiated two kinds of sense of surprise: "physical tempo" and "psychological tempo." Physical tempo means extremely fast assessment of the situation, based on watching the external situation (e.g., the opponent's movements, distance, and his weapon movements). Psychological tempo, however, is based on noticing the signs that reflect the opponent's state of mind—signs of: a temporary lowering of attention; hesitation; concentration on preparing an attack; etc. Barbasetti thought that psychological tempo was inborn and could not be changed, and that physical tempo could be improved by various exercises. In my opinion, "psychological tempo," although very difficult to develop, may be, and very often is—like various kinds of motor response—improved by carefully and intelligently chosen exercises. There are some fencers who practically can "read" the opponent's mind and assess his state of concentration. This helps the fencer very much in taking the opponent by surprise.[8]

The most important factors concerning "fencing surprise" can be summarised in the following concise points:

- In our discussion on "fencing surprise," instead of time and moment, we have stressed the importance of a complex tactical situation, comprising many various factors (which, like all material phenomena, take place in time).

- "Sense of surprise" is an integral part of any bout, and an essential factor in the result of the bout.
- "Sense of surprise," "sense of timing," is inborn but should be cultivated in fencers, by perfecting technique, motor responses, and tactics together.

The conscious strengthening of a fencer's resistance to unexpected and dangerous situations, requires a high automatization of movement—a very high degree of acquisition of sensory-motor skills. Thanks to this, a fencer need not concentrate his attention on how to execute a given movement or set of movements, but rather on which movement or set of movements to choose in a given situation.

The constant tempo and character of movements (rhythm, direction, amplitude, and speed) makes the correct assessment of the situation, and choice of counter-action, comparatively easy. Every change in rhythm, speed, strength, and amplitude of movements, interferes with the correct assessment of the tactical situation. This causes the decision to be either delayed or incorrect. The most important factor in taking an opponent by surprise is change of rhythm and speed. This is why—although it may sound paradoxical—good reaction to a moving object is a sign of a fencer's talent and good form.

The above is probably connected with various processes of inhibition and excitation in the brain cortex and requires further and detailed study by physiologists and psychologists.

References

[1] Battesti, P., Prost, L.: *Traité d'Escrime – Fleuret.* INS, Paris 1963
[2] Laskowski, K.: *Sportowa szermierka na bagnety.* GKKF, Warszawa 1951,
[3] Kevey, J.: *Szermierka na szable.* GKKF, Warszawa 1951.
[4] Ozoray-Szenker, Z.: *Szermierka na szable.* Sport i Turystyka, Warszawa 1952,
[5] Cléry, R.: *L'Escrime aux trois Armes.* Amphora, Paris 1965,
[6] Bertrand, L.: *Cut and Thrust.* Athletic Publications, London 1927,
[7] Kotarbinski, T.: "Z zagadnien ogólnej teorii walki," in: *Haslo dobrej roboty.* Wiedza Powszechna, Warszawa 1968, p. 54
[8] Barbasetti, L.: *Das Stossfechten,* Wilhelm Breumüller: Wien und Leipzig, 1900

5. Elementary Conception of Motor Responses in Fencing

"A tennis player may have highly efficient techniques but may lack skill in tennis because he does not perceive the right moment to use those techniques. A skilled footballer, or any other games player, must take action which is appropriate; and therefore the skill involves interpreting the needs of the situation and making the right decision, as well as carrying out the necessary movements. In games, decision making is a vital part of the skill."

--Barbara Knapp

"At every instant the motor activity must be related by, and appropriate to the external situation. . . what is learned is not a series of individual acts. . . what we learn at tennis is not a set of strokes but how to make strokes appropriate to the moment."

--Barbara Knapp

INTRODUCTION

All physical exercises, movements, strokes, and actions which are the form and content of various disciplines of sport, display certain traits which are characteristic of conscious, voluntary activity. Such activity occurs most often in the form of sensory-motor response—commonly called reaction.

Simple reaction is a responsive action: it is a reply in which one knows or foresees a stimulus which is about to occur and for which one prepares an adequate response in a specific way. Take, for example, the sprinter's start. The athlete knows the aim of his movements, he knows how to execute them, and he knows the stimulus. He is waiting for the stimulus: the pistol shot. To this known signal, he responds with a well-known, well-learned, and often-repeated movement—the start. Another example of simple reaction: in a sabre lesson, the fencing master commands, "On my opening—change of position from quinte to seconde—you execute direct cut to head." The beginning of the fencing master's movement acts as a signal for the execution of the cut to the head.

Before I go into further discussion on sensory-motor responses and their application in fencing, I shall try to present a simplified scheme of the most important processes of reaction (Figure 5.1).

The structure of reaction consists of:

1. Receiving a known conventional stimulus (signal).
2. Appreciation, or realisation, of the stimulus.
3. Execution of the appropriate movements.

We can distinguish three periods of sensory-motor response:

1. Preparatory period, which contains: a) waiting for the stimulus and b) preparation for an appropriate movement.
2. Latent, or central, period.
3. Executive, or final, period.

The latent period of reaction, lasting from the appearance of the stimulus to the beginning of the action, takes a very short time but it is very important, indeed. It strongly influences the speed and manner of execution of a movement or action. The athlete is still immobile, but very dynamic and important processes are taking place in his brain cortex.

The latent period may be divided into:

1. Sensory part of the latent period of reaction: receiving the stimulus (signal).
2. Associative part of the latent period: realisation that this is the stimulus for action.

3. Motor part of latent period: excitation of the motor area of the cortex and a flow of motor impulses along the nerves to the appropriate muscles.

The executive (or final) period of reaction consists of the time from the beginning of the movement (action) to its completion. It is visible and therefore appears, to a superficial observer, to be the most important phase. It should be understood, however, that the actual movement is prepared by, and depends on, the first and second periods of reaction.

A motor response is a sensory-motor skill (motor habit), executed and applied as a reaction to a stimulus. Figure 5.1 depicts a simple model of a sensory-motor response.

Fig. 5.1 – A Model of a Sensory-Motor Response

Preparatory Period	Latent Period	Executory Period (Executiion of a Given Stroke)

The preparatory period lasts from the signal, "attention" (or situation which causes an increase of attention), to the appearance of the stimulus. The latent period lasts from the appearance of stimulus to the beginning of movement. The executory period lasts from the beginning of movement to its completion. When we say "reaction time," we mean the time of the latent period. The time of motor response comprises the time of the latent period and the time of the execution of the movement.

Most authors distinguish and describe only simple, choice, and differential reaction. In my opinion, however, we must distinguish seven varieties of motor responses: simple reaction, choice reaction, differential reaction, reaction to a moving object, switch-over reaction, intuitive reaction, and reaction to a pre-signal. All these varieties of motor responses are very important in fencing and other combat sports, as well as in team games. In fencing, they form the basis of various technical-tactical capabilities, like control of distance and choice of footwork, recognition of the threatened line, choice between parry and stop-hit, choice of the appropriate parry, intuitive choice of an action, and the ability to change one's intention during a foreseen action as a reply to the opponent's unexpected movement, etc. The most important varieties are: simple motor response and choice motor response.

SIMPLE MOTOR RESPONSE

The essence of simple reaction is: a known, foreseen stimulus/a known, foreseen response. For example: in a laboratory, on the appearance of a red light, you must press a button; in a fencing lesson, when the coach announces, "On my step forward (the known, expected stimulus), you execute direct attack with lunge (foreseen response)"; in a fencing bout, when one expects or provokes a given movement by the opponent and reacts to it with a previously foreseen and planned action.

Figure 5.2 shows the structure and essence of simple reaction.

In simple motor response, the process of reaction is not very complicated. There is only one well-known stimulus (signal) to which one replies with one well-known foreseen movement. In the preparatory part of simple response, two important psychological processes occur: a) waiting for the expected stimulus (signal) and b) preparing the reply: motor program of a foreseen action.

By careful observation and laboratory experiments, it has been found that there are three main types of simple motor response:

Fig. 5.2 – A Model of Simple Sensory-Motor Response

1 | A	2 | B	3 | C
Waiting for an Expected Stimulus	a b c	Execution of a Foreseen Movement

1 Signal, "Attention!" "Ready!" or change of external situation which causes a higher demand of attention.
2 Appearance of the stimulus.
3 Beginning of the movement/action.
A Preparatory period.
B Latent (central) period.
C Executory (final) period.
a Sensory part of the latent period (noticing the stimulus).
b Associative part of a latent period (recognizing the expected stimulus—"This is the cue we were waiting for!").
c Motor part of the latent period (sending executory motor impulses to muscles).

the differences lie in the preparatory period. The noted differences have an impact on the latent and executory periods of reaction and—above all—on the duration of the latent period.

1. Sensory type of motor response

During the preparatory period, the athlete concentrates, above all, on perceiving the signal (e.g., the sprinter waiting for the pistol shot or a fencer waiting for the expected movement of his opponent's blade.)

Waiting for the signal stimulates those parts of the brain cortex which are concerned with analysis of auditory stimuli (sprinter) or visual and tactile stimuli (fencer). Other areas of the cortex—among others, the motor areas—are very faintly active or slightly inhibited. The athlete, concentrating all his attention on waiting for the signal, is not well prepared for a speedy, energetic and well-coordinated execution of a given action since, as stated above, the motor areas of his brain cortex are slightly inhibited. The duration of the latent period in a sensory type of reaction lasts from 160 to 170 thousandths of a second.

2. Motor type of motor response

During the preparatory period, the whole attention of the fencer, boxer, etc. is concentrated on preparing the execution of the foreseen action. The excitation which occurs in the auditory or visual receptor is very quickly transmitted to the part of the brain where analysis is made, and from there it goes to the association centers. When it comes to the motor area of the brain cortex (the motor program being already well-prepared), the impulses go very quickly through to the effector organs—the muscles. These reactions have the shortest latent period, lasting from 100 to 125 thousandths of a second.

These types of reaction, however, have a certain drawback because, not infrequently, mistakes occur. The athlete, by mistake, takes another stimulus for the one he is awaiting. That is why false starts or premature actions of the blade occur. For example, a fencer who is waiting for his opponent's attack and has prepared a parry-riposte (anticipated defensive action), mistakes a slight movement of his opponent's blade for the commencement of the attack and parries too early.

3. Intermediate type of motor response

Lastly, there exists a sort of mixed, intermediate type of reaction, when there is a certain equilibrium of excitatory and inhibitory processes in the sensory and motor parts of the cortex during the preparatory period. The fencer divides his attention between carefully watching for the appearance of the stimulus and preparing the motor program of the expected action. The latent period of such types of reaction take from 140 to 150 thousandths of a second.

In discussing the above reactions, times have been given for latent periods only. It is obvious, however, that the various types of electric apparatuses which measure the speed of a fencer's reaction when he reacts to a given signal (e.g., a light) by responding with a foreseen action (e.g., direct thrust with lunge)—simple reaction—are measuring the total time of motor response: that is, the latent period along with the executory period of reaction (execution of the lunge). Of course, in laboratories, there are many apparatuses which measure only the latent period of reaction. The famous "Magic Box"—invented by Master Geoff Hawksworth of Dukinfield and demonstrated at the fencing master courses in London some years ago—measures the time of latent and executory periods, together.

Choice Motor Response

Choice sensory-motor responses are those required when there is a possibility of many varied stimuli and many, or at least several, varied replies, and further, when we do not know which of the stimuli will act nor with which reply (which action) we should react to a given stimulus, because to each stimulus there may be a varied number of reactions. As I explain to my students, "We know all the answers—we just don't know which question will be asked."

Choice reactions are very important and they occur in all combat sports—like fencing, boxing, judo, wrestling—and in games like tennis, badminton, basketball, soccer, and volleyball.

A fencer acquires quite a large repertoire of the various sensory-motor skills (motor habits) of fencing actions—offensive, defensive, and counter-offensive—and, meeting his opponent on the piste, he usually knows what he should use, what style of fighting he should prepare against his opponent. He will base his general plan of action on his experience of meeting his opponent previously on the strip, or by observing the opponent's style of fencing. But what he does not know, and cannot know, is which action at a given moment his opponent will use. He, therefore, must observe his opponent's movements, preserving a general preparedness for action, and must be ready for a quick, precise and adequate response to his opponent's movements. This is why choice reactions should not resemble a motor type of simple reaction. One should not concentrate on preparing a motor programme of a given action because one does not know what the opponent will do; to every movement of the opponent, one must respond with a different counter-action.

Examples from practice may illustrate the difference between simple and choice reaction:

- A fencer notices that his opponent frequently uses a reverse (circular) beat as a preparatory movement. He resolves to derobe by counter-disengagement on the next beat. This is an example of a simple reaction used in a bout—a known stimulus with one foreseen reply.

- While preparing a defensive action, a fencer resolves "If my opponent attacks by a simple movement, I will parry. If he attacks using a compound attack, I will stop-hit." This is a choice reaction.

- The fencer has no idea what his opponent will do and, on the opponent's action, he chooses the appropriate counter-action. This is also a choice reaction.

The structure of choice reaction is more complicated than that of simple reaction because it differs considerably in both the preparatory and latent periods. In simple reaction, a fencer already knows in the preparatory period what action he will execute in the executory period; in choice reaction, on the other hand, the fencer chooses his reply only after the appearance of the signal (stimulus) and only then—in the latent period—does he choose the appropriate motor program.

In the preparatory period of choice reaction, there are two important processes:

a. A high level of attention and perception, trying to assess the development of the tactical situation and, above all, the opponent's movements, and

b. A general readiness for action (unlike simple reaction, not just waiting for one foreseen signal, but trying to be prepared for any situation).

In the latent period of choice reaction, we distinguish the following parts:

1. *Sensory phase* of choice reaction: noticing the (unforeseen) stimulus.

2. *Selecting the stimulus from others acting at the same time*: i.e., a fencer receives a constant stream of stimuli—watching his opponent's legs, weapon action, movement and general behaviour and, to a lessor degree, various external factors in his environment—and yet selects one particular movement which will be important to him as a signal for reaction.

3. *Recognising the selected signal* (closely connected to the previous part): the fencer classifies the selected signal as belonging to a certain group of actions which is usually connected with the secondary signalling system. This, of course, is not expressed in words but it is a split-second realisation of his opponent's intention (perception on a higher—conceptual-functional—level; not only perceiving, feeling, etc., as with a foreign language we do not understand, but perceiving and understanding what is going on).

4. *Differentiating stimuli and selecting the motor program of a chosen action*: the fencer has to distinguish one given signal from among others which are sometimes similar and act at the same time. This is very important for understanding a tactical situation and the opponent's intention—his plans—and, above all, for choosing an

adequate stroke. After recognising the opponent's movement, the fencer chooses the appropriate counter-action and selects, from a long-term memory store, the appropriate motor programme.

5. *Motor part of the latent period of choice reaction*: mobilisation and activation of the motor area of the brain cortex and the sending of appropriate motor impulses to the effector organs—the muscles.

Figure 5.3 illustrates choice reaction.

In a slightly simplified manner, we may say that in the latent period of choice reaction, there are the following parts:

1. Sensory part,
2. Selection of stimulus,
3. Recognition of stimulus,
4. Choice of stroke.
5. Motor part of latent period of reaction.

Figure 5.3—A Model of Choice Sensory Motor Response

	1	2
Watching the opponet; a high level of attention and perception; watching for stimuli. General readiness for action	a b c d e	Performing the chosen stroke

1 The appearance of an important stimulus (signal).
2 he beginning of the execution of a chosen stroke.
a Sensory part of choice reaction—reception of the stimulus.
b Isolating the stimulus from among others acting at the same time.
c Identification of the stimulus—qualifying it to a given group of actions.
d Perception of a given stimulus, in connection with other stimuli acting at the same time; assessment of the situation and understanding the opponent's intentions; choice of appropriate action; programming execution of the action.
e Motor part of choice reaction—sending motor impulses from brain to muscles.

As a result of the more complicated structure of the latent period of choice reaction, the time increases and is usually slightly more than 300 thousandths of a second. In a well-known activity, choice reaction lasts a comparatively short time and, with fencers of great competitive experience, the latent period of choice reaction is very short, indeed, and very often it is nearly as short as among competitors engaged in the sensory type of simple reaction.

It is worth remembering that simple reaction and choice reaction varies with different people, and it is not developed to same extent in each individual. There are fencers with very fast simple reactions and slow choice reactions, and vice versa. There are also fencers with both very slow simple and slow choice reactions.

Of course, the ideal for a fencer is to have fast simple and fast choice reactions. One example is Jerzy Pawlowski of Poland, Olympic sabre champion and winner of many medals in Olympic Games and World Champions. In his brilliant bouts, he took advantage of simple, choice, and other varieties of motor responses.

However, one can achieve very high results, indeed, with only average simple, but very fast choice reactions—provided one can adapt one's fencing style and tactics as the occasion requires. A very good example of a fencer whose great assets in fencing included very highly developed choice reactions was Jacob Rilsky of the USSR, who was three-time world sabre champion. Also, one may be very successful with fast simple reactions and average choice reactions: Polish foilist Witold Woyda—who won two gold medals at the Olympic Games in Munich and won many medals at World Championships and Olympic Games—based his tactics, to a large extent, on extreme speed of simple reaction and great speed of movement (in other words, very fast simple motor response).

Simple and choice responses must be carefully distinguished from simple and compound actions. A compound action may be a simple reaction—for example, when a fencer executes a compound attack on a signal which he was expecting, such as a "one-two" (attack by feint of disengagement-disengagement) executed on his opponent's expected pressure on the blade. Conversely, choice reaction may result in a simple action selected from several possible movements in answer to an unforeseen stimulus.

Fencing masters, stressing the importance of speed in fencing, often use the expression "speed of reaction" and "speed of execution" (or "speed of movement"). It is obvious that, by "speed of reaction," they really mean length of the latent period of reaction; and, by "speed of execution", they mean the length of the executory period of reaction.

Other Varieties of Motor Responses

As I have mentioned above, there are other varieties—apart from simple and choice—of sensory-motor responses—all very important in fencing bouts, forming the basis of technical-tactical abilities.

Other than simple and choice reaction, we may distinguish the following sensory-motor responses:

1. *Differential reaction* – when one has to differentiate between stimuli which are very similar to each other, and act accordingly.

2. *Reaction to a moving object* – This is not only important in tennis, soccer, volleyball, etc., but also in fencing; one assesses the trajectory and speed of a given object—soccer ball, tennis ball, epee, etc.—and reacts at the appropriate moment—not too early and not too late. This is why, in fencing, change of rhythm and, especially, acceleration of the final part of an attack is so very important and constitutes an important factor of taking the opponent by surprise (timing, *l'à propos*).

3. *Switch-over reaction* – change of a preconceived action during its execution as a reaction to the opponent's unexpected movement.

4. *Intuitive reaction*—a sensory-motor response based on "statistical intuition."

5. *Reaction to a pre-signal*—reacting, not to the opponent's final movement, but to a "pre-signal"—when the opponent, by a certain gesture or change of position, betrays his intention.

All varieties of sensory-motor reactions are concisely presented in Table 5-A.

Figure 5.4 presents the essentials of reaction to a pre-signal.

Fig. 5.4 – A Model of Sensory-Motor Response to a Pre-signal

1 2 3 4

Waiting for the movement of the attack. Preparing the parry.		Executing the movement (parry)
Preparatory Period	Latent Period	Executory Period

1. Signal, "attention," or change of situation which stimulates the fencer's attention and vigilance.
2. Appearance of pre-signal (change of position, unwitting betrayal of opponent's own intention).
3. Appearance of "proper" stimulus (in this case, the opponent's attack).
4. Beginning of movement; the fencer—sometimes not fully consciously—begins to parry, as a reaction to the pre-signal, before his opponent really starts the attacking movement.

It is obvious that when a fencer reacts to a pre-signal, he starts his movement earlier than if he had reacted to the "real" stimulus. It should be noted that the beginning of the movement is earlier, though the latent period takes the same time, because the latent period starts sooner—before the "real" signal.

All the varieties of sensory motor responses are described in more detail in Chapter 15.

Being surprised is a privilege of youth. Yet—in spite of my "advanced" age—it never ceases to astonish me that many coaches, in individual lessons and other exercises, only pay attention to, and teach, how to quickly and correctly execute a given fencing stroke. They are completely oblivious to the fact that the speed, accuracy and success of a fencing action depends, not only on the executory period, but also—and to a large extent—on the preparatory and latent periods of sensory-motor response.

For example,

1. A very accurate, fast, and well-chosen fencing action is not good and not effective if it is started too late (bad perception, long latent period of reaction).

2. A fast and accurate movement which is started early is also to no avail if it is inappropriately chosen. If, for example, my opponent executes an attack—cut to head with lunge—and I, very early, quickly, and beautifully, take parry two (wrong choice of action), I shall, of course, be hit.

3. A well-chosen and early-started action—even if it is slightly slow—may be successful (fast reaction—short period of latent period).

So, it is obvious (and obvious things—as I often say—are the most difficult to notice) that the fencing master and pupil should pay attention to all three periods of sensory-motor response, i.e., early and correct perception of stimulus, fast choice of appropriate action, and early, fast and correct execution of the action.

Table 5-A – Main Varieties of Sensory-Motor Responses

Variety of Response	***Essence of Response***	***Situation in a Lesson***	***Situation in a Bout***
Simple Reactions	Known signal or stimulus—known response: known and foreseen action as reply to expected movement.	Execution of a given stroke as a response to coach's previously-announced movement.	Fencer expects a certain movement from the opponent, having a prepared motor program of the response.
Choice Reactions	Unknown sig-nal—pupil responds appropriately: pupil does not ("We know all the answers, but not which question will be asked.").	Choosing from previously-announced and previously unannounced actions.	Fencer responds to the opponent's unexpected offensive movements or adapts his offensive actions to the opponent's defensive actions, foreseen actions and partly foreseen actions.
Differential Reactions	Differentiating between very similar stimuli	For example: on coach's false preparatory attack, pupil disregards; on real attack, parries; on correctly executed head cut, parries; on head cut with hand raised—stop cut.	Fencer assesses whether attack is real or false, simple or compound—whether the cut is executed correctly or with exposed arm.
Reactions to a Moving Object	Perceiving and anticipating the trajectory and speed of a moving object (in fencing, the opponent's weapon)	Learning and perfecting orientation in space and time.	Fencer foresees the path of the opponent's weapon and reactions——for example, parry or beat— at the appropriate time: not too early or too late.
Switch-over Reaction	Change of original intention while executing a foreseen (first or second intention) action, in reply to the opponent's unexpected movement.	The pupil practices foreseen attack (or other actions) and the coach, from time to time, changes his predicted	For example: the fencer wants to hit the opponent with a feint attack, but the opponent unexpectedly stop-hits instead of parrying; the fencer then changes his original intention and applies counter-time.

Variety of Response	Essence of Response	Situation in a Lesson	Situation in a Bout
Reactions to a Moving Object	Perceiving and anticipating the trajectory and speed of a moving object (in fencing, the opponent's weapon)	Learning and perfecting orientation in space and time.	Fencer foresees the path of the opponent's weapon and reactions——for example, parry or beat— at the appropriate time: not too early or too late.
Switch-over Reaction	Change of original intention while executing a foreseen (first or second intention) action, in reply to the opponent's unexpected movement.	The pupil practices foreseen attack (or other actions) and the coach, from time to time, changes his predicted	For example: the fencer wants to hit the opponent with a feint attack, but the opponent unexpectedly stop-hits instead of parrying; the fencer then changes his original intention and applies counter-time.
Reaction to Pre-signal	The pupil does not react to a "real" signal/ stimulus, but to a pre-signal (e.g. preliminary movement, change of position, unwitting betrayal of the opponent's own intention).	For example: attack on the coach's "careless" movement, betraying the desire to start an attack.	For example: the fencer executes a fast attack in the moment when his opponent, by an unnecessary movement, betrays his own intention of launching in attack.
Intuitive Reaction	A response based on "statistical intuition".	Exercises "lottery à la Borsodyi" (see Chapter 15).	The fencer makes decisions, not so much based on observation or very penetrative perception of opponent's movement, but based on not fully conscious intuitive mental-emotional processes shaped by hundreds of similar situations in practice and competition.

6. Motivation and Arousal in Fencing

"Motivation is a basic factor of rational and goal directed activity."
--Tadeusz Ulatowski

"Motivation does not bring results unless a person realizes the aim of the activity and the practical means of achieving the goal."
--Wlodzimierz Szewczuk

BASIC INFORMATION ABOUT MOTIVATION AND AROUSAL

"Tenez votre fleuret comme vous tiendrez un oiseau: pas trop fort pour ne pas l'étouffer, assez fort tout de même pour ne pas le laisser s'échapper."
"Hold your foil as if you were holding a bird in your hand: not too hard, so as not to choke it, but at the same time hard enough, so as not to let it escape."
--Justin Lafaugère

If one had to enumerate the most characteristic features of modern, top-level sport, one could probably point out: 1) strict specialization in a given branch, or event, of a sport (in fencing, one chosen weapon); 2) profound individualization of training; 3) the ever-increasing role of competition and the drive to achieve the highest possible results; 4) the increased role and number of sporting events.

Considering the increased role of competition—the struggle for better and better results, the increased number of big international events, and the ever-increasing prestige attached to Olympic and World Championship medals—it is a small wonder that all leading coaches, including fencing masters, try to discover and analyze not yet fully-exploited factors and aspects of training in order to increase its quality and effectiveness.

I would add here that the increased effectiveness of training seems particularly important nowadays, since it is difficult to achieve better results by a mere increase of the time devoted to training or an increase of general training loads. The problem is, then, to increase the effectiveness of training—in other words, to do more, and do it better, in the same amount of time.

The contents, speed, and precision of training; the retention of learning in the process of training; the competitor's preparedness, participation and results in competition—in other words, all of a fencer's activities—are influenced by an immense number of factors, such as: age and sex; state of health and basic capacity for effort; certain psychological dispositions; energy fitness and coordination abilities; the range of sensory-motor skills (motor habit patterns) acquired in childhood; approach to the sport; training and fighting; knowledge of results at a particular stage of training; forms, methods, and choices of exercises applied in training; successes and disappointments, victories and defeats; dimensions of personality, various traits of temperament; organization and conditions of training; level of the fencing master's knowledge and his practical abilities; and many, many others.

However, among all the factors very markedly influencing the effectiveness of training and the results achieved in competition, one must especially mention motivation and arousal.

Motivation includes the totality of our motives—factors which drive us to a certain activity (ambition; the desire to do something, to achieve something; the striving to achieve a goal; the desire to fulfill certain needs). Motivation—connected, above all, with fulfilling different needs—influences our behavior, activities, and attitudes.

Arousal means a state of activation of the central nervous system (especially the brain cortex), autonomous nervous system, and the organism as a whole. Richard H. Cox writes,

> To understand arousal is to understand what basic changes take place in the body when the organism is activated. When we speak of arousal, we are talking about the degree of activation of the organs that are under the control of the autonomic nervous system.[1]

In activation, a vital role is played by the cerebral cortex, hypothalamus, and reticular formation. Arousal may be understood as a continuum that ranges from from deep sleep (a very low level of arousal) to an extreme state of excitement (a very high level of arousal).

It has been proven beyond any doubt that for efficient activity—perceiving, thinking, remembering, learning, performing, decision-taking—an optimal level of arousal of the entire brain cortex (and not only the sensory part, to which impulses from receptors arrive) is vital. This is achieved in the following way: part of the sensory impulses from receptors to the brain, pass through the reticular formation; here they undergo a certain "transformation" and, thus "transformed," they activate the entire cortical matter.

Extroverts differ from introverts with respect to achieving optimum arousal.

In extroverted subjects, the reticular formation has a certain inhibitory action, and thus the cortex is often not activated enough. In order to raise the arousal of their cortical matter, extroverts are always stimulus-hungry, very lively, very active, talkative, noisy, and fond of changes.

An introvert's reticular formation promotes a flow of impulses into the entire area of the cortical matter, which can lead to a high level of arousal. So, introverts—contrary to extroverts—try to avoid a large amount of stimuli, are not very talkative, not very lively, and avoid noisy company in order to preserve their optimal levels of arousal.

Extroverts and introverts form a very important issue in sport—concerning, especially, the principle of individualization, communication between pupil and coach, motivation, education, teaching-learning technique and tactics, performance at competitions, etc. I hope to discuss this subject in detail in my next book which—with the help of the gods—I will publish in the US.

The effects of various levels of arousal and motivation are so similar that some authors equate these two terms. This is not quite correct: motivation is a psychological process, and it is directed toward fulfilling certain needs connected with cognitive and emotional processes. Arousal, on the other hand, is a physiological process, and it is not directed: the same external signs of arousal—like palpitation, increased blood pressure, increased heart rate, sweating, trembling, etc.—occur in different situations. Arousal may be the same, irrespective of the contents of motivation.

Nevertheless, in the great majority of cases, with an increase of motivation comes an increase of the level of arousal. One may even say that the effects of arousal and motivation are, mostly, very much the same (see below). An extremely high level of motivation generally produces a very high level of excitation—but as I have mentioned above, not always.

For example:

- A surgeon performs a very complicated operation on a very important person. His motivation to perform it successfully is extremely high, and yet he tries, and manages, to keep his level of arousal relatively low, knowing very well that too-high arousal would negatively affect his skill, and consequently, the final result of the operation.

- Similarly, a top-class fencer is fighting for the gold medal. His level of motivation, desire to win, ambition, and motivation for success are extremely high, and yet he must manage to keep his level of arousal on a lower level.

In spite of their immense value in training, many fencing masters and competitors often do not understand the significance and role, or the mechanisms and effects, of motivation and arousal in training and competition. As a result, they may commit many errors in teaching, learning, coaching, and competing.

Motivation, stating it simply once more, is a set of drives connected with definite values and needs, stimulating human beings towards activity in a certain direction, to achieve a certain goal.

One may distinguish positive motivation, (the desire to learn, to win, to achieve something) from negative motivation (trying to avoid something, being afraid of defeat or failure, etc.).

Motives may be either inborn (like all physiological needs) or acquired (like psychological and social needs). We may also distinguish physiological motives (the desire to fulfil physiological needs like sleeping, eating, drinking, having sex, etc.) from sociopsychological motives (the need for domination or submission; the need of affiliation, friendship, recognition, achievement, an active life, etc.).

Motives may also be fully conscious and recognized (the person understands and knows exactly what he needs and wants to attain) or not fully realized, subconscious motives (e.g., a coach tries to be very domineering, very sharp—he gives a string of orders, often shouting; he likes to punish his pupils; etc.—saying that he does it for the good of his pupils, while, in reality, he is—without fully realizing it—trying to compensate for an inferiority complex, lack of self-confidence, and, sometimes, laziness).

Taking another set of criteria of classification, we may distinguish—and this is of extreme importance—intrinsic from extrinsic motivation. Intrinsic motivation means that we want to do something (e.g., reading, learning, swimming, fencing, working in a garden) because it satisfies us, gives us pleasure and we think it is good and beneficial for us. Extrinsic motivation means that we do something, not so much for its own sake, but because we have to, or because we expect some gain—money, rewards, security, prizes, recognition, etc.—that will provide us with satisfaction.

A student may study very hard because he loves his studies and wants to increase his knowledge (intrinsic motivation), or he may study in order to pass his exams, obtain a grant or scholarship (extrinsic motivation), or get a good job. Many people play tennis, swim, run, or fence, for fun, fitness, health, and enjoyment (intrinsic motivation), and some cultivate the same activities professionally, to make a living (extrinsic motivation).

Usually, the effects of intrinsic motivation, apart from sheer pleasure, are positive. We do something much better (exactly, effectively, successively, and without undue fatigue) when it is what we like, what gives us pleasure. For example, a musician who loves the violin may practice and play for hours without feeling fatigue—on the contrary, being very satisfied and in an excellent mood. Einstein, apart from many hours of heavy work as a scientist, spent many hours playing violin, sailing, and walking in the mountains; and was not tired. On the contrary, these activities gave him great pleasure, a feeling of fitness, energy, and optimism. The effectiveness of compulsory activity is usually less positive.

Some readers may protest, giving examples of outstanding professional tennis, basketball, or soccer players, who cultivate these sports for enormous amounts of money. Here I have to explain that we distinguish—and this, again, is very important—two functions of extrinsic motivation: one is positive and one is negative—the informative function and the control function.

The informative function of extrinsic motivation means that money, awards, and publicity, "inform" the athlete, coach, club, press, and public about the talent, efforts, success and achievements of a given athlete.

The control function of extrinsic motivation means that the athlete is forced to train very hard, to attend various training camps, and to take part in many competitions, because he is obliged to, he is paid for it, and he has to obey orders. His activities and actions become externally directed and controlled; he ceases to be his own master. This function of extrinsic motivation has a definite negative influence on human dignity, personality, and competition results.

The best combination is strong intrinsic motivation *supported by* the informative function of extrinsic motivation. This set of motives occurs among well-known, top-class, professional athletes.

The salient features and assets of intrinsic motivation, and the resulting activity, can be briefly summed up as follows:

a. Activity (exercises, competitions, and everything connected with fencing) that is influenced by intrinsic motivation forms a source of pleasure, joy, and satisfaction.

b. One does, efficiently and eagerly, what one likes and what gives one pleasure.

c. Intrinsic motivation encourages activity; it is conducive to a deep and many-sided analysis of our possibilities, training, results in competitions, etc., and gives insight to new and more efficient ways of solving the problems connect with cultivating fencing.

Even a very high level of intrinsic motivation does not always diminish the efficacy and results of our activities. A high level of intrinsic motivation may not lead to too high a level of arousal.

1. Intrinsic motivation diminishes the perception of fatigue and helps the process of recovery after heavy effort.

2. Intrinsic motivation leads to a high level of interest in one's sport (cognitive factor) and a

love of one's sport (emotional factor)—which influence each other positively, increasing, at the same time, concentration and selectivity of attention.

Summing up the value and meaning of intrinsic and extrinsic motivation, we should state that: The most efficacious and socially valuable motivation is intrinsic motivation.

In high-level competitive sport and in professional sport, good results are created by a combination of intrinsic motivation with the informative function of extrinsic motivation.

However, the control function of extrinsic motivation does not produce good results and its social and educational value is very low.

It should be stressed that there is a great diversity of motives for cultivating sport. An immense number of different factors attract people to sport: the desire to be successful, to display one's value, to gain social recognition; the sheer pleasure of movement and effort; the fascination with a given discipline of sport; the promotion of health; the maintanence and development of motor fitness; the contact with water, snow, forests, and mountains; the social contact; and finally, the satisfaction of many different (often not fully-conscious) socio-psychological needs, like domination, friendship, aggressiveness, affiliation, etc.

One can notice marked differences of motives between people cultivating high-competitive sport (element of fight, rivalry, recognition, success, achievement) and those cultivating recreational sport (active rest, joy of movement, psychological relaxation, promotion of health and fitness, social contact). The results of a great deal of research seem to indicate that, in the cultivation of sport—especially the high-competitive variety—the most important factors are socio-psychological.

Human behavior is usually multi-motivational (stimulated by many different motives)—meaning that one activity may, at the same time, satisfy several needs, which may be biological (need for food, drink, oxygen, reproduction, etc.), psychological (need for affection, for domination, for belonging, etc.) or social (need for achievement, recognition, cooperation, productive work, etc.). For example, a simple activity as attending a big dinner not only satisfies our basic biological need for food and drink, but also our need for meeting interesting people, exchanging ideas, relaxing, talking, enjoying good wine, discussing training and competitions, etc.

Likewise, there may be many motives which attract a person to cultivate fencing: sheer pleasure of physical activity and effort; desire to be fit, strong and fast; the need for recognition; desire for an outlet for aggression; a competitive attitude and desire to compare oneself with others; self-realisation and the need to develop one's personality; fascination with the history of fencing and its athletic modern version of today; desire for self-esteem and higher social status; etc.

Motivation plays a particularly important part in a fencer's activity—both in training and competition, as previously mentioned. A fencing master who does not understand the influence of motivation on our activity, and the effect of motivation on the level of performance, may, and usually does, commit many serious mistakes in his teaching and coaching.

At competitions, one can often see a coach exciting his pupil to produce extra effort, exclaiming, "Come on, you have to score one more hit!" "We need you to win!" "We are counting on you!" etc. This usually has a bad effect on a competitor who is already very highly motivated, nervous, and anxious, and sometimes in a state of panic (when, for example, the last hit decides his, or his team's, victory, or his advancement to the final). Such "advice" increases the intensity of a fencer's motivation and arousal, far beyond its optimal point (see below) and does more harm that good.

For many years, many scientists did extensive research and conducted many tests, trying to assess the influence of motivation and arousal on the efficacy of human activity (see below). Before I present the famous laws of Yerkes and Dodson, and other views on motivation and arousal, I will present the results of observations and empirical experience of some thoughtful and prominent coaches.

A high level of arousal and motivation has a negative influence on the efficacy of activity, when:

- The movements, sensory-motor skills, and capabilities are still not fully acquired;
- The acquired motor skills and capabilities are difficult, complicated, and demand particular accuracy of

execution, and fast and accurate perception of many external stimuli;

- The movements require particularly precise control of speed, strength, differentiation of rhythm, and hand "stability" (e.g., watchmaker, surgeon, marksman, archer, fencer);

- There is a need for lightning-speed choice of action in the quickly changing and unpredicted situations of a fight or game (choice motor responses, open motor skills; in combat sports, athletic games, etc.);

- The competitor already feels pre-competition fever, competition anxiety; there are fear-producing stressful situations, a high motive of avoiding failure, fear of defeat, high prestige and value of the competition, a great feeling of responsibility for the result;

- In such cases of too-high motivation and arousal, to demand a higher effort, to excite an already overexcited competitor, to throw a cascade of advice and shout meaningless slogans is a sign of—excusez le mot—sheer stupidity.

The positive influence of a high level of motivation and arousal occurs when:

- The application of large amounts of strength, especially power (strength plus speed) is necessary (e.g., weightlifting);

- Sensory-motor skills and technical-tactical capabilities are perfectly mastered and "easy" for a given athlete;

- The application of high speed—especially in simple motor responses—is necessary;

- The athlete must perform certain closed (intrinsic) sensory-motor skills of motor type.

I. THE YERKES-DODSON LAWS OF MOTIVATION AND AROUSAL

Early in the previous century, two American psychologists, Yerkes and Dodson, conducted extensive research by performing many most interesting experiments on human beings and animals, trying to assess the influence of the level of motivation and arousal on human performance. They described and explained the results of the experiments on the interrelationship between the level of arousal and motivation, and the efficiency of performance, in two laws, known as the First and Second Yerkes-Dodson Laws.[2] Since that time, many psychologists have continued to conduct similar experiments, which have confirmed the accuracy of Yerkes' and Dodson's findings. One may say that, apart from scientific experiments, even everyday observation and common sense can lead us to believe that there is a certain correlation between the intensity of motivation (ambition, desire to do something, fulfilling one's needs, etc.) and arousal, on one side, and efficiency, quality, and results of activity, on the other.

The First Yerkes-Dodson Law

According to the first Yerkes-Dodson law, a higher intensity of arousal and motivation increases efficiency and effectiveness of activity—but only to a certain point. When the level of motivation increases beyond a certain optimum point, then the efficiency of activity begins to decrease, and when the level of motivation is very high, the standard of performance becomes very poor. Sometimes too much arousal and motivation act destructively on our performance. (See Fig. 6.1).

Life gives us many examples illustrating they ways that Yerkes' and Dodson's laws are valid. It is enough to look around and reflect on human desires, activities, and the results of our work. For example, a student who does not have a strong desire to study (low level of motivation), has poor results and low marks. On the other hand, an extremely ambitious student may work a lot, possess a great knowledge and want to impress his professor at the exam; but he wants so much to be brilliant and display his range of knowledge, that in front of the professor at the examination he can hardly utter a word. This is the destructive influence of too-high motivation and arousal.

Fig. 6.1
First Yerkes-Dodson Law:The Interrelationship between the Level of Arousal & Motivation and Efficacy of Performance

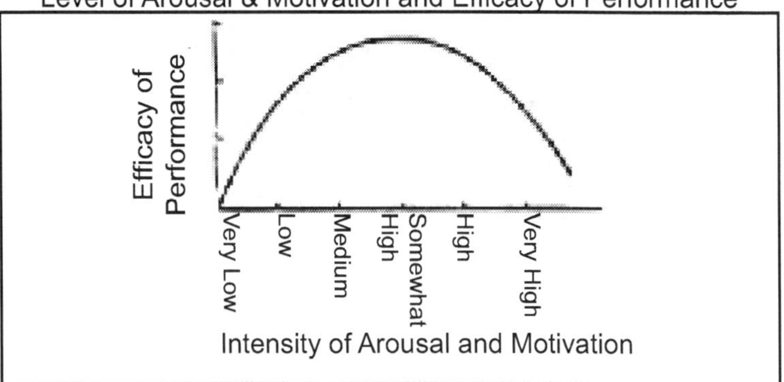

In sport, we very often observe the negative influence of too-high arousal and motivation when the stakes are high. For example: a tennis player who misses a simple shot, a soccer player who cannot score into an empty goal, or an excellent fencer who performs technically and tactically far below his normal potential and abilities. Sports journalists generally do not understand the paralyzing effects of too high a level of arousal and motivation in very important competitions, and often criticize the coach: "The coach stated that the competitor was very well prepared for these championships, but he must have made a mistake."

During nearly seventy years of fencing activities—both as a competitor and a fencing master—I have personally observed many striking examples of how too high a level of motivation negatively affects the process and results of a bout. To quote only one: At the World Championships in Brussels, 1953, an outstanding Hungarian sabreur, Pal Kovacs (many times a medalist in World Championships and Olympic Games), had already gathered six victories and was to fence the last bout against the French fencer, Jacques Lefevre. The victory would assure the much coveted gold medal. The much more experienced Kovacs soon led 4 – 1 and needed only one hit to become World Champion. Now I observed how he became very nervous and excited; his arms and legs trembled and his movements had become chaotic and uncoordinated. Lefevre hit him three times in succession, equalizing the score, 4 – 4. Now Kovacs made a desperate and badly executed attack and received a stop-hit, well in time—but the director (out of pity) awarded the hit against the Frenchman!

Numerous laboratory experiments, empirical experience, and everyday observation of human life and human activities, indicate that the appropriate level of motivation and arousal (ambition, excitation, desire to win, desire to learn something, being interested in something) helps to achieve better results of activity. In fencing, the optimal level of motivation accelerates the process of learning and ensures better acquisition of motor skills and their successful application in a bout, which leads to more efficient fencing. The best results in training and competition are achieved when there is a proper relationship between the level of activation and the level of difficulty. Too-strong excitation, too-high motivation, the desire to win at any cost, feverish ambition—especially in very important competitions—all bring about lower performance.

We know from our own experience that when we want something desperately, when something seems terribly important to us, we sometimes go to pieces and perform our task far below our normal possibilities. The following example may illustrate the point: we open the door to our homes hundreds of times, automatically, without thinking about it and without any difficulty; however, were the apartment on fire, such a simple and often-repeated activity might become terribly difficult. The nervous tension could make putting the key into the lock nearly impossible.

As I have already mentioned, the Yerkes-Dodson Laws have been, throughout many years, verified many times, and confirmed by means of numerous, ingenious experiments, conducted both on human beings and animals (the observed mechanisms of learning in animals are similar to those in human beings).

Here is an example of one such experiment. Three groups of rats were taught the route of a maze (at the end of a properly chosen route there was food). Group A consisted of rats who had eaten recently; they were not hungry and their level of motivation (to find the way to the food) was rather low. Rats of Group B had their last meal eight hours earlier and began to feel hungry, so the level of their motivation and arousal may be described as optimal. Rats of Group C had not eaten for thirty-six hours and, consequently, were desperately hungry (too high a level of arousal and motivation). The rats from Group B, with an optimal level of motivation, learned the correct route of the maze after a few trials. The rats of Group A—with a low level of arousal and motivation—required more time and trials to find the correct way in the maze. The hungriest rats from Group C, with very high motivation and arousal, had much more difficulties learning the path of the maze (it took them much longer and many more trials) than the rats from Group B.

The Second Yerkes-Dodson Law

Skillfulness and efficiency of activity depends, not only on the level of activation, ambition, desire to win, etc.—in other words, it does not depend only on the level of motivation and arousal—but is influenced equally by the level of difficulty and complexity of the task which one wants to perform (learning something, acquisition of a new motor skill, execution of an action, solving a tactical problem, winning a bout, etc.).

According to the second Yerkes-Dodson law, when solving and executing comparatively easy tasks, one achieves high skillfulness and efficiency of learning and performance if the level of motivation and arousal is high; efficient performance of difficult tasks requires a lower level of motivation and arousal.

If we represent schematically on a graph (Fig. 6.2) the interrelationship of optimum motivation and arousal, and the level of difficulty of a task, the optimal motivation for easy tasks, well-acquired skills, is on the right side of the graph and, conversely, the

Fig. 6.2 – The Second Yerkes-Dodson Law: Interrelationship between a) Level of Arousal & Motivation and b) Task Difficulty

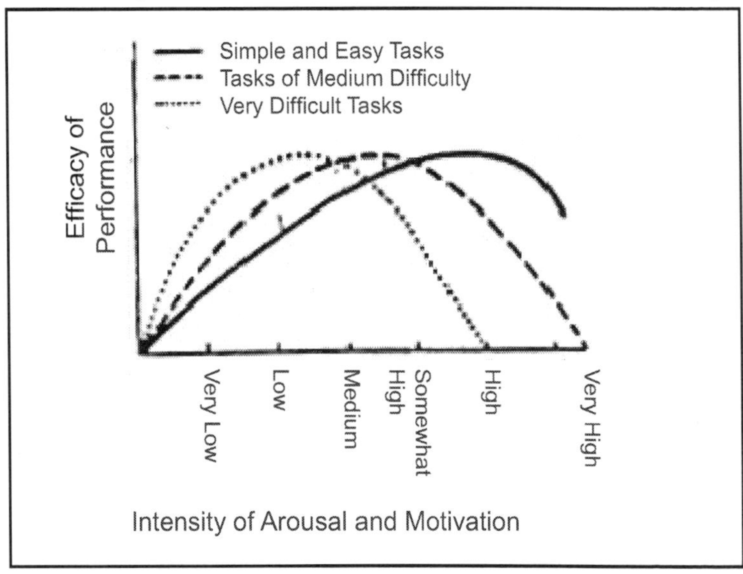

optimal level of motivation and arousal for complicated, difficult and complex tasks is on the left. In practice, it means that while learning a simple task or executing an easy and well-acquired skill, even very high motivation and arousal—and even a state of anxiety and nervousness—do not lower the efficiency and results of the performance. For example, one may quite effectively perform simple and well-known tasks like washing the dishes, vacuuming the floor, etc., even though one is very nervous, anxious, and thinking with great intensity about some serious problems. In the same state of anxiety, it would be impossible to solve mathematical problems, play chess, or fence a bout with an opponent. In other words, the more difficult the task we want to learn or perform, the lower the required level of arousal and motivation.

The second Yerkes-Dodson law has an equally important role in fencing—both in the process of training and in competition. In accordance with the second law, a low level of motivation and arousal is necessary for learning difficult, complex actions. Equally, while applying complicated actions in a bout, the more complicated and difficult the task, the lower the level of motivation conducive to good results.

Yerkes and Dodson express it this way: "... an easily acquired habit, that is, one that does not demand difficult sense discrimination or complex associations, may readily be formed under strong stimulation, whereas a difficult habit may be acquired readily only under relatively weak stimulation."

A very high level of motivation and arousal—when learning and applying easy motor skills with relatively simple structures—has a positive influence on the speed of acquisition of sensory-motor skills and their efficient application in a bout. On the other hand, the same level of motivation may exert a distinctly negative influence on the efficacy and results of activity when learning difficult, complicated, and dangerous movements—and even more so while executing them at competitions. This variable level of optimal motivation for the application of difficult motor skills and complicated technical-tactical capabilities in competitions, becomes more obvious and more pronounced in difficult and extreme situations: when one hit decides a bout winning a medal; when the team's result depends on the last bout; when the opponent leads with one minute left to the end of the bout; when one must win to be promoted to the next round.

Sometimes we can see opposite effects of high motivation and arousal in the same bout. Suppose a competitor with poor technique, a very modest range of actions, and very simple tactical solutions ("the warrior" style of fencing: see Chapter 8), is matched against a fencer whose technique is very correct, versatile, and complete (the "technician" style of fencing). The warrior, fencing in a state of high excitation, full of fighting spirit and determination, very often causes serious trouble, intimidates, and even beats the technician, whose high level of motivation causes too-late, and not always appropriate, reactions, inhibits boldness, and sometimes even lowers the technical level of his actions—which had been his strong point.

This is an example of the positive influence of high arousal and motivation on the fencer with simple technique and tactics (the "warrior" type) and the negative influence of high arousal and motivation on fencer of complex technique and tactics (the "technician" type). In other words, the same level of high motivation and arousal positively influences the performance of easy and simple tasks, and negatively influences the performance of difficult and complicated tasks—in accordance with the second Yerkes-Dodson law.

Quite often, in fencing competitions, games, and other spheres of human activity, one may see the paralysing effects of an extremely high level of motivation and arousal (nervousness, great desire to win, fear of losing, responsibility for the result in a particularly important event, etc.). Too high a level of arousal and motivation may affect even very highly trained and experienced competitors, especially when the competition is very important and prestigious. On the other hand, it often happens that a competitor, after losing a few bouts and realising that he is eliminated (the level of motivation and arousal markedly drops), suddenly achieves the peak of his performance and surpasses himself.

Application of the Laws of Arousal

Profound understanding of the Yerkes-Dodson Laws not only widens a coach's theoretical knowledge, but is of paramount practical value. So let us consider how to apply, in practice, the knowledge of these laws: what to do, how to educate, how to train a fencer in such a way that introducing new actions and abilities will not lower his performance under the influence of high motivation and arousal.

The influence of various levels of arousal and different component parts of motivation (contents, direction, level; intrinsic and extrinsic motivation; achievement motivation—see below) is highly differentiated and specific. The specificity of the influence of motivation and arousal on the competitor manifests itself as follows:

- Each athlete has his own optimal level of arousal and motivation, which ensures his most efficient performance.

- The optimal level of arousal and motivation for each competitor may undergo certain changes during the day (some athletes are better in the morning, some in the afternoon, and some in the evening).

- Different branches of sport are best performed at different levels of arousal and motivation (for example, billiards and shooting require a low level of arousal, whereas weight-lifting demands a high level of arousal). See Fig. 6.3.

- Even in the same branch of sport, certain actions are best executed with a low level of arousal (e.g., shooting a penalty in soccer; a compound counter-attack by feint of derobe – derobe, in fencing) while other actions are best executed with a high level of arousal (e.g., a bold, fast, surprising attack). See Fig. 6.3.

- Athletes with a strong type of nervous system (high endurance of nervous cells) act most efficiently with a high level of arousal; athletes of a weak type of nervous system act efficiently with low levels of arousal (this

Fig. 6.3 – Optimum Level of Arousal for Different Kinds of Activities, and Different Branches of Sport

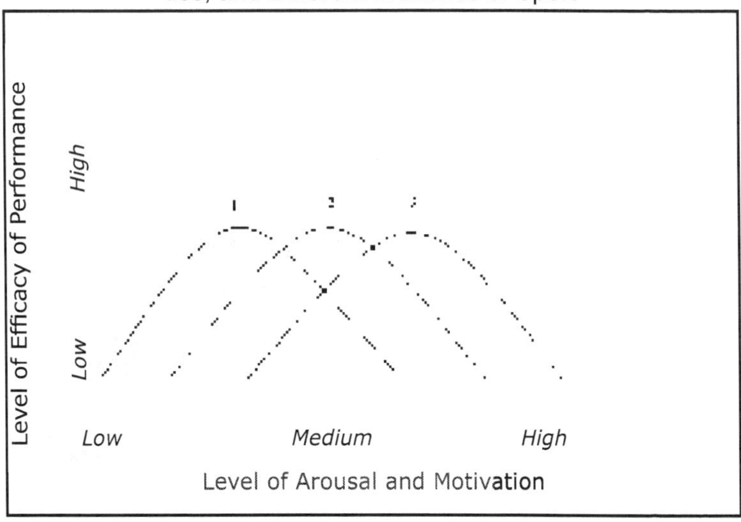

According to the second Yerkes-Dodson law, for motor skills and activities demanding a high level of attention, reaction, choice of action, and very precise movements, the optimal level of arousal is rather low. For rather easy, simple skills demanding strength and speed, the optimal level of arousal is high.

1. Shooting, archery, golf, billiards, figure skating, penalty shooting, etc.
2. Fencing, tennis, badminton, volleyball, etc.
3. Weight-lifting, rugby, boxing, hockey, etc.

Fig. 6.4 – Optimal Level of Arousal for Efficient Activity in Various Stages of Training

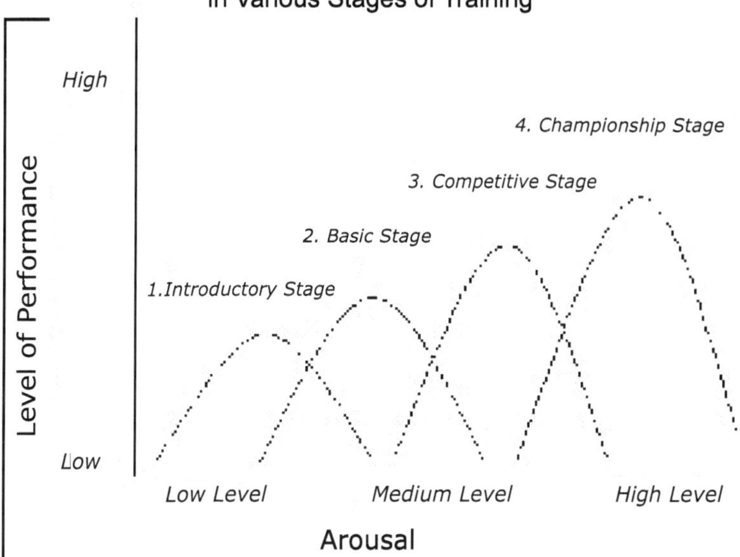

According to the second Yerkes-Dodson law, the optimal level of arousal and motivation increases with the level of skill (acquisition of motor skills and technical-tactical capabilities). This means that, as a fencer becomes more trained and experienced, and his motor skills and capabilities become more securely attained, he will be able to perform at increasing levels of arousal.

is why—among other things—"weak" types often do better during practice, whereas "strong" types do better in competitions).

One can conclude—taking into consideration that, as years of training pass, and a fencer enters higher stages of training with better and better acquisition of motor skills and fencing specific capabilities—the optimal arousal, occurring in practice and competitions, differs in different stages of training. This means that the higher the stage of training, the better a fencer is able to perform at higher levels of arousal (see Fig. 6.4), in accordance with the second Yerkes-Dodson law.

V. A. Vyatkin expressed the opinion that the strength of the nervous system determines the quality of motor performance—including those in sport activities—indirectly, through motivation.[3] Depending on the strength of the nervous system (capacity of nervous cells), the level of motivation acts differently on different athletes. Thus, during practice (lower level of motivation and lower arousal), athletes with a weak type of nervous system often show a high level of performance, but, in competition (high level of motivation, responsibility for results, difficult situations), they achieve much lower results—the quality and efficacy of their activity is markedly lower. Strong types act efficiently in difficult situations, and their results in competitions are not infrequently higher than during practice.

A characteristic feature of the performance of "weak" types is not only that they achieve poorer results in competition, but also that their results are very inconsistent. Observations and interviews seem to indicate that situations of competition cause, among weak types, nervous tension, too-high arousal, diminishment of self-confidence, fear of defeat, and competitive anxiety. For strong types, a high feeling of responsibility, emotions connected with participation in competition, a high level of arousal and motivation, all stimulate energetic and efficient activity.

Generally, one may state that fencers of "warrior" type act most efficiently and effectively when their level of arousal and motivation is very high, whereas fencers of "technician" type act most efficiently and effectively when their level of arousal is relatively low (see Chapter 8). There are—and it is a rather rare occurrence—some outstanding fencers who perform efficiently and effectively, and achieve the highest results, when their level of arousal and motivation, and the level of difficulty, are extremely high.[4] A good example of such a type might be Poland's Ryszard Parulski—world junior sabre champion, world senior foil champion, world championship gold medal winner in senior team epee, and many-time finalist and medallist of Olympic Games and World Championships—who fenced at his highest, world-class level when his arousal was very, very high, when he was angry and had quarrels with the referee, opponent, and colleagues (now, by the way, he is a very prominent lawyer—a good example of a successful combination of high-competitive sport and an outstanding professional career).

Generally, however, too high a level of arousal—especially combined with a strong fear of defeat—has a negative influence on efficacy of performance, diminishing speed and accuracy of perception and reaction, handicapping various qualities of attention, retarding decision-taking, leading to inaccurate, clumsy, or even chaotic execution of movements. In other words, it negatively affects all three periods of sensory-motor response (see Chapter 5)[5] A fencer with too low a level of arousal sees "too much": he notices plenty of stimuli, both relevant and irrelevant; he sees not only the opponent, but also the referee, the scoring machine, the scoreboard, the public, etc. The awareness of too many stimuli delays choice of action, since the time for transforming information becomes too long. It is not unlike the driver on the road with a low level of arousal who notices not only traffic, cars, and road signs, but also houses, restaurants, trees, billboards, etc. There is too much information, delaying his correct assessment of the situation and his decision-taking, and, as a consequence, he may crash into a tree or another car.

A competitor with optimal arousal perceives only the relevant stimuli: he assesses the distance, the opponent's movements—trying to guess his intentions—and since the amount of stimuli is rather limited, he has time to transform the information, take the proper decision and execute the chosen action in time. A fencer with too high a level of arousal has a very narrow field of perception and does not perceive—or perceives too late—some relevant stimuli. That, of course, leads to defeat.

So, if the coach notices in training—and, especially, in competition—a pupil's distractibility (a sure sign of too high a level of arousal), he must try to apply the adequate means to lower the fencer's excitation.

To make it clear, we come back to the comparison with the driver (fencing is a mirror of life). A driver with an optimal level of arousal only perceives relevant stimuli: the road, road signs, and traffic. His decisions and reactions are fast and correct. A driver with a very high level of arousal does not perceive some of the relevant stimuli—which, of course, may lead to an accident.

II. AROUSAL AND MOTIVATION IN THE DEVELOPMENT OF YOUNG FENCERS

Too high a level of arousal and motivation exerts a particularly negative influence on the cognitive-motor activity of children. This is extremely important because nowadays, in many branches of sport (including fencing) coaches—and the entire system of training—put too-early, one-sided, and too-strong emphasis on rivalry and competition, which exploits, too much, the vital strength of young athletes, and also does not facilitate stable, accurate, and labile acquisition of motor skills.

Some coaches frequently forget that the main object of the first, introductory, stage of training is not "production" of a young champion, but proper preparation for the next stages of training and the achievement of high and stable results in adult age. Such procedure (too-early and one-sided concentration on rivalry, competition, and results) leads nowhere because if young athletes win medals in the youth and cadet categories, but then achieve much worse results as juniors and seniors, it means that the system of training is wrong (see Chapter 11). I know many examples of coaches who have produced winners in very young age categories and yet have not educated a single good fencer over twenty years old.

In certain branches of sport based on closed motor skills (gymnastics, figure skating, diving, etc.) where judges give points assessing complexity, difficulty, fluency and precision of execution, gracefulness and beauty, appropriate rhythm of movements—it is obviously necessary to introduce new elements of technique, new and difficult sequences of movements and complicated abilities—without them, the competitor would have no chance of achieving good results. The increased level of difficulty, of course, makes the competitor vulnerable to the negative influence of a high level of motivation and arousal.

Some coaches of fencing, boxing, wrestling, and team games (sports based on open motor skills; where individuals or teams directly oppose each other) express the opinion that in order to avoid the negative influence of a high level of motivation and arousal, it is effective to teach a very narrow range of motor skills (motor habit patterns) and very simple tactics. Competitors make up for the limited technical-tactical abilities (and, in our case, their simple style of fencing) with great ambition, fighting spirit, boldness and aggressiveness (i.e., an intensity of motivation and arousal which is right for easy tasks, but would "kill" more refined technique and tactics). Such a solution initially brings early successes but, in the end, often turns out to be short-sighted. In the further development of a competitor—as he gradually achieves higher results and is bound to meet more and more experienced and versatile opponents—sooner or later, he is forced to increase his fighting repertoire, to increase his technical and tactical capabilities; in other words, he will have to make his technique and tactics more versatile and complicated—which, of course, makes them more difficult to apply. Besides, compensating for low level and simplicity of technique and tactics only by aggressive tendencies and a high level of arousal and motivation, inevitably leads to a one-sided, uneconomical style of fighting, and early exhaustion of a competitor's vital stamina and energy.

In my opinion, there is a better solution of how to avoid the negative effects of a high level of excitation and motivation on a competitor's performance and results—at the same time, teaching a wide range of motor skills, many different fencing strokes, a fencer's reactions, and various tactical capabilities.

The first step towards finding the proper solution is to realize that feeling, or sensing, the level or degree of difficulty of any task, is something totally subjective and depends on personal assessment of a difficulty and on the degree of acquisition of a motor skill and tactical capabilities. Changing a tire may be a dramatically difficult task for a young girl who is just learning to drive a car, while the same task is something childishly easy and routine for a professional driver. In a circus, the performance of a trapeze artist is liked by the audience when it appears difficult, complicated, and dangerous. Circus artistes perform under a high level of motivation: the desire and necessity to execute difficult and dangerous tasks, the desire to be applauded by the public, the desire to be approved by the director, professional pride, etc.; and, at the same time, their breath-taking and neck-breaking somersaults in the air must be executed with precision to a fraction of a second, full coordination, gracefulness and lightness. In other words, a difficult and dangerous, extremely fast and precise movement—by way of persisting, long-lasting exercises—must become an "easy one" so that its quality (and the safety of the artists) is not negatively affected by the necessarily high level of motivation and arousal.

In many professions, activities, and branches of sport, the "difficult" movements must become "easy" ones, from the performer's (violinist's, magician's, illusionist's, juggler's, contortionist's, tightrope walker's, artistic gymnast's, figure skater's, ballet dancer's, billiards player's, fencer's, etc.) point of view. Opponents' actions in combat sports and team games produce additional difficulty. The conclusion seems obvious: athletic training ought to be programmed and conducted in such a way that difficult and complicated movements, and other necessary abilities, become, for a trained athlete and competitor, easy ones. Of course, this does not apply only to the mere execution of a movement (motor skills and technical capabilities). It applies as well to "reflex,"unforeseen application of a given stroke in a bout (technical-tactical capabilities), decided on the spur of the moment, as well as to rational, foreseen, efficient, and correct application of a given action in a bout, on the basis of observations, reconnoitering of the opponent, foreseeing his movements, and planning one's own actions (tactical capabilities).

III. OVER-LEARNING

One of the methods which ensures correct execution and efficient application of difficult movements in fighting conditions under the pressure of high motivation is the so-called over-learning method. It consists of using difficult movements, together with sequences of other strokes, in complicated, changeable conditions, with great speed and for long periods of time. If, for example, a fencer practices artificial, complicated, and difficult fencing phrases—for example, containing, in different settings, ten thrusts by disengagement—most probably using one thrust by disengagement in competition, in an adequate tactical situation, will not be too difficult for him. A "difficult" stroke will become, for this fencer, a subjectively "easy one"—not deteriorating under pressure of high motivation and arousal (see Chapter 14).

A kind of over-learning method was introduced in the first half of the 19th Century by the famous French master, Jean Louis de Montpellier (who also was one of the coaches who introduced and insisted on using the sixth parry to defend the high outside line). He introduced the so-called "reprises"—a method demanding very fast, very accurate, fluid execution of a sequence of fencing strokes, all foreseen and pre-announced. These "reprises"—the perfection of complicated, compound sets of fencing movements, executed fast, "in one breath"—became very popular in the second half of the 19th Century in different schools.

The experience of many generations of eminent fencing masters of the 19th and 20th centuries, and their pupils' style of fencing and results, seem to confirm the efficacy of the over-learning method. I would like to add that many very eminent fencing masters, very often and successfully, have applied, and still apply, the over-learning method (though, perhaps not calling it that); for example: Giuseppe Mangiarotti, Livio di Rosa, and many of today's leading French coaches.

It has been stressed several times in this chapter, that a very high level of motivation—both positive (great desire to win) and negative (being afraid of defeat)—in competitors, very often leads to a lowering of standard and efficiency of performance. One may counteract this by a properly-conducted warm-up before the competition, the fencing master's verbal assurance and attitude, etc. (see Chapter 16)—but most important in this respect is training itself. An athlete's training should ensure that objectively difficult motor skills and special abilities become for him subjectively easy ones, and that he may execute them in fighting conditions with the ease, lightness, and precision of an expert pianist, ballerina, or acrobat performing before an audience. In order to achieve this, one should use the already-mentioned over-learning method, alternating it quite frequently with well-known, well-acquired, easy exercises which give the competitor certainty of execution and confidence in his skills, abilities, and possibilities, and pleasure in displaying his skill.

IV. OTHER ASPECTS OF MOTIVATION

Naturally, motivation is not the only factor influencing the course of results of sports training and achievements in competitions, but it is so important and essential—and at the same time, so misunderstood—that one should devote plenty of time, thought, and attention to its shaping.

Shaping the right kind of motivation—productive and valuable from the social and educational point of view—and its appropriate level (according to the actual level of the competitor's abilities at a given stage of his fencing career, and the proper relationship between his aspirations and his actual level of possibilities) is a very important, difficult, and delicate task of a fencing master.

Since motivation is a set of factors propelling us towards activity in a defined direction in order to fulfil our needs, its development must essentially consist of shaping the appropriate needs, aspirations, values and drives related to sport and activities outside sport.

Of particular importance—especially in the first stage of training and in the process of teaching and perfecting sensory-motor skills of a given discipline of sport—is sport enjoyment and love of one's chosen sport.

An athlete's attitude towards his sport should include, not only the desire to achieve certain goals (valuable and attractive as they may be: higher social status, going abroad, gaining money and recognition, being fit and healthy, etc.), but also a pure and spontaneous enjoyment of cultivating a given sport, of performing exercises and taking part in competitions. In other words, he must be mainly interested in his sport, without "interest."

Instrumental motivation, without a feeling of sheer enjoyment of the game, has only limited value. The eminent Soviet fencing master, Vitali Arkadyev, stressed the point by saying, "A coach's first duty is to make his pupil a fencing fanatic," and "Soviet fencers achieve such great success because they are lovers of their sport." (In the 2002 World Championships in Lisbon, the Russian fencers won six gold and two silver medals, showing that there is still truth in Arkadyev's words today.) Barbara Knapp also stressed the importance of this aspect of motivation by expressing the opinion that, "It is highly unlikely that a person could achieve significant results in a given game or sport, if his or her motivation did not include the need of perfecting his or her own physical fitness, as an aim in itself."[6]

In positively motivating pupils, an important role is played by judicious application of the principle of gradual increase of knowledge and level of difficulty, which includes taking into account perceptive possibilities and a pupil's state of preparedness at a given stage of training. Too-easy tasks are simply boring and decrease the level of motivation. Too-difficult tasks have discouraging effects on pupils and very often decrease the level of motivation. Presenting tasks, obviously too difficult and much above the capabilities and possibilities of a competitor at a given stage of training, exerts a particularly negative influence on pupils with great ambition and a great need for achievement and recognition. Such competitors do not even try—or do not even begin to try—to perform a too-difficult task, being afraid, often subconsciously, of failure and a feeling of defeat.

Similarly, if, in training bouts, a young and inexperienced fencer opposes a far better and experienced competitor, his reactions may take two opposing forms: knowing the marked superiority of his opponent, he may give up any attempt to fence seriously and, consequently, his level of performance will be very low; or his reaction may be different—he may want so desperately to do well against a much superior opponent that his level of motivation will be too high, so that of course, he will not be able to fence well.

Rivalry, competing, and comparing oneself to others, constitute some of the most important factors in contemporary top-level sport, and one ought to take advantage of these facts in the process of training. But here, a few words of caution. Very sharp rivalry, used in teaching and training, constitutes an excellent stimulus for pupils with strong nervous systems, high levels of aggressiveness, fencers of "warrior" type, and for people with many traits of a Machiavellian personality. For such people, rivalry is a very efficient way of extracting maximum effort. But methods containing strong elements of rivalry must be applied with moderation, carefully, tactfully, and gradually, when dealing with people who are shy and easily intimidated, who have rather weak nervous systems, who are strong introverts, or who belong to the "technician" type of fencer. In the latter case, one should introduce rivalry in such a way as to gradually mould and shape pupils' confidence in their own capabilities and possibilities—and only after they have gained confidence, should sharp rivalry be introduced.

The coach's influence on stimulating and shaping the right kind and level of a pupil's motivation ought to be many-sided and varied. The important thing is to employ, not only one, but a whole array of encouragements, challenges, and motivational influences, such as:

1. Well-organized training:
    - Interesting and varied exercises presented in colorful and attractive ways;
    - Stressing the usefulness of the exercises in instilling a love and interest in fencing.
2. The coach's verbal approval and encouragement:
    - Application of praise and prizes, if necessary;
    - Constructive criticism;
    - Warnings and punishments;
    - Appeals to a fencer's ambition;
    - Setting and explaining goals to be achieved.
3. Loyalty, affiliation, cohesiveness, and identification with the club, team-mates, coach, and country.
4. Presentation of the direct and indirect benefits and assets obtainable from the sport.
5. Stressing the meaning of sport as one of the ways to a person's self-realization and as a means of enabling fulfillment of numerous physiological, psychological, and social needs; etc.

One-sided motivation, overly stressing the importance of the material benefits connected with top-level sport and high-level achievements, may sometimes have negative consequences, for example:

- It may paralyze a competitor, lowering the standard of his performance and decreasing his results—when, for example, in exchange for major sports results, the competitor is promised big material profits.

- It ceases to be effective when a certain level of attainment is sufficient to keep a certain standard of life and enjoyment of privileges connected with belonging to an Olympic squad.

Some coaches willingly use, and abuse, negative motivation by means of punishments, curtailment of certain privileges, warnings, reprimands, financial sanctions, etc.—all of which are very easy to apply. It reminds me of a little-known Napoleonic saying: "It is easier to control people by means of their vices than by means of their virtues." Of course, it is much easier to bribe or to punish people than to educate them—although, obviously, it is sometimes necessary to resort to these negative means. Nevertheless, exaggerated and one-sided reliance on warnings, punishments, curtailment of privileges, etc., is not very effective and of small educational value.

One has to realize that no one has ever been taught anything positive or cured of any bad habits, merely by being subjected to punishments and negative motivation.

In shaping pupils' motivation and instilling positive dimensions of personality, long tradition recommends the need to overcome difficulties and cope with difficult situations. This reminds me of a well-known statement by Pope John Paul II: "The most precious gift that a man can offer God is suffering." This does not appeal to me, much like the practice of some coaches who load their pupils with difficult, unpleasant, and even painful tasks, claiming that it is developing their "will-power." I think that life brings enough frustration, pains, diseases, and accidents that we do not need to seek self-martyrdom. St. Augustine's words, ""Unconstrained curiosity is far better than severe discipline" appeal to me much more.

The negative attitudes of many coaches, described above, could be expressed as follows: "You have to do, not what you would like or enjoy doing, but what is necessary or what you have decided to do." Now, I think, a far more practical attitude would be: "Enjoy and be willing to do what is necessary." As with the majority of educational advice, this one is also easier to formulate than to apply in practice. In spite of that, I am of the firm opinion that we should strive to educate our pupils in such a way that performing their duties, fulfilling training tasks, etc., becomes for them a need at the same time that it is a pleasure. It is far "healthier" than developing "will-power" by unpleasant tasks because, as we know, we are better able, and more willing, to do those things that we enjoy doing, that give us pleasure and satisfaction. Such an attitude brings out more initiative and new ideas, and allows for longer sustained effort.

V. MOTIVATING CHILDREN

> *"In the operation of sport programs, the motivating power of joy should not be overlooked. Second, it is important to understand the nature of the sources of enjoyment. . . ."*
>
> --Tara K. Scanlan and Jeffrey P. Simmons

The coach, training children and youth (the introductory stage of training), should try to answer the following questions:

1. What level of arousal and what contents, direction, and level of motivation are most suitable and valuable for children?

2. Which motivating factors can be employed to provide children with joy and satisfaction?

3. How to ensure their versatile development and future good results in competition—through the appropriate motivation?

4. How to shape the motivation of children, educating and training them and, at the same time, developing their self-efficacy, diligence, active and conscious at-

titudes, and cultivating their passion and interest in a chosen branch of sport?

The key to the efficacious motivation of children and youth is to understand their needs and help them in the rational fulfillment of those needs. Realizing this task, we have to remember:

- The motivation of children and youth differs in many respects from the motivation of adults.

- Motivation in sport activities differs at different stages of training.

To appropriately shape the motivation of children—its contents, direction, level, social value, and value for a given branch of sport—one has to know and understand well the children's needs, interests and aspirations, and influence them appropriately.

Above all, one should remember that it is sport for the children, and not children for the sport.

A factor of immense importance in motivating children and youth—and also adults!—is the ability to set the appropriate main goals (which may even be far-reaching in time) and, resulting from them, more detailed and concrete tasks. Setting different tasks influences the attitudes, behavior, and activities of young athletes in many different ways. Among them, it may produce:

- The desire to demonstrate one's abilities, skills and possibilities—a competitive attitude, a high level of motive of success—that is, ego-involvement.

- Concentration of their entire attention on activity itself—a mastery approach, self-improvement, an increase of one's skills and abilities—that is, task-involvement.

One can gather from much research, discussions and observations that children's participation in sports activities fulfils many of their needs (see below) and constitutes a rich source of enjoyment and happiness. Children cite many different motives and reasons for cultivating sport, such as:

- Rivalry and comparing oneself with others;
- Learning and perfecting one's own skills and abilities;
- Comradeship and friendship;
- The activity itself;
- The fun of applying acquired skills;
- Play;
- Competition;
- Comparing oneself with one's own ideal;
- Prestige;
- Prizes and signs of recognition;
- An outlet for emotions and physical energy.

According to the results of interesting research by L.M. Wankel and P.S. Kreisel, young boys, as a source of fun and enjoyment in sport, enumerate: [7]

Intrinsic factors;

- Executory factors;
- Enjoyment of the game itself;
- Personal achievements;
- Applying the acquired skills in a game.

Slightly less appreciated are the social factors:

- Being a member of a team,
- Contact with friends.

The least appreciated are extrinsic factors:

- Results and consequences of activities;
- Victories and achievements;
- Receiving prizes;
- Providing pleasure for others (the coach, family, colleagues, teachers).

Very interesting research on the sports enjoyment of children and youth—an important factor in motivating and educating, and in the process of training, itself—was conducted by T.K. Scanlan and R. Lewthwaite.[8] Their research once more supported the view that sport enjoyment is not only the result of intrinsic motivation (although, it is very important!), but is also connected with extrinsic factors, as well as with some factors that deal with achievement and some that do not.

Intrinsic factors connected with achievement are: perception by an athlete of his own value, skills, abilities and competence. Such factors might be strengthened by a feeling of self-efficacy in executing and applying given actions.

- Extrinsic factors connected with achievement influence self-esteem, self-efficacy and satisfaction (feedback—assessment by others, praise, recognition by others).
- Intrinsic factors not connected with achievement (they are a pleasure due to the activity itself): pleasant emotions during exercises and competitions.
- Extrinsic factors not connected with achievement (they are connected with non-competitive aspects of sport): contact with colleagues, friendship, meeting important and interesting people (e.g., an outstanding, great coach; an enthusiastic official; etc.), visiting other towns and countries, sightseeing, visiting museums (the latter having educational value, as well).

Knowledge of these problems will allow a reflective coach to apply the appropriate leadership style, fostering, among pupils, interest and love for his branch of sport, and appropriately influencing his pupils' motivation.

In our sport, I should also add, a very attractive and valuable motivational factor is the colorful, interesting, and exciting history of arms and fencing.

From my many years of fencing activity, observations, readings, talks, and research, I have come to the conclusion that in motivating children, the following motives are particularly important:

1. Play, entertainment, and an outlet for emotional and physical energy.

2. Ensuring the proper level of arousal.

3. Feeling of self-efficacy and competence.

Shaping of "far-reaching" motivation, setting short- and long-term goals and tasks (training, and results in the stages of training, are most important, in contradiction to very fast, one-sided training with only the thought of achieving good results in the next competitions—"victory at any cost").

Shaping enthusiasm, a love for fencing (emotional factor), and deep interest in fencing (cognitive factor).

VI. ACHIEVEMENT MOTIVATION

> *"The study of achievement motivation concerns goal-directed behavior, including the causes, direction, and consequences of this activity. It concerns how individuals approach, engage in, and respond to achievement activities as well as the reasons why they engage in certain achievement behaviors."*
>
> --Carole Ames

A trait of all living organisms is rivalry—which displays itself in expansionism and fighting. Even plants "fight" for water and access to sunlight. Rivalry is necessary for the development of the economy, social life, science, culture, literature, art, sport, etc. A lack of rivalry leads to a stand-still.

Sport is noble and sublime, and governed by specific rules and principles of fair-play—with an aspect of rivalry. Without rivalry, there would be no sport—especially high-competitive sport.

One should, then, appreciate rivalry—but not overemphasize it, especially when children are concerned. "Victory at any cost" is an attitude not to be advocated.

Different people show very different attitudes, behaviors and needs in situations of rivalry. The set of a person's motives, attitudes, and aspirations, connected with a situation of rivalry, forms, in a way, a stable dimension of personality—achievement motivation.

From among the numerous motives forming achievement motivation, many authors consider most important the motive of success (desire to fight, belief in one's own success, an active and optimistic attitude) and the motive of avoiding failure (fear of defeat, lack of confidence, pessimistic attitude). According to these authors, the result of a bout is determined by the predominance of a motive of success over a motive of avoiding failure. This is correct, although it does not explain everything in these matters—there are other factors which also determine the result of a fight.

D.C. McClelland and J.W. Atkinson distinguish the following component parts of achievement motivation (See Table 6-A):[9]

- Motive of success (Ms: motive of rivalry, desire to compete and fight, self-confidence);

- Motive of avoiding failure (Maf, FOF: fear of failure, avoidance of risk);

- Probability of success (Ps: perception of the possibility of success, expecting success), inspiring value of success (Is: contentment, joy of victory);

- Extrinsic motivation (Me: prizes, recognition, benefits, money);

- Motive of avoiding success (Mas, FOS: fear of success, fear of the expectation by others of further success (this requires explanation: when a young fencer achieves, unexpectedly, a very early success, he or she might be afraid that "everybody"—coach, colleagues, family, journalists, club authorities, etc.—will expect further good results and, in case of poorer results, will be disappointed);

- Generally, the need of achievement (nAch) embraces achievement motivation.

In Table 6-A, the reader will notice that the need of achievement, the need of success, the need to prove one's value, all form the basis of achievement motivation, which is composed of several different motives.

Many authors stress—and rightly so—the immense value of self-confidence and self-efficacy. I think that the main difference between "healthy," efficient motivation—motivation of success—and motivation of fear of failure, is self-confidence.

One could, surprisingly, quote many cases when excellently trained and prepared competitors lost important bouts against rather poor opponents, precisely because of a low level of self-confidence and a high level of a motive of avoiding failure (fear of defeat and its consequences). So it is a very important—and, at the same time, difficult—task for a fencing master to motivate his pupil in such a way that he gains self-confidence and believes in his possibilities. It is much easier to teach a pupil how to kick a penalty, how to throw a ball into a basket, or how to execute thrust by counter-disengagement with an epee, than it is to instill self-confidence.

J.T. Spence and R.T. Helmreich conducted very interesting research on women's motives and attitude towards work and family.[10] They distinguish four main attitudes, which we might call the main attitudes in achievement motivation. The results of their tests are applicable to the motives and attitudes of athletes. Below, I present these four main attitudes regarded as signs of achievement motivation in sport (in our case, fencing):

1. *Emphasis on "murderous" effort, exhaustive work.* Some competitors (and coaches) see the main source of success only in the quantity of work and exhaustive effort, minimizing the value of technique, tactics, proper methods, and psychology. Such competitors

Table 6-A – Component Motives of Achievement Motivation, According to Atkinson and McClelland

Component Motive	Explanation	Symbol
Need of achievements	Achievement motivation	nAch
Motive of success	Desire to participate in competitions and rivalry situations	Ms
Motive of avoiding failure	Fear of failure; motive of avoiding—or the postponement of—rivalry situations; fear of defeat	Maf (FOF)
Probability of success	Perception of probable success; expecting success	Ps
Inspiring value of success	Perception of satisfaction and joy due to success	Is
Extrinsic motivation	Prizes, praise, recognition; symbolic and financial rewards; publicity; social advancement; etc.	Me
Motive of avoiding success	Fear of success	Mas (FOS)

(Based on the work of H. R. Arkes and J. P. Garske: Psychological Theories of Motivation, Monterey, 1982)

and coaches consider only the quantity, and not quality, of training. There are coaches who take delight in treating their students instrumentally, imposing "Prussian military drills" where the only measure of the value of the exercises is the level of sweat and fatigue of the pupils—and some fencers, strangely enough, love it and consider it an infallible means to success.

2. *Task involvement/mastery involvement.* The competitors love their chosen sport, and enjoy taking part in exercises and competitions. Their main object is precise knowledge of fencing, improvement of their skills and capabilities, and progress in technique and tactics. The competitors get great satisfaction from improving their skills and self-efficacy, and not only from competition results. Such a fencer, even after he has lost a bout, may still feel satisfaction if he thinks he fenced well and demonstrated some progress in his technique and tactics. This is a typical attitude—and a variety of achievement motivation—of the "technician" type (task involvement; see Chapter 8).

3. *Rivalry.* Competitors with a strong need for rivalry and achievement like to show their superiority in competitions. Such fencers are not interested in the fine details of technique and tactics—they want to fight and win, often using very simple actions based on speed, surprise and aggressiveness. This is a typical attitude and motivation of the "warrior" type (Again, see Chapter 8).

4. *Independence and self-reliance.* Fencers who value independence and self-reliance rely less on a group and more on themselves. They do not want to obey, passively and blindly, the coach's orders and instructions, but want to, consciously and actively, co-direct—with the coach—the process of training. They enjoy the acquisition of new knowledge and abilities; they like to assess and control the course and results of their training and the participation in competitions; they like to discuss, with the coach and colleagues, the problems connected with training, their tasks, and their results in competitions.

These are four extreme types. They do exist in reality—but there are many fencers who are a "mixture" of these types.

Many coaches are of the opinion that the most important, and most successful, motive is the motive of rivalry (a high level of a motive of success, the desire to fight, the desire to win, and belief in success) and an emphasis on intense effort (in other words, the attitudes and motives described in points 1 and 3, above). However, my many years of practical experience, observations, notes, and analytical meditation, lead me to the conviction that the surest sources of success are in the combination of the following motives: motive of rivalry (optimal level of a motive of success—not mania-like "success at any cost"), mastery motive (task involvement, self-improvement), and motive of independence and self-reliance (points 2 and 4, above, with an optimal level of point 3).

Most generally speaking, the motives connected with rivalry, competitions, and achievements, may be divided into three main groups:

- Demonstrating one's skills, capabilities, value, and competence (capabilities and attitudes necessary in competition).
- Concentration on tasks.
- Gaining social recognition.

The first and third of the above-mentioned groups correspond to ego-involvement; the second group corresponds to task-involvement.

For fencers with a very strong motive of rivalry (ego-involvement), success is victory; demonstrating their skills and capabilities; defeating opponents.

Fencers with task-involvement value the improvement of their fitness, skills, and capabilities (which do not, necessarily, have to be connected with victory); such athletes—in accordance with the theory of an ultimate goal (long-term goal)—do not get easily discouraged by lost bouts or failures.

For competitors with marked ego-involvement, who value rivalry and competition, bad results may have a totally different effect, depending on the levels of the motive of success and the motive of avoiding failure:

1. For fencers with a high level of the motive of success who are optimistic, like rivalry, and believe in themselves, bad results do not have a negative influence. They still believe in their possibilities and expect good results in the next competitions. Such types may begin to have doubts about their talent and future successes only after a long series of very bad results.

2. On the other hand, athletes with ego-involvement, but a very pronounced fear of defeat, react very negatively to bad performance and bad results in competitions.

Recently, as shown by Carron's extensive research, the great majority of leading athletes heavily emphasize and value rivalry.[11] The motive of self-improvement (task involvement) strongly connected with intrinsic motivation, is less marked—but one should not underestimate it, as it is very important, both from the educational and competitive point of view.

The increased frequency—especially among top fencers—of an accent on rivalry is understood as a logical consequence of the very essence of high-level, competitive sport; and it is strengthened, also, by the markedly increased role of publicity, mass-media, various ranking lists, a large number of big international competitions, the rising importance of Olympic Games and World Championships, honors, prizes, etc. One should, however, take care to prevent extrinsic motivation—especially its control function—from lowering the importance of intrinsic motives and the social and educational values of sport.[12]

VII. THE FENCING MASTER'S MOTIVATION

> *"The coach wants the athlete to identify himself with the coach but the most effective way is for both to identify with a common goal."*
> --James E. Counsilman

The motives of a coach's attitudes and activities are as various and versatile as those among competitors. Coaches represent different dimensions of personality, have different temperaments, display various attitudes, and adhere to different leadership styles (see Table 9-A). In a flood of very different motives (love of fencing, need of achievement and recognition, desire to educate, etc.), three groups of motivation are most important, and probably most frequent:

1. Attempting to provide one's pupils—and oneself—with happiness, pleasure, entertainment, active rest, psychological relaxation, and an adequate level of arousal (as mentioned above, each person, and each activity, demands a different, optimum level of arousal—especially of the brain cortex).

2. Taking care of pupils' education; developing their personalities, their all-round and specific functional-motor, psychological, and social development.

3. Striving to ensure the best results, records, victories, and achievements for the athletes and team under one's care. This very often constitutes the main (and, sometimes, only) goal of a coach's activity—this holds true for, above all, a coach of "warrior" type, whose main object is rivalry, fierce fighting, and success; such a coach, very often, treats his pupils as "instruments" to fulfil his own motives and ambitions.

All three of these main groups of motives, goals of a coach's educational activities, are important and necessary (but without maniacal overemphasis on results). One should, however, take care that the "accent" be properly distributed, taking into account the place of work, the pupil's age, the level of competitive preparedness and fencing skillfulness, etc. And so, in a school or children's fencing club, the most important are, obviously, the first and second of the above-mentioned groups; in an ordinary fencing club (which includes children, adults, recreational and high-competitive fencers) and on the national squad, the most important is, of course, the third motive (but even with strong emphasis on competition and results, one should not forget about sport enjoyment and educational influence).

In schools, various youth organizations, or children's fencing clubs, it is also important to take care of the versatile, many-sided development of the pupils, comprising:

- Functional-motor development; enhancement of the state of health; development of resistance to fatigue, difficulties and diseases; heightening of functional and adaptive possibilities; installation of stable habits of motor activity.

- Shaping of psychological processes (perception, various qualities of attention, choice of action), educational influence, development of pupils' feeling of self-worth, self-confidence, and self-efficacy; preparation for life and work in society.

In all branches of physical culture—in schools, in recreational sport and high-competitive sport—the coach should not forget about promoting arousal, entertainment and enjoyment. This is very evident and understood in the training of children and in recreational sport (sport for all), but one should not forget about it in high-competitive sport. One should avoid "martyrdom" attitudes and excessive stress on murderous effort, a great load of work, and exhaustive fatigue.

The personality, motivation, knowledge, and practical capabilities of a coach can be seen distinctly in his style of leadership. We may distinguish the following leadership styles: dictatorial, directive, formal, cooperative, and friendly. The best socially, educationally—and ensuring high and stable competition results, in the long-run—are the cooperative and friendly styles.[13] From the social and educational point of view, the worst style is the dictatorial one. As James Counsilman aptly notes, "It is extremely difficult for an intelligent, mature athlete to form an identification with a coach who sets himself up as a dictator, and whose authoritarian manner must be accepted unquestionably."[14] It is obvious that, without co-operation, empathy, and reciprocal respect between the coach and pupil, it is extremely difficult to achieve high results.

VIII. MOTIVATING COMPETITORS

"Be very careful in educating because an error committed in teaching is considered a premeditated crime."
--Rabbi Yehuda

"The basic problem in motivating athletes during practice seems to be how to make a period of physical stress a pleasant and rewarding experience. An athlete should look forward to practice with anticipation, and should not merely consider it a period of drudgery that is a necessary prerequisite for him to perform well in competition."
--James Counsilman

Summing up what has been said about motivation and arousal—and their influence on performance, results, and the pupil's attitude—final conclusions may be presented in the following points:

First, motivating and educating a competitor depend, not only on the coach's words, but also—and to a large extent—on his attitude, behavior, personal example, and many other factors, such as: a well-planned and -organized process of training; a process of recovery; efficient application of the principle of individualization; team cohesion; the coach's role; respect for the pupil's personality; promotion of the pupil's initiative; inspiration of the pupil's interest and love of fencing. Here it is very important to remember that various motivational factors may have a completely different influence on different competitors (for example: in many respects, one should use different methods of inspiration and training for extreme types of introverts and extroverts or for "warrior" and "technician" types).

Of course, even ably applying the best motivational, educational and training methods, we cannot make a great champion from a pupil devoid of any fencing talent (as I say jokingly to my students, "Even I cannot make a falcon out of a sparrow."). But, we can—apart from great champions—educate and produce good "medium-level" fencers who will enjoy cultivating fencing, and will be good partners in exercises and competitions for other, more talented, fencers.

Extremely important—and, at the same time, very difficult—is the adequate, skilful, and efficacious motivation of a competitor, as far as contents, direction, and level of motivation are concerned. The application of various motivational factors ought to be adapted to the fencer's age, stage of training, and personality dimensions (extroversion, introversion, emotional stability or instability, traits of temperament, etc.). Besides, different needs and motives are prominent in physical education in schools, in recreational sport, in physiotherapy, in high competitive sport, and in professional sport. Shaping adequate motivation—in the broad sense of the word—relies on the development of adequate aspirations, needs, ambitions, and goals in a pupil's activities in sport and outside of sport.

As already stressed many times, the coach should pay great attention to a pupil's intrinsic motivation, united harmoniously with the informative function of extrinsic motivation. Primitive, one-sided application of extrinsic motivation, with a strong emphasis on its control function, is bad from the educational and social point of view, and very often does not lead to high, stable results.

In each stage of training, one has to remember, and promote, sport enjoyment. The coach should emphasise such attitudes, needs and motives, which cause the fulfilment of training tasks to be a pleasure, not perceived as an external constraint and pressure. It is well known that we work, act, and learn, much more efficiently and effectively when what we do gives us pleasure. It is astonishing how many coaches do not appreciate, or forget about this fact.

A joint discussion on training tasks and results tasks is a very important and efficacious way of inducing the right motivation of a competitor. Such a discussion favorably influences the competitor's conscious and active attitude.

Concerning achievement motivation: the interaction between the coach and team is very important. In this respect, the most important factors are: an optimal level of motive of success, plus task involvement and a feeling of one's independence and shared responsibility with the coach and team-mates. All of this has a favorable influence on self-confidence, and self-confidence acts positively on a fencer in the difficult situations of competitions, lowers the motive of avoiding failure, lowers the fear of defeat, and prevents a too-high, destructive level of arousal.

Each competitor differs—sometimes very markedly—regarding abilities, personality dimensions, traits of temperament, and also the contents, direction, and level of achievement motivation. The coach should treat athletes with a high level of fear of defeat and emotional instability very carefully and with special attention. When dealing with such competitors, the coach should avoid sharp criticism and should, rather, slowly and patiently install self-confidence and a belief in oneself and one's possibilities.

One of the elementary qualities of sport is the strongly visible factor of rivalry and competitiveness. When dealing with children, the coach should not exaggerate the importance of this factor. Children between the ages of 10 and 14 develop at very different rates, and undue accent on sharp rivalry and pressure to achieve very high results may cause the loss of many talented children whose natural development is rather slow, but who might—and very often do—achieve excellent results after a few years. I know a surprising number of cases in which very young fencers made very slow progress at first, but then, after a few years, achieved top international results. Besides, one should not forget that the set of traits, qualities, skills and capabilities necessary for successful participation in competition in childhood (introductory stage of training) is very different from such a set for a fencer of adult age (competitive and champion stages; see Chapter 11). With children, the coach should, rather, stress the importance of training tasks over results in competitions. The coach should also stress self-improvement—assessing one's own abilities, capabilities, and progress (without comparing it to that of others). Concerning more advanced competitors, result tasks (the planning of certain concrete results in competitions) should be emphasized with competitors of the "warrior" type; while training tasks (e.g., improvement of coordination abilities, acquisition of new motor skills or tactical capabilities) should have priority when dealing with competitors of the "technician" type.

Generally, in motivating his pupils, the fencing master, above all, should apply the following sets of motivational incentives: the possibility of fulfilling many different needs by cultivating fencing (in this respect, fencing is a wonderful sport, and it is much easier to motivate fencers then swimmers, runners, or cyclists); intrinsic motives and sport enjoyment connected with the informative function of extrinsic motivation; the coach's personality and personal example (love of fencing, deep knowledge, practical abilities, punctuality, empathy, ability for interpersonal communication, sense of humor, ability to teach, friendly and cooperative leadership styles, etc.); assignment of main goals and tasks; knowledge of results and their assessment; variability and versatility of exercises; competition, as a motivational factor.

The American psychologist Albert Carron, classifies various motivational factors as follows:

- Situational factors (extrinsic), easily changed: symbolic prizes, goals and tasks, ways of conducting exercises, social reinforcements, the coach's leadership style;

- Situational factors (extrinsic), not easily changed: the presence of other people, participation in competition, the team and team cohesion;

- Personal factors (intrinsic), easily changed: initiative, assessment of the results of activity, interest in a given activity, expectations of others, self-confidence;

- Personal factors (intrinsic), not easily changed: trait anxiety, state anxiety, need of achievement, style of attention (narrow-wide, external-internal).[15]

The same way of treating different pupils may sometimes have dramatically different consequences; this is one of the most important conclusions of contemporary research on motivation. It ought to be a challenge for those coaches who think (and act accordingly) that by applying one method of teaching and educating—irrespective of the personalities of the pupils—they can achieve the best level and kind of motivation in all athletes and the best results in competitions; this, of course, is wrong. Everybody demands individual treatment that takes his personality into account.

The coach should remember—and draw practical conclusions from—the fact that, although motivation and arousal are strongly connected with each other, and their effects are very often similar, motivation and arousal—contrary to some authors' beliefs—are not the same. Motivation is directed toward the fulfillment of certain needs and is connected with cognitive and emotional processes, whereas arousal manifests itself as certain physiological processes and signs (increased heart rate, high blood pressure, tremor, paleness, frequency of micturition, activation of certain endocrine glands, high activity of the sympathetic system, etc.). Also, it is possible to keep the optimal level of arousal with a very high level of motivation which, of course, is very important in competition: a fencer is determined to win, does everything for it—high level of motivation—and yet manages to keep his arousal at the optimal level, avoiding too high a level of arousal, which would spoil his performance.

The fencing master—in accordance with the principle of unity of theory and practice, and cognition and action, ought to know and understand well the essence and significance of various motives and take advantage of them in his coaching and educational activity. As I have mentioned, each motivational factor has its own meaning, and various motives interact and influence each other. For example, the introduction of a system of setting goals and tasks increases the competitor's level of motivation and leads to an improvement of the training system and competition results. This, in turn, gives a fencer satisfaction, improves self-confidence, and results in persistence in trying to attain far-reaching, future goals and tasks. Application of additional, positive social reinforcements (such as words of praise) increases a competitor's intrinsic motivation, love of fencing, and interest in participation in practice. Similarly, progressively better results give joy and satisfaction, and strengthen self-efficacy and self-confidence which, in turn, facilitate the achievement of still better results in competitions.

Perception of one's own value constitutes a constant component part of intrinsic motivation, and is strengthened by nearly all motivational factors. Contrary to what some coaches think, negative reinforcements—criticism (tactful and objective!) of errors and inefficiencies—also constitute, especially for intelligent and ambitious people without inferiority complexes, a very efficacious motivational factor.

Applying, if necessary, critical remarks, drawing attention to errors and mistakes, the fencing master must realize that a pupil's perception of self-worth depends, to a large degree, on how others perceive him and how they co-operate with him. This is why athletes expect the coach's belief in them, and positive reinforcements—praise, recognition, personal interest in the competitor, a friendly style of leadership, empathy.

An equally important factor is the proper assessment of a competitor's results, which influences the way the athlete perceives the causes of his achievements and defeats.

All motivational factors act on a competitor, not separately, but in conjunction with each other, defining, finally, the contents, type, direction, and level of motivation. Let us remember that—as Napoleon said—"Ambition is the engine that moves the world."

Let us also remember that cooperative and friendly leadership styles facilitate the creation of an athlete's feeling of co-responsibility and independence. An extreme dictatorial style of leadership is not only ineffective, socially bad, and brings bad results in competitions, but offensive to human dignity.

As a final summary of this rather long chapter, I shall again quote James Counsilman, a swimmer, coach, psychologist, author, and scientist whom I greatly admire (among other things, for his fantastic talent for motivating athletes in such a "monotonous" sport as swimming):

"Not every swimmer or every coach can be a winner. With intelligent, hard work, each can achieve the best that is within him or within his team, and this is the standard he'll be measured by, by both other persons and himself.

My self image is more important to me
Than what my neighbor's opinion might be."

References

1. Cox, R.H. *Sport Psychology – Concepts and Applications.* C. Brown Company Publishers, Dubuque 1990.
2. Yerkes, M. and J. D. Dodson. *The Relation of Strength of Stimulus to Rapidity of Habit Formation.* "Journal of Comparative Neurology and Psychology", No. 18, 1908.
3. Wiyatkin, W.A. *Rol tiempieramenta w sportivnoy dieyatielnosti.* Fizkultura i Sport, Moskva 1978.
4. Czajkowski, Z. *Taktyka i psychologia w szermierce.* AWF, Katowice 1984.
5. Czajkowski, Z. "Motywacja i pobudzenie w działalności sportowej." *Rocznik Naukowy* 19 vol. VIII, AWF Gdańsk, 1999.
6. Knapp, B.: *Skill in Sport: The Attainment of Proficiency.* Routledge and K. Paul, London 1970.
7. Wankel, M.L., Kreisel, P.M.J. *Factors Underlying Enjoyment in Youth Sport.* Journal of Sport Psychology No. 7, 1985.
8. Scanlan, T.K., Lewshaite, R. "*Special Psychological Aspects of the Competitive Sport Sport Enjoyment for Youth Participants Predictors of Enjoyment.*" *Journal of Sport Psychology* No. 8, 1986.
9. Mc Lelland, D.C., Atkinson, W.J. *The Achievement Motive.* Harper and Row, New York 1953.
10. Spence, J.T., Helmreich, L.J.: *Masculinity and Feminity.* University of Texas Press, Austin 1978.
11. Carron, A.V.: *Social Psychology of Sport.* Ithaca 1980.
12. Czajkowski, Z. "Palat." *Sport Wyczynowy* No. 1-2/2003.
    ___________. "Co wpływa na sprawność uczenia się i stosowania nawyków w walce?" *Sport Wyczynowy* No. 3-4/2003.
13. Czajkowski, Z. "Skrajne style kierowania zespołem sportowym." *Sport Wyczynowy* No. 7-8/2003.
    ____________."Motywacja osiągnięć – nastawienie na „ja" i nastawienie na zadania." *Sport Wyczynowy* No. 3-4/2001.
14. Counsilman, J. *The Science of Swimming.* Prentice Hall Inc., New York 1975,
15. Carron, A.V. *Psychology of Sport* Ithaca 1980.

7. The Main Types of Fencers: Tactics and Psychology

"Everyone in his heart believes that he is a good psychologist, even though he may modestly confine the outward expression of that belief to the statement that he is a good judge of character. This is natural, for people are endlessly interested in their own personalities, and find their neighbors' almost as fascinating a study."

--Derek M. Dunlop

Recognition of some of the most common types of fencers, and a broad classification of them—with regard to their tactics and personality—is extremely useful, both for the competitor and for the fencing master.

For the competitor, knowledge of the most characteristic tactical types of fencers—and the ability to recognize them—is useful and necessary because:

1. He may classify himself and better understand his own personality so he can take an active part in his own training—particularly as regards exercises of tactical preparation.

2. Knowledge and recognition of his own tactical type will help him choose the style and tactics most suitable for his own temperament and dimensions of his personality, in general.

3. The same knowledge will help him assess the type of the opponents he meets on the strip, which will help him choose the right tactics.

For the fencing master, knowledge and understanding of tactical types, as well as knowledge of the pupil's personality, is of immense help in his general education activities and especially in choosing and conducting technical and tactical exercises. (This, of course, is closely connected with the practical application of the principle of individualization of training.) Fencing coaches should take care to train and teach their pupils, give them tactical advice, and generally educate them along certain tactical lines—taking into consideration the personality, traits of temperament, physique and potential of each pupil; paying special attention to dimensions of personality (extrovert, introvert; emotional stability; traits of temperament; etc.) and specific manifestations of their motor responses (see Chapter 4, as well as Chapter 15).

Style is the adaptation of a typical technique to the individual traits and requirements of a fencer. A fencer's style of fencing and the tactics he uses in competition reflect his personality, motivation, level of arousal, and temperament. This is why, in fencing, style and tactics are highly individualized, although influenced to some extent by the fencing school and the master. The influence of the fencing master may be very marked and many-sided; it embraces technique, tactics, style of fencing, motivation and attitude towards fencing and competing.

Thus, style of fencing and tactics are influenced by the competitor's personality traits, by the fencing school and by the personality of the coach. Fencing school and coach are important factors and very easily noticed in a bout, but the individual traits of a fencer (personality, higher nervous functions, "philosophy" of life, etc.) are definitely more strongly pronounced.

In the '50s, the top Polish sabreurs were subjected to a vigorous but extremely one-sided system of training by Janos Kevey, who completely failed to take into consideration the principle of individual approach. The result was that they shared several common characteristics in style and tactics: great mobility on the strip, constant use of maximum speed, simplicity of actions, fencing at a very long distance, frequent use of extremely acrobatic fleches, etc. Yet in spite of this uniformity of school and training, the differences in style and tactics between particular individuals immediately struck the eye.

I noticed the same thing among Hungarian fencers: the three superstars of Hungarian sabre of that period—Pal Kovacs, Aladar Gerevich, and Rudolf Karpati—showed many of the typical characteristics of the Hungarian school, but they differed among themselves by their personality, temperament, and style of fencing. For example, Kovacs, in his offensive actions, relied mostly on fleches; Karpati used, nearly exclusively, lunges and advance-lunges; and Gerevich used, with equal ease both lunges and fleches. It is true, however, that when the fencing master has a very strong and dominating personality, this leaves an unmistakable imprint on a fencer's technique, style, tactics and behavior.

CHARACTERISTIC TYPES OF FENCERS

I. Active vs. Passive

From the psychological point of view, taking into consideration general attitudes in a bout, one can distinguish two extreme types: the active fencer and the passive fencer (and, of course, there are many intermediate types).

The Active Fencer

This fencer attempts to impose his initiative on his opponent, attempts to control and dominate the progress of the bout, and usually does not wait very long before launching an offensive action. An active fencer usually tries to create convenient tactical situations, generally displays a preference for offensive rather than defensive actions (although, there are some active fencers who create situations for the use of their own parries), likes to accelerate the fencing phrase, and is very mobile and full of initiative.

The positive characteristics of a typical active fencer are:

- A high degree of motivation;
- A high level of motive of success;
- Combativeness (fighting spirit);
- A strong desire to win;
- Purposefulness of action;
- Tenacity;

- Quite often a large variety of actions;
- Decisiveness in fighting;
- A low level of motive of avoiding failure.

On the other hand, an active fencer may display these negative qualities:

- A certain lack of caution and patience—sometimes an excess of arousal and lack of self-control;
- A certain lack of very concentrated and judicious observation of the opponent;
- Lack of careful planning of his bouts and, sometimes;
- A certain superficiality in understanding the tactical situation.

Paradoxically, the psychological and technical base of the very active, mobile and successful actions of an active fencer is confidence in his defense. It means that while preparing his offensive actions or beginning to attack, he is ready to parry or counter-attack an unexpected action from the opponent. On the other hand, an active fencer who relies a lot on parries and counter-attacks is usually able to launch a very fast, unexpected attack.

The Passive Fencer

This fencer is inclined to leave the initiative to the opponent, usually particularly favors defensive actions, and prefers extensive and careful maneuvering on the strip, waiting long and patiently for the chance to score a hit. The passive fencer would rather take advantage of the opponent's mistakes than attempt to create tactical situations, himself. In his passivity and caution, he very often misses good opportunities for scoring a hit (for example, by an unexpected, fast, simple attack). He is usually well concentrated, but his bouts are neither lively nor spectacular and among his weak points are, sometimes, a pronounced lack of courage and a delay of decisions.

These two types, active and passive, are, of course, the most typical extremes. In reality, various mixed types—intermediate fencers with a tendency either toward the more active or passive attitude—are met. These two types are mainly determined by the fencers' traits of personality and the psycho-physiological properties of their central nervous systems. Usually, active fencers are found among strong excitatory types (cholerics) and among lively types (sanguines). Although every fencer will show a tendency toward an active or passive way of fencing, it is still very important for the fencing master to know his pupils temperament (by using observation and applying simple tests) and direct the "tactical education" accordingly.

II. Foreseen Actions vs. Improvisation

From the point of view of tactics (in the most general sense: applying learned fencing actions in a bout), and taking into consideration the ways of choosing and applying fencing actions, two extreme types can again be distinguished: the fencer of foreseen actions and the fencer of improvised actions.

The Fencer of Foreseen Actions

This fencer is fond of actions which are previously decided on and thought-out—premeditated actions. He carefully observes his opponent and tries to seize an opportunity to use a previously planned and thought-out action. For example, a sabreur has noticed that his opponent exposes his forearm while attacking or making exploratory movements. He decides to execute a stop-cut and may wait quite some time for a chance to use this premeditated foreseen action. This type of action is, in a way, less risky and more sure in its execution as it entails a state of preparedness, greater self-confidence, better technical execution of a stroke and—with an already chosen motor program—it may be applied earlier and faster. On the other hand, a competitor of foreseen actions may very often lose the chance of scoring a hit with an action on the spur of the moment, dictated logically by an unforeseen development of the situation. A fencer of foreseen actions may have a predilection for first or second intention actions, or use them both. The fencer on foreseen actions mostly relies on simple motor response.

The Fencer of Improvised Actions

The fencer of lightning-speed improvisation and unforeseen actions, fences without any preconceived plan of action. He does not wait for the chance to use an action that is planned and thought-out. He tries to take advantage of the movement of the weapons, his own and his opponent's, as well as the change of distance, for immediate execution of various actions, carried out as sensory-motor responses, and dictated by the situation on the strip and the course of the fencing phrase. These actions are executed on the spur of the moment and are based on technical-tactical abilities which, in turn, are based on various types of specific sensory-motor reactions.

The assets of this type of fencer are:

- A variety of actions;
- Richness and spontaneity of his repertoire;
- The ability to prolong or break off, if necessary, a fencing phrase;
- The ability to take a lightning-speed decision, or to change his intention while executing an action;
- Great speed of orientation and reaction;
- Speed and accuracy of his perception;
- Great motor coordination (motor adaptability and motor educability); and usually
- A very good feeling of surprise—"choice of time."

These abilities depend on a mobility and adaptability of the nervous processes (ensuring, in case of need, a quick switch from excitatory to inhibitory processes and vice-versa), good operative memory, good speed of operative thinking and very good, and fast, sensory-motor responses.

The shortcomings of this type of fencer are:

- Inability to penetrate the thoughts and intentions of his opponent;

- Inadequate analyses of the opponent's style and tactics;
- A certain superficiality of observation;
- Lack of plans of action;
- All of which, very often, lead to missing certain chances to score hits by taking advantage of noticed, and expected, mistakes and weaknesses of the opponent.

A fencer of improvised actions uses mostly choice reactions and, also, differential, switch-over, and other varieties of reaction.

In practice, again, we meet with a variety of intermediary types. Both extreme types of fencers can, and do, achieve very high results. The best results in fencing, however, are obtained most easily, and in a spectacular manner, by a competitor with the ability to act as necessity arises—sometimes in a preconceived way and sometimes in an improvised way, together with a combination of traits of the active type.

The style of fencing, tactics and, especially, the way of applying actions in a bout, must be cultivated according to the personality and temperament of a given fencer. Certain extreme shortcomings can be compensated for by conscious work on one's self—self-education—and special choice of exercises. For example, a very active, lively fencer with great mobility and lability of nervous processes will obviously, and rightly, base his tactics on lightning-speed improvisation, using mainly unforeseen actions. In order not to be too one-sided, he must devote a certain amount of time and energy to cultivating patience, caution, tactical observation and, from time to time, preconceived actions. The same goes—but in the opposite direction, of course—for a rather passive, cautious fencer who has a predilection for preconceived foreseen actions.

III. Cooperative vs. Contradictory Tactics

As regards the way of conducting a bout and, especially, reacting to the opponent's moves, one may distinguish: the fencer of "cooperative" tactics and the fencer of "contradictory" ("cutting-through") tactics.

The Fencer of Cooperative Tactics

This is a fencer of long and complex phrases. Having understood the tactical conception of his opponent, he reacts, to begin with, in apparent compliance with the opponent's intentions, but ends with an extra movement, unforeseen by the opponent. The opponent, noticing the initial success of his action and losing his caution, is lured into a trap and finally hit.

For example:

Example 1 The fencer foresees the opponent's compound attack consisting of two feints and the final stroke. He reacts to the feints by successive parries—which is what the opponent expected—then unexpectedly adds still another parry and scores a hit with the riposte.

Example 2 The opponent repeats several times, in succession, a quarte pressure on the blade. The fencer realizes that the opponent wants to draw his attack by double disengagement in order to parry the attack and hit with the riposte. Therefore, he executes the opponent's desired attack as a false attack with a rather short lunge, then parries the opponent's riposte and score a hit with a counter-riposte (thus executing one variety of second-intention attack). This is, of course, a sometimes rather risky form of tactics—one may not rightly guess the opponent's real intentions—but it is very often successful at leading the opponent into a trap.

The Fencer of Contradictory, or Cutting-Through, Tactics

This is a fencer of simple and short phrases. Having understood his opponent's intentions, he does not co-operate with him, even in the first stages of the action, but applies, at once, some uncomplicated, fast action which immediately spoils the opponent's plans.

Example 1 Against an expected attack with feints, the fencer of contradictory tactics will not react by parries, but will execute a stop-hit or a stop-hit with opposition.

Example 2 A foilist, having guessed that his opponent wants to provoke him into making an attack by double disengagement, will not comply with his wishes but will instantly disengage and execute a counter-sixte beat followed by a straight thrust.

A fencer of cooperative tactics takes delight in long, complicated phrases. His style of fencing is complex, often containing exploratory exchanges of parry-riposte and various tactical traps. Such a style of fencing is usually spectacular and pleasant to watch.

A fencer of cutting-through tactics prefers and applies short, simple movements leading to short, uncomplicated phrases. The exchanges of strokes, as well as the bouts of such fencers are usually very short.

There are, of course, versatile fencers who use, in turn, both cooperative and cutting-through tactics.

IV. Wide vs. Narrow Range of Actions

Another important criterion of classifying the tactical types of fencers is the range and variety of actions actually applied by them in competition. From that point of view, we may distinguish: the fencer of a wide range of actions and the fencer of a narrow range of actions.

The Fencer with a Wide Range of Actions

This "many-sided" fencer is a one who uses a wide variety of actions in a bout. Variety in actions may be expressed by all or some of the following elements: applying offensive, defensive and counter-offensive actions; using various types of attacks; taking decisions in a tactical fight in various ways (using foreseen, unforeseen and partly foreseen actions); using various kinds of parries or counter-attacks; applying simple and compound actions; alternatively using, in defense, parries and counter-attacks; etc. The variety of tactics, however, does not consist only in applying a large range of real actions—though this, naturally, is very important—but also in using the variety and cleverness of preparatory actions (see Chapter 3). There are some versatile fencers who use, actually, a limited repertoire of actual actions but prepare them with incredible ingenuity and variation.

The Fencer with a Narrow Range of Actions

This "one-sided" fencer is one who always uses the same, very limited number of actions in a bout. His strong points are extreme confidence, and perfection in executing his actions. On the other hand, his tactics are very easily deciphered by an experienced opponent, who usually finds no great difficulty in counteracting them.

Tactical one-sidedness, the application of a very limited number of actions in a bout, may result from inadequate technical training that includes only simple and foreseen actions. Fencers of lightning-speed improvisation must, of necessity, use a rich and varied repertoire of actions resulting from constantly changing situations in the course of the bout.

V. Cautious vs. Risk-Taking

The Cautious Fencer

A vital characteristic of a cautious fencer is a very high level of concentration. He is very careful not to take any risks, waiting patiently for a "sure" opportunity to score. He is usually a rather passive type of a fencer; he does not display initiative, but tries to take advantage of the opponent's mistakes.

The Risk-Taking Fencer

This fencer is the extreme opposite of the above; he does not concentrate enough, is not very watchful, and is always inclined to take a risk. Very often, he does score a hit by his bold and courageous actions but, equally often, receives "easy" hits as a result of not being observant enough.

VI. Offensive vs. Defensive

The Offensive Fencer

The name easily describes his qualities—the offensive fencer relies mainly on attacks and other offensive actions, very often using a cascade of false and real attacks.

The Defensive Fencer

As the name implies, he is more cautious, relying mainly on defensive and counter-offensive actions.

Of course, in practice, one does not see only these typical examples, but many various types. Also—and this is very important—a fencer may be described and classified using not only one, but several criteria of classification. For example, fencers may have combinations of traits such as the following:

Fencer A: Very active, uses lightning-speed improvisation, unforeseen actions, wide variety of actions, cautious type.

Fencer B: Active, uses foreseen actions, a defensive fencer, very cautious, uses a whole variety of defensive actions.

Fencer C Very active, offensive fencer, uses a small unforeseen variety of strokes, very incautious and risky.

Etc., etc.

VII. INCREASING THE NUMBER AND VARIETY OF ACTIONS

The number and variety of actions used in a bout by a competitor can be increased by:

1. Special tactical exercises, developing the capability to apply various actions in similar situations.

2. Advising the pupil to apply, in loose play, strokes learned in the lesson and, even more important, to use strokes applied in loose play when in competition.

3. Systematizing the fencer's knowledge of fencing theory and tactics with a strong emphasis being put on the application of principles of an active and conscious approach and the principle of unity of theory and practice, as well as the principle of transfer of skills (from lesson to loose play, from loose play to competition).

To correctly assess a fencer's tactical type and style, a coach uses, of course, careful observations of training bouts and competition, and may also use special tests. Below are a few chosen examples:

- The coach notes a pupil's variety of actions in a lesson in comparison to his variety of actions in training bouts and in competitions. This is very important because it happens quite often that a fencer acquires a rich repertoire of strokes in a lesson, but only uses a few of them in a training bout, or a fencer uses rich and versatile technique in training bouts but, in competition, his range of strokes and tactics is very narrow and limited. It must be stressed once more that, really, a fencer has learned a given action or capability if he is able to apply it successfully in competition (principle of transfer of skills).

- The coach carefully and systematically observes and records the range (number of different actions applied in a competition) and efficacy (number of given actions which score hits) for all athletes and all bouts in a competition. This allows a coach to notice and assess various changes and trends in fencing in all weapons. I started such observations, noting all the hits at the 1948 Olympic Games in London, and have repeated such recordings for many years at World Championships, Olympic Games, World Cups, etc. The result of these observations have allowed me to characterize changes in the technique and tactics of various weapons and also the strong and weak points of leading foreign and Polish fencers (see Chapter 10: "Directing the Process of Training, taking Competition and an Athlete's Personality Dimensions as a Model").

- Similarly, the coach watches and records the range and efficacy of actions for one individual fencer. It may happen that a fencer, in a series of bouts, executes a hundred attacks, out of which only twenty are successful; whereas another fencer, in the same number of bouts, uses forty attacks and scores with them twenty-five times. It might happen that a fencer, who applies many unsuccessful attacks, rarely relies on parry-riposte, and yet his percentage of hits scored by parry-riposte is very high. Such—of course, more detailed and frequent—analysis of the range and efficacy of various actions performed by a given fencer in competition, gives a wealth of information about his strong and weak points and helps direct attention to the actions and capabilities the fencer must improve.

- Fencers are asked to, for a certain period of time (e.g. two weeks), record all the successful offensive actions in training bouts—describing the tactical character of the actions. Such a record gives deep information about the tactical type and skills of a given fencer.

Here are two real-life examples:

1. Fencer K.P. – An overwhelming number of his attacks were first intention foreseen actions; a small percentage were attacks, originally foreseen, but with a change of intention during their execution. It reflected his fencing style: he was a very fast, well-coordinated foilist with very fast reactions. He was sure of his technique and reactions, so he did not need to use second intention attacks and did not "bother" to employ open-eyes attacks. He used mostly foreseen first intention attacks, but if the opponent managed to make an unexpected movement, he—relying on his fast reaction—could change the final part of the attack with ease.

2. Fencers A.D. – An overwhelming number of her attacks were second intention (second intention counter-riposte, second intention counter-time). Most of her first intention attacks were not simple, but compound (with feints). There was not a single attack with open-eyes or change of intention. She was a very intelligent, diligent, enthusiastic fencer, but of a phlegmatic temperament with low mobility of her nervous processes; she was rather slow in reaction and slow in movement, but with a good understanding of fencing and tactics. With such characteristics, she could not rely on very fast, surprising simple attacks, or partially foreseen actions (open-eyes and change of intention). Her slow reaction and slow movements were compensated by a high state of concentration and cleverly applied second intention actions.

The above-presented classification of fencers and the examples of observational tests, although very sketchy and simplified, may be of great help to a coach, as well as to a fencer who has to take stock of his opponent and prepare a plan of action before a bout.

The individualization of training and tactics, and the attempts to classify various types of fencers, although sometimes neglected by modern coaches, constitute nothing new. The famous Italian master, Salvador Fabris, wrote in 1601, "Sapersi governare contre i grandi, i picoli, i deboli, i forti, e contro i collerici e i flemmatici." ("Know how to deal with the large ones and the small ones, the weak ones and the strong ones, and against the choleric ones and the phlegmatic ones.")[1]

References

1. Fabris, S.: *de lo Schermo, overo scienza d'arme*, Copenhagen 1606.

The Professor at His Blackboard
I: Theory

8. The Main Types of Fencer: The "Warrior" and the "Technician"

"Sports rivalry ought to be wiped out."
--Father Stanislaw Rucinski

"Winning isn't everything—it's the only thing.."
--Vince Lombardi

In the previous chapter, the most commonly occurring types of fencers are described. The differentiation of these types is based on style of fencing, tactics, repertoire of strokes, etc. (active or passive fencer; offensive or defensive fencer; fencer of foreseen or of unforeseen actions, etc.).

In the present chapter, I describe and analyze two extreme types of fencers: "warrior" and "technician" (it should be understood that these names are rather arbitrary). I identified these two types many years ago after long and careful observation of many training sessions and competitions.[1] As we know, every classification must have one clear criterion. Here, the identification of "warrior" and "technician" types is based, above all, on the fencers' achievement motivation, strictly connected and associated with their attitudes towards sport, in general, and towards fencing, training, competitions, tasks, results, the coach, colleagues, and opponents (see Chapter 6).

It must be conceded at the outset that these two types represent extremes; in reality, there are many fencers who display characteristic traits of both types in varying proportions,. It is also worthwhile to notice that the attitude of my "technician" type corresponds, more or less, to what the majority of sport psychologists describe as "task-involvement;" while the attitude of my "warrior" closely resembles one type of an "ego-involvement" personality—namely the one characterized by a strong desire to compete, to achieve successes, to get recognition, to show one's superiority, and all of this with a very high level of a motive of success. There are also types with highly competitive attitudes who are strongly afraid of defeat (a high level of a motive of avoiding failure); these types will not be discussed here.[2]

Differentiating and recognizing various types of fencers is extremely important for the efficacy of the training process—especially in applying the principle of individualization, when the coach must take into account his pupils' dimensions of personality, traits of temperament, intelligence, emotional stability or instability, extroversion or introversion, as well as their attitudes towards fencing, exercises, competition, results, etc. (In this book, I only briefly mention the importance of individualization, but I hope to publish another book in the US, in which a very big and comprehensive chapter will be devoted to this topic.)

Even a fencer or coach who is not very experienced should realize that a very important consideration in the individualization of training—one of the most important—is the pupil's attitude towards fencing, fighting, etc. It never ceases to astonish me that in the majority of fencing textbooks, so little attention is paid to it. Yet, it is obvious that diagnosing and recognizing "technician" and "warrior" types—as well as various intermediate types—allows for individual treatment and different, appropriate training methods, as well as different educational approaches. We, of course, must remember that what is good for one type may be dramatically bad for another.

By watching the practices of other branches of sport and discussing the problems of training with coaches from other sports, one may conclude that similar types also occur in other sports and games—especially combat sports.

I. A GENERAL DESCRIPTION OF THE "TECHNICIAN" AND "WARRIOR" TYPES

"From among all that differentiates a human being from lower representatives of the animal world, and that differentiates people amongst themselves, nothing is more complex, interesting, and fascinating than human personality ... The structure of personality has no limit to its dimensions. One has got a warm heart, is magnanimous, open-hearted, and joyful; the other one is cold, mean, reserved, and spiteful; the third one is carefree, easygoing, polite, and unreliable; and the fourth one, on the other hand, is anxious, tense, quarrelsome, but reliable."

-- R. Tilleard-Cole

Personality is a dynamic complex, in which the various characteristic functions interact. The recognition of dimensions of personality is immensely difficult. It is, however, of primary importance to the fencing coach. When trying to recognize the pupil's personality and his predispositions for fencing, as well as when choosing various educational methods, one should start—in my opinion—with defining which traits of "warrior" or "technician" manifest themselves in a given pupil.

What is the difference between these two types?

For a "technician," fencing range (number of given actions applied in a competition) and efficacy (number of given actions which score hits) is a complicated branch of a sport containing certain elements of art. It is entertaining and fun; it serves the many-sided development of personality; it teaches new skills, abilities, and capabilities; it gives new feelings and experiences; it promotes mental development and gives plenty of rich emotions.

A "technician" believes that one should study fencing, learn about it, and enjoy its beauty. He is an advocate of systematic, precise, technical and tactical education. He always strives to better his abilities and widen his knowledge. A "technician" is interested, not only in what has direct application in competition—in the form of concrete motor skills and technical-tactical capabilities—but in everything that widens his knowledge and cognitive horizons regarding fencing: the development of weapons and the history of fencing, fencing literature, the classification of fencing actions and fencing terminology, etc. Competition, for a "technician," is a conflicting game of minds, emotions, and learned, acquired, correct and accurate movements of the weapon. He often pays attention to the aesthetic values of fencing—the beauty of the movements and exchanges.

For a "warrior," fencing is, above all and nearly exclusively,, a fight. He cultivates fencing in order to fight, hit his opponent, and win. A "warrior" does not pay much attention to learning technique; he is not interested in the theory of fencing and tactics; he does not appreciate the beauty of movements or the cleverness of tactical play. His main object, bordering on obsession, is to hit his opponent at any cost, and by any means.

And so, if a typical "technician" says, "The hit is not so important, but the way you achieve it is," then a "warrior" maintains, "It does not really matter how you score a hit, the importance is the mere fact of the hit."

A "warrior" is, then, very ambitious, aggressive, and sure of himself. For him, the most important aspects of fencing are: comparing himself to others, sharp rivalry, and striving—by means of good results in competition—for higher social status.

II. ATTITUDE TOWARDS, AND PERCEPTION OF, PRACTICE, LESSONS, TRAINING BOUTS AND COMPETITIONS

A "technician" constantly learns. He tries to increase his skills, abilities and dexterity in yielding weapons. He tries to learn new strokes and fencing actions. Let me quote a statement of a prominent Polish boxer, G. Skrzecz, which depicts a typical "technician" attitude: "I spar to learn, not to fight."

During my first visit to Budapest, in 1952, I watched, with certain surprise and great admiration, the great Hungarian sabre stars—Aladar Gerevich, Pal Kovacs, Rudolf Karpati, and others—practicing with great concentration, devotion, enthusiasm, and obvious joy, paying attention to the smallest detail of the technical execution of strokes and applied tactics.

A "warrior," in a lesson, sees only bouting situations; he wants to score a hit at any cost. Complicated, very accurate, precise technical exercises are, for him, boring and tiring. An Italian sabreur—a typical "warrior"—once said to me, "I don't care at all what I look like on the strip. It doesn't matter what they say about my style. The only thing that matters is that I get touches."

A "technician" treats competitions not only as rivalry, but also as a valuable occasion to learn something new—to try newly acquired skills and capabilities. For him, results—comparing his own to that of others—are not so very important; at least, that is what he says. A "technician" assesses his progress, his strong and weak points, without necessarily comparing himself to others. Even if he loses a bout, he may be satisfied: if the opponent was very good; if he thinks that he fenced well; or if he noticed improvement in his fencing.

For a "warrior," as already mentioned, participation in competitions means only—and above all—acute rivalry. All that matters is whether he wins or not. He values the victory irrespective of how it was obtained, with what style, by what means, or against whom it was won.

III. STYLE OF FENCING

A "technician" relies on well-acquired and thoroughly learned fencing actions, and willingly applies certain complex sets of strokes. He often uses, not only offensive, but, equally, defensive and counter-offensive movements; his movements are efficacious, economical, well-controlled, and pleasing to the eye. He uses a wide variety of tactical solutions: first and second intention actions, foreseen and unforeseen actions, etc. In the same situation, he may use different actions (e.g., defending against an opponent's attack in low line, he may alternatively use: parry two, parry eight, stop-hit from above, stop-hit in opposition, etc.).

A "warrior" is aggressive, mobile, energetic, fast, and relentless; he bases his actions on surprise ("timing") and speed, often using simple actions, mostly offensive actions; he often uses "cutting-through" tactics (see Chapter 4 and Chapter 7). He does not care whether his movements are precise—they are often "ugly," sloppy, inaccurate and uneconomical. In a fight, a "warrior" uses a lot of energy, "jumping" around the strip, trying to catch the opponent by surprise. His repertoire of actions is rather limited and "stereotypical"—he always reacts to the same situation in the same way. A high motive of success and high level of arousal increases the speed and efficacy of his actions, which are often based on simple reaction (easy, well-acquired movements demanding speed are usually executed well and efficiently in a high state of arousal (see Chapter 6).

IV. ATTITUDE TOWARD VARIOUS TACTICAL SITUATIONS, THE OPPONENT'S MOVEMENTS AND INTENTIONS

There is a huge difference between a "warrior" and "technician" in the way they perceive and react to tactical situations and the opponent's intentions and actions, although this difference is hard to perceive.

A "technician" very often pays most of his attention to himself—his own actions and intentions. His actions are usually well-executed, but sometimes may not be well-adapted to the actual tactical situation, distance, the opponent's movements, etc.—which, of course, decreases the chances of success. He may, for example, think, "Now, I am going to execute an attack—quarte-beat and double disengagement," oblivious to the fact that his opponent relies mostly on circular parries, and so the "technician's" attack will be unsuccessful. He also pays great attention to the quality—the correctness and "beauty"—of his movements.

A "warrior"—quite to the contrary—does not "see" his own movements; he does not pay attention to whether they are nice and correct, or ugly and unorthodox. All of his attention is concentrated on assessment of distance, the opponent's movements, and the quick recognition of the opponent's mistakes (e.g., inaccurate assessment of distance, exposing the forearm in epee or sabre, signs of lowering of attention, etc.) in order to take immediately advantage of them. Generally, a "warrior" does not try to create situations to facilitate the use of a preconceived action, but, relying on his speed and mobility, capitalizes on his opponent's mistakes. The consequences of such attitudes and tactics are—apart from speedy and effective exploitation of the opponent's mistakes—a limited range of actions, tedious maneuvering on the strip, and a certain tactical one-sidedness.

V. ACHIEVEMENT MOTIVATION, EMOTIONS, ATTITUDE TOWARD THE OPPONENT

A typical extreme "technician" usually does not show a high level of fighting spirit—the opponent is, for him, a partner. He may even lose a bout with satisfaction, saying that the fight was "nice and interesting," or that, although he lost, he learned a lot. The motivation of an extreme "technician"—especially his achievement motivation—is not quite appropriate for rivalry in competitions; this is often why an extreme, one-sided, "technician"—with a high level of task-involvement and too low a level of motive of success—obtains results far below what one might expect from observing his skill in practice.

For an extreme "warrior," the opponent on the strip is a real enemy, at whom he is angry (he nearly hates him). He tries to hit him, at any cost. Fighting on the strip is, for him, not a sporting rivalry, but a real "life and death" fight. His achievement motivation (especially motive of success), self-confidence, ambition, and strong emotions, help him to fight and overcome fatigue. He is not afraid of strong opponents, or of famous, well-trained, and experienced fencers. He does not respect them; he does not notice—or pretends not to notice—their values, dexterity, and strengths.

A typical "warrior" attitude was expressed by a very well-known Soviet sabreur, Victor Sidyak, to a journalist's question, "Do you have any fencing heroes, or any competitors whom you especially admire?" He replied, "I leave looking for heroes to my opponents. A good fencer always looks for the weak points of his opponents, not the qualities that deserve admiration." A similar opinion was expressed by the great Italian sabreur, Mario Aldo Montano, "It was never important for me to look nice on the piste. Really, the only things that count are scoring touches, defeating the opponent, and winning."

Completely different attitudes and values were demonstrated by the Italian, Michele Maffei, and the very famous Polish sabreur, Jerzy Pawlowski.

The object of a fencing bout is, of course, scoring hits, avoiding being hit, and defeating the opponent. Technique, tactics, and the entire system of training serve this purpose. Participation in competitions is an efficacious and stimulating way to compare one's values, assets, skills, and capabilities with those of others; it constitutes, in a way, a sign of optimism and self-efficacy, since only one fencer may win and defeats cause unpleasant emotions. Because of this, a "warrior" feels excellent at competitions, whereas a "technician" is in a slightly less happy situation. Of course, a "technician" also appreciates victory, but his satisfaction and contentment is, rather, due to self-assessment of his skills, capabilities, and his style of fencing, and not so much based on only competition results, or the assessment of other people. The ruthlessness in a fight which a typical "warrior" would impose is, for a "technician," unpleasant and difficult to accept. An extreme "technician" type does not consider competitive success as the final, most important, and only object of cultivating fencing. Defending himself against the possibility of defeat, the "technician" uses the "shield" of his technical capabilities, elegant fencing, and "philosophical" attitudes towards victory and defeat.

What is the attitude of a technician towards a warrior, and vice versa? Contrary to the well-known saying that one values more what one does not possess—or, "The grass is always greener on the other side"—extreme representatives of both types do not seem to like and respect each other (perhaps—as frequently happens—it is a sign of a hidden form of jealousy?). A "technician" says of "warriors" and their style of fencing: "barbarian," "primitive," "jumper," "that isn't fencing," etc. A "warrior" does not have a very high opinion of technicians and their style of fencing either: "gymnast," "trained monkey," "anti-talent," "it's a show and not a fight," etc.

Incidentally, in the very long history of fencing, the "warrior" and "technician" types have been differentiated for many years, though by different names. It is a very interesting fact that even at the turn of the 20th century, when a highly stylized, artistic, and very conventional way of fencing with foils was predominant—when the beauty of movements and style of fencing was often appreciated more than efficacy—there were fencers of the "warrior" type. Then they were called "ferrailleurs" (literally "scrap-iron dealers, junkyard wariors") or "naturalists." They were treated with a certain forbearance, not to say disregard—but many fencing manuals of that period gave advice on how to fence against "ferrailleurs."

VI. COMPETITION RESULTS AND DEVELOPMENT PERSPECTIVES OF THE "WARRIOR" AND "TECHNICIAN"

Now an obvious question appears: What are the competition results of the two extreme types of fencers, and what are their perspectives of development?

At the beginning of their fencing careers, in the first stage of training, at a very young age—and even among juniors—fencers of "warrior" type possess a visible superiority. They achieve early results and keep up this tendency for quite some time. They get satisfaction from their results as well as from their style of fencing and ways of training.

A "technician," initially, is in a much less fortunate position: his results—often for a very long time—are far below his expectations and skill level. His efforts are directed to acquiring, learning, and applying various fencing actions, and only to a lesser degree to beat his opponents. Very often, at the beginning, he must pass through a period of disappointment when his precisely learned and thought-out actions are brutally stopped and annihilated by the fast and rather primitive "warriors." A "technician," at the beginning of his fencing career, often loses to opponents obviously technically weaker than himself. This often invokes the surprise of "connoisseurs": "How could he lose with such overwhelming technical superiority?" A "technician" may then begin to doubt his talent and capabilities, and sometimes even doubts the competence of, and training methods used by, his fencing master ("You've taught me many varieties of a beautiful lunge and very fine yielding of the blade, and yet others fight and hit me."). The final reactions of a "technician" to initial failures may be of two varieties:

To avoid constant disappointment and the unpleasant emotions connected with defeat—which mostly occur while fencing against "barbarians"—he stresses the aesthetic value of fencing, depreciating the importance of results and victories; subconsciously cultivating the attitude: "Me—Leonardo. You—caveman."

By means of further persistent effort to perfect technique and tactical capabilities, conscious self-development of fighting traits, and by gaining competition experience, he arrives at the stage in which the efficacy of his actions in competition markedly increases. He begins to ably take advantage of his technical superiority, and gradually achieves better and better results. In this case, the "technician's" way to high achievements is slow, but successes become more stable and long-lasting.

A "warrior" also has his troubles and problems. His aggressive, active, offensive attitude on the strip brings him early successes, and he and his coach often do not realize that the achieved results do not correspond to the level of his technical capabilities (the results are "higher" than his capabilities)—but the series of good results to which he was accustomed may come to an unexpected end. This may occur when his aggressiveness becomes weaker and his extremely active and mobile style of fencing, and rather modest repertoire of actions, causes undue fatigue. In the long run, even the full exploitation of his natural abilities, spontaneity, and impulsiveness, ceases to be sufficient and a lack of a good technical base makes widening the range of his applied actions, and the versatile application of known actions, difficult.

A "warrior" always applies the same actions; he is always waiting for the occasion to apply them—which is very tiring (he is obliged to fence with the utmost energy, effort, and concentration, from the very first bout in a competition). A disregard of technique and precise, basic education, by a "warrior" (and, sometimes, also by his fencing master!) very often leads to the emergence of technical errors, which are difficult to correct once they have become automatic.

Because, at the beginning of his career, a "warrior" usually begins to achieve good results very early, stagnation of his good results come as a shock to him; especially since, very often, he does not understand what is causing it. In such a situation, the logical conclusion for a "warrior" ought to be systematic, strenuous effort to develop his technical capabilities and increase the range of learned fencing actions. But that is precisely what a "warrior" does not like! Besides, as is generally known, improvement of faultily learned movements (changing a motor skill) is extremely difficult once they have become automated; and even "eradicated" mistakes are committed in competition under the influence of emotions and high arousal, when attention is concentrated on tactics (what to do and when to do it, but not how it is done).

VII. RESULTS OBTAINED BY "WARRIORS" AND "TECHNICIANS"

By careful analysis of the course of the athletic careers of outstanding fencers—from various countries, at various times, and in various weapons—one may reach the following conclusions:[3]

1. The greatest achievements in the Olympic Games, World Championships and other great international tournaments, and long-lasting high athletic form and long-lasting sustainability of high results, are generally shown by fencers with a high level of technical, technical-tactical, and tactical capabilities, and psychomotor abilities, with very good, precise, basic education, who display many traits and characteristics of a "technician" and some adequately developed (inborn or learned) traits of a "warrior." Such fencers often display rich tactics based on impeccable, "elegant" technique. Such traits were possessed by the legendary stars of international fencing; to name only a few: Christian d'Oriola, Jean-Claude Magnan, Edoardo Mangiarotti, Aladar Gerevich, Jerzy Pawlowski, Rudolf Karpati, Victor Zhdanowich, Egon Franke, Yakov Rylski.

2. Outstanding results in international competitions, equal to those of the above-mentioned group, are also achieved by athletes with a marked prevalence of "warrior" traits who are able to supplement their aggressive motivation with the appropriate technical capabilities, often developing a very specific, unorthodox style of fencing. For example: Ilona Elek, Tibor Berczelly, Victor Sidyak, Grigory Kriss, and others.

3. However, fencers with extreme, one-sided traits of a "technician" or "warrior," mostly do not achieve very high results in international competitions. A "technician" with too low a level of fighting spirit and motive of success, becomes an average fencer with correct technique, whose style of fencing is nice to look at, but

> not efficacious. A "warrior" who does not improve his technique, and does not widen his repertoire of actions, after a period of initial successes, soon reaches the ceiling of his possibilities: his repertoire of actions becomes ossified; he becomes an unrelenting, fierce, but mediocre fencer and, very often, finishes his fencing career relatively early.

I myself am a strong champion of many-sided, versatile training, developing technical and tactical capabilities, cognitive and psychomotor abilities, promoting sport enjoyment and a deep interest in fencing, while, at the same time, enhancing the right set of achievement motivation (see Chapter 6). Many prominent coaches—who we might call "technicians" with a sound proportion of "warrior" traits—have displayed similar view and attitudes.

The traits and attitudes of a "warrior" are inborn, but they are developed by coaches who we may also call "warrior" types. These coaches do not worry about their pupils' education or the development of their personalities. "Warrior" coaches treat their students instrumentally, and their only aim is "victory at any cost"—for their own benefit and glory. If coaches of "technician" type can be described as people who love fencing in themselves, then the "warrior" coaches are people who love themselves in fencing.

A wide variety of negative factors--difficulties, threatening situations in competitions, responsibility for results, referees' mistakes, a high level of arousal, and all stressful situations—may cause, among "warriors," heightened mobilization, aggressive attitudes, boldness, and even recklessness, increasing the efficacy of their actions. The same situations, among some "technicians," may negatively influence their efficiency: deteriorating speed and accuracy of perception and reaction, lowering self confidence, etc.

The above-mentioned phenomena may be explained in the following manner:

1. In accordance with the Second Yerkes-Dodson Law, high motivation and an elevated level of arousal may exert a negative influence on efficacy and results of activity, in situations where motor skills are very fine, difficult, and complicated (this means that the same

level of arousal, good for "warriors" may already be too high for, and negatively influence, "technicians"). Thus, high arousal and motivation, ambition, and great responsibility for results, hits a "technician" first. The same level of arousal may be optimal for a "warrior," whose style of fencing is based on simple motor skills and primitive tactics. As I mention in other chapters, the best remedy for a "technician" is to make difficult tasks easy, by using the over-learning method (see Chapter 6).

2. The great majority of "warriors" possess a strong nervous system (nerve cells with a high capacity of effort and high resistance to fatigue), whereas, among some "technicians," one meets individuals with rather weak nervous systems. As we know—and it has been stressed many times—difficulties, threatening situations, and rivalry, increase the efficacy of actions of competitors with strong nervous systems, and decrease the efficacy of actions of fencers with weak nervous systems. My observations, in this respect, have been verified by much scientific research.[4] Besides, competitors with weak nervous systems much more often display their states of anxiety—which may also diminish the quality and efficacy of actions.

VIII. PRACTICAL ADVICE FOR COACHES

These observations and considerations imply that a fencing master, in his coaching—which, of course, includes education—should not act against the nature of a given competitor, but should rather ably apply the principle of individualization of training, taking advantage of an athlete's strong points and tendenciess while minimizing his weak points and negative traits.

It is necessary to ensure the pupil's active and close cooperation in enhancing the right direction, kind, and level of motivation, and in building and developing his style of fencing, taking into account his dimensions of personality, temperament, and psychological and tactical tendencies.

Coaching a fencer who mostly displays traits of the "technician" type, the fencing master should take advantage of the pupil's good points—his assets (fondness of systematic effort, desire to deeply understand fencing, intellectual approach towards training, task-involvement, a high level of motor coordination—which helps in the acquisition of sensory-motor skills)—at the same time influencing his fighting spirit, enhancing his motivation, and carefully and gradually introducing difficult situations, psychological pressure, and elements of rivalry.

When coaching a fencer with overwhelming "warrior" traits, the fencing master should take advantage of the pupil's inborn aggressiveness, strong desire to compete, love of rivalry and fighting, and—making use of the difficult situations of bouts and rivalry—create good and variable bases of technique, gradually enriching his range of acquired and applied fencing actions and capabilities.

One should not, however, strive to impose complete uniformity—nor conformity of fencer's styles and tactics to either of these two contrasting types. It is not desirable and, anyway, it is impossible to attain. What really matters is taking advantage of the good points and assets of both types, and balancing their qualities, assets, and weak points. A "technician," just the same, will base his fencing style on technique and an "intellectual-technical" variety of tactics. A "warrior" will base hers mainly on fighting spirit, speed, sense of timing, boldness, and an impulsive style of tactics. For fencers of both types, appropriate training and supplementary influences will help them become more versatile and efficient fencers.

In applying the principle of individualization in tactical preparation (and in the entire process of training, as a whole), it is important to differentiate various traits of temperament and—influencing these temperamental traits—various qualities of the nervous system, mainly the strength of neurological processes and, especially, the strength of excitatory processes.

Among pupils with a weak nervous system, difficult conditions of exercises and, especially, situations of competition and rivalry cause intimidation, confusion, a lack of self-confidence, and certain difficulties in acquiring motor skills and capabilities. Pupils with a strong nervous system enjoy difficult situations, rivalry, and exercises demanding high speed and orientation in time and space.[5]

The early introduction of rivalry can cause problems for a coach. Competitions, ranking lists, point systems, and other complicated systems of rivalry (sometimes bordering on absurdity), may give young "warriors" heir first successes—due only to mobility, speed, aggressiveness, and other "warrior" traits. But these successes may cause a coach serious difficulties in giving the pupil the necessary many-sided training and education.

To pupils who do not appreciate the importance of technique and tactical capabilities, who try to avoid the sometimes difficult exercises which ensure basic skills, a coach should try to explain that, although rivalry and competition are very typical and important factors of sport, there are also other values which one should appreciate, like: developing one's personality, cognitive processes, motor control and adaptability, and other factors, such as aesthetic ones. A coach should educate his pupils in such a way—developing such qualities and attitudes—that fencing is not only a kind of rivalry, but fulfils a very valuable educational role and gives pleasure and sport enjoyment; a very one-sided, aggressive attitude may only appeal to a small bunch of bloodthirsty people, who in any case may not be the champions of the future.

References

1. Czajkowski, Z.: *Taktyka i psychologia w szermierce,* AWF, Katowice 1984.
2. Czajkowski, Z.: "Motywacja osiągnięć – nastawienie na „ja" i nastawienie na zadania," *Sport Wyczynowy* No. 3-4/2001.
3. Czajkowski, Z.: *Teoria, praktyka i metodyka szermierki – Theory, Practice and Methodology of Fencing,* AWF, Katowice 2001.
4. Czajkowski, Z.: *Sprawozdania z zawodów (reports on competitions),*
5. see ref. 2.,

9. The Knowledge, Skills, Personality, and Work of the Coach

"A good teacher is always a most diligent pupil."
--Maxim Gorky

"I have learned a lot from my teachers, much more from my colleagues, but the most from my pupils."
--Rabbi Yehuda

A COACH'S SKILLS, KNOWLEDGE AND TASKS, AND THE ESSENCE OF HIS WORK

A coach's work is extremely varied—conducting training; teaching sensory motor skills and tactics; developing pupils' energy abilities, fitness, and motor coordination; and, also, developing his pupils' personality.

The relative importance of the various skills and abilities of a coach depends, to a large degree, on where he works. In high-competitive (elite) sport settings, the primary emphasis is on achieving high results in competitions. In recreational sport, the emphasis is on fun, health, active rest, and keeping up the over-all level of fitness. In schools and youth sport centers, the primary object is ensuring the versatile development of children and youth, ensuring a high level of functional and adaptive possibilities, providing sport enjoyment, and giving the young pupils a sense of self-confidence and competence as well as optimizing their level of arousal. To achieve these objectives, the coach must constantly try to keep up his personal fitness, develop his performance skills, and enrich his knowledge of sport (psychology, physiology, methodology of training, etc.). Of course, the coach should always strive to educate and influence his pupils positively.

Certain coaching skills and methods are the same in all branches of sport and some are different and specific to a given branch of sport. In figure skating or acrobatics, for example, the coach's main objective is to teach the very precise execution of many different motor skills, full of finesse and expression. In track-and-field events and other sports where physical (energy) fitness is of primary importance, the coach must first develop energy abilities and one specific closed motor skill (technique of execution). In combat sports and team games, energy abilities and motor coordination serve as a basis for rich technique, tactics, and psychomotor abilities (psychological processes closely connected with motor performance). Here, open motor skills, tactical abilities, various qualities of attention, speed and accuracy of perception, and speed of decision are important.

One unique coaching philosophy does not exist. High results are achieved by coaches of different personalities, different temperaments, different methods of training, and different leadership styles. There are, however, certain common traits among the most successful coaches:

1. A wide knowledge, both general and specific, which is constantly improving and widening, combined with the application, in practice, of various branches of sport science, psychology, and other basic subjects.

2. A high level of technical skills, which ensures a high level and efficacy of the practical teaching of sensory motor skills.

3. A high level of the ability to convey knowledge, practical skills, and various abilities to pupils; a strong command of methods of perfecting energy and coordination abilities; profound knowledge of methodology.

4. Management and leadership abilities.

5. The ability to educate, inspire, and motivate pupils; here, a coach's personal example is most important. Of paramount importance is the unity of what a coach says, what he does, and his attitude toward sport, work, and his pupils.

6. An innovative approach, constant perfecting of one's own abilities, seeking new knowledge, watching and noticing the changes occurring in sport.

7. The ability to plan, program, and organize the process of training, controlling its results, exact and penetrating observations of competitions, applying the important principles of training (principle of specificity, transfer of skill, individualization, etc.); the ability to conduct exercises in an interesting and colorful manner; fostering the interest and love of their discipline of sport among athletes; the documentation of training and competitions.

8. Effectiveness in co-operating with officials, other coaches, school administration, psychologists, journalists, etc.

9. Sharing knowledge and experience with other coaches and instructors, trying to develop one's own branch of sport, writing and publishing textbooks, reports, essays, and instructions on the subject of their sport. The latter point is very often underestimated and yet it is very important indeed. Preparing a report or article forces a coach to analyze various actions of training and competitions.

A COACH'S MOTIVATION

In a coach's professional activities, one may distinguish many different motives (rivalry motives, motives of social approval, financial motives, etc.). There are, however, three main groups of motives which must be distinguished and considered:

1. Achievement of highest possible results by his pupils.

2. Ensuring the pupils' feeling of fun and enjoyment, optimal level of arousal, motor activity, and feeling of competence.

3. Ensuring the young athletes' versatile development, education; developing pupils' independence and self-efficacy. Taking care of health and psychological, social, and intellectual development.

All three groups of motives are very important in all kinds of physical education and sport activities, but the first set of motives is obviously most important in high level competition sport; the second predominates in sports for youth and children, and educational sports; while the third is foremost in physical education in school (cognitive-motor education).

IS THERE ONE UNIQUE, IDEAL COACHING PROFILE?

The answer to this question is, definitely, NO. I would suppose that every great coach chooses and walks his own path. Coaches of very different personality and temperament, using quite different methods of training and quite different styles of leadership achieve good results. Great coaches are not devoid of certain week points. They achieve high results, not because they lack weak points, but because of great development of their strong points and possibilities. One can give many examples of famous coaches who achieved very high results in various branches of sport and whose views and methods were quite different.

Generally, people assess a coach's quality by his pupils' results in competitions. My own opinion is that a great coach is one who:

- Ensures his pupils great results in competitions;
- Properly educates his pupils and develops their personalities;
- Tries to develop his discipline of sport, introducing new knowledge and new methods;
- Shares his knowledge and skills with others, teaches younger coaches and instructors, and presents his knowledge and experience in the form of books and articles.

In spite of many marked differences between various great coaches, there are certain features and qualities which are common to all of them:

1. Great love of their sport— creative passion.

2. Introducing new knowledge and new methods.

3. Taking advantage of the knowledge of other sports, but not copying blindly.

4. A strong personality with a powerful influence on his pupils.

5. Perfect acquisition of the technique of his sport, inspiring demonstrations, and an interesting, versatile, and colorful manner of conducting exercises.

6. Self-assurance and self-confidence; a belief in the rightness of his views and efficacy of his methods, but, at the same time, an open approach to other views and methods.

7. The gift to convey his knowledge and abilities to others.

8. A wide general interest in sport (in spite of great concentration on his own branch of sport); a good coach may be a maniac, but not a monomaniac!

9. A great talent for teaching; the desire and ability to convey his knowledge and experience to others—both in the form of practical exercises and in writing books.

10. Great creative energy, perseverance in activity, and enthusiasm for his work.

LEADERSHIP STYLES

The variety of different coaching profiles is reflected, among other things, in different leadership styles. One may distinguish the following coaching leadership styles:

1. Dictatorial style—extreme form of formal and directive styles—the coach behaves like a dictator: he does not explain anything; he does not care about the pupils' opinions and feelings; he simply gives orders. He ap-

plies negative reinforcements, often treating his pupils instrumentally.

2. Directive style—the coach distinctly plays the part of the superior and leader. He lectures and gives orders, and the athletes listen and follow the orders, but the tone is not as severe as in the dictatorial style.

3. Formal style—the coach and athlete co-operate, concentrating on the achievement of consecutive training tasks.

4. Cooperative style—This style may be applied even with young pupils: the coach directs the course of training but he explains his decisions; he takes into account the pupils' feelings, doubts, questions, and opinions; he stimulates student initiative and independence.

5. Friendly style—This style may be applied with adult, intelligent athletes: there is friendly cooperation and a marked emotional linkage.

One may achieve good results applying various styles of leadership, but definitely the most efficacious and most educational are the Cooperative and Friendly styles (see Table 9-A).

COMPETITION PROFILE & INDIVIDUALIZATION OF TRAINING

I do not support the currently very fashionable theory of the, so-called "champion profile." I think that great athletes, Olympic medalists—like great coaches—although possessing many similar traits, may and do differ in many important respects (extroversion-introversion; traits of temperament; technique and tactics; offensive and defensive types; various somatic traits; etc.). My opinion is that:

- Training and competitions—like theory and practice; like cognition and action—should not be separate, water-tight compartments. An athlete must see, in training, certain situations which occur in competitions; and, in competition, he must recognize certain situations experienced in the course of training.

- In planning and conducting training, one must take into account what actually happens in competitions—which actions are most commonly used, which are most efficacious, what style of fencing, etc., is prevalent and most successful.

- Apart from modeling the training on a competition profile (see Chapter 10), one must take into consideration the athlete's qualities, dimensions of his personality, traits of temperament, technical and tactical style, etc.

- The entire process of training ought to be based on a knowledge approach and not a procedure approach. This means that you must know perfectly the characteristics of your branch of sport, choose certain tasks and, according to them, choose the appropriate training methods and training loads.

- In the long-reaching plan of training, the athlete must overcome the following "difficult situations":

Table 9-A – Extreme Leadership Styles in Coaching

	Dictatorial Style	Cooperative and Friendly Style
Essence and Main Characteristics	The coach makes all the decisions on his own, without consulting anyone. He does not explain his intentions or motives; he does not explain his methods of training; he does not discuss with his pupils the goals and tasks in the process of training, in the club or training camp. The athletes obey his orders and execute them.	The athletes cooperate in creating general training plans and forming tasks for consecutive training stages. Not only are they informed about what they have to do, but they have a certain influence on the coach, who listens to their questions, doubts, and proposals. The coach wants the athletes to precisely understand the essence and goal of all exercises and to be able, by themselves, to assess the quality of their performance, and application of learned actions in competition. The athletes co-operate in directing the process of training.
Coach's Approach	The coach concentrates only on rivalry, competition, and successes (the latter of which, he treats as his own).	The coach, appreciating the value of competition and results, tries, at the same time, to develop athletes' personalities, their upbringing and education. He is interested in an increase of his pupils' abilities, skills, and knowledge.

Table 9-A – Extreme Leadership Styles in Coaching—continued

Main Feature of Coach-Pupil Relationship	The coach treats his pupils instrumentally; their results serve solely to fulfill the coach's ambition and to gain certain benefits (recognition, social status, prizes).	The coach treats his pupils as partners, taking into consideration their feelings and views. He takes care of their development, emotions, satisfaction, progress, and results in competition.
Coach's Perception of the Athletes	According to McGregor's "X" theory (see below).	According to McGregor's "Y" theory (see below).
Empathy	No empathy.	A lot of empathy; cooperative and friendly relationships
Most Important Factors of Achievement Motivation	A very high level of motive of success; overwhelming emphasis on very intense effort; aggressive attitudes in competition (opponent is your enemy; the ends justify the means).	Task and self-improvement involvement; feeling of independence and responsibility; fascination and interest in the chosen discipline of sport; optimal (not mania-like) level of motive of success. The opponent ought to be treated as partner and colleague, not enemy.
Psychological Basis	Psycho-analytical psychology and behavioral psychology.	Cognitive psychology—appreciating and stressing the social humanistic values of sport; also taking into account emotions and emotional intelligence.
Difficulty; Range of Application	Easy to apply—much easier than cooperative style—especially when dealing with aggressive unsubtle athletes. Certain elements might be applied with children and young athletes in cases of poor discipline and tactless behavior, especially with large groups and during training camps.	This style is quite difficult to apply. It requires from the coach a good deal of experience, knowledge of pedagogy, and tact and patience. The most effective style when dealing with intelligent and cultured persons. The coach develops positive dimensions of personality and endeavors.

Table 9-B
Theories "X" and "Y" of the Perception of Human Nature by Superiors

McGregor's Theory X	McGregor's Theory Y
People naturally dislike work and effort, and avoid them as much as possible.	Physical and mental effort is as natural and pleasant to people as rest and play.
One needs to force people to work—by controlling, checking, supervising, directing, and threatening them.	People can direct their own lives and work, themselves; they are able to check the fulfillment of the tasks with which they identify themselves.
The average human being prefers to be directed and controlled, externally; tries to avoid responsibility; and has no ambition.	The average human being, in favorable conditions, not only willingly accepts responsibilities, but actively seeks them out.

a. Learning a given amount of sensory motor skills and abilities.

b. Transferring these skills and abilities from exercises into training bouts.

c. Transferring skills and abilities from training bouts into small competitions.

d. Transferring skills and abilities from small competitions to big and highly important competitions.

The smoothness and ease with which a fencer transfers his skills and abilities from Point A to Point D depicts the efficacy of his process of training.

WHAT COACHES SHOULD AVOID

In their activities, coaches must avoid: constant repetition of the same exercises and the same way of doing things (monotony causes fatigue, loss of interest, poor performance, and lack of motivation); blind copying of others; clichéd actions and movements; actions and movements which have no application in competition; "functional fixation"; failure to notice changes in rules, technique, tactics, ways of refereeing, and methods of training.

In connection with the contents of Table 9-A, it is necessary to explain, even very briefly, McGregor's "X" and "Y" theories. D. McGregor classified a supervisor's attitude toward subordinates (e.g., a teacher to pupils, a director to employees, head of a medical ward to nurses, a coach to athletes, etc.) into two categories, which he called Theory 'X' and Theory 'Y'[1]

Theory "X," from the point of view of the coach, presents a very negative picture of human-beings, while theory "Y" presents a very positive and optimistic picture.

It is obvious that, depending on the theory to which he adheres, the coach will either choose a dictatorial or cooperative style of leadership.

Table 9-B presents the most essential points of McGregor's "X" and "Y" theories. As I have mentioned above, after studying McGregor's theories, one may conclude that a dictatorial coach perceives his athletes according to "X," whereas a cooperative and friendly coach, perceives his pupils in accordance with "Y."

Fig. 10.1

TRAINING	→	PERFORMANCE

Simple attempts to direct and control the process of training: hypothesizing a direct relationship between results in competitions and training load (range, contents, intensity and frequency of exercises).

Personally, I think that, apart from the coach's dimensions of personality, traits of temperament, pedagogical views, knowledge, and even working conditions, a very important influence on the choice of a style of leadership is exerted by the three following interconnected features:

1. Whether the coach's motivation is solely connected with fulfilling his own needs (recognition, domination, profit, competence, etc.), or whether he equally takes into account the athletes' needs (recognition, competence, achievement, arousal, affiliation, friendship, material benefits, etc.);

2. Whether the coach's views on human nature and his attitudes towards his pupils, are in accord with McGregor's "X" or "Y" theory;

Fig. 10.2

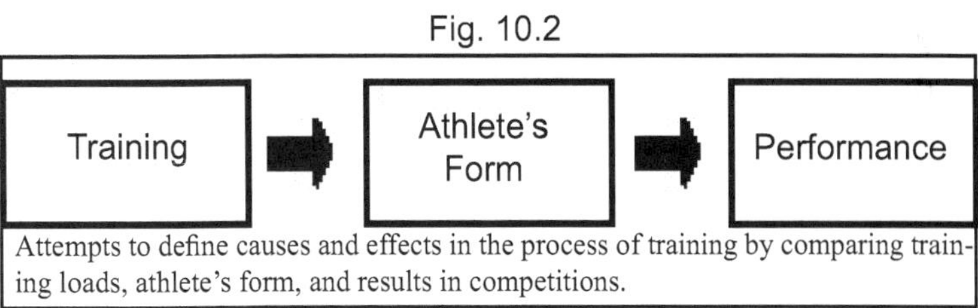

Attempts to define causes and effects in the process of training by comparing training loads, athlete's form, and results in competitions.

3. Whether, generally, the coach's attitude towards other people—including, of course, his pupils—is positive, friendly, constructive, helpful, respectful, cooperative, etc., and if he has interest in their well-being.

I am inclined to think that a typical dictatorial coach tries, above all, to fulfill his personal needs; treats his athletes instrumentally; perceives people in accordance with theory "X" (though, of course, he need not know it); and does not necessarily like his students.

Nota bene: I was recently very surprised to notice that a very famous former Soviet fencer, several times world champion, does not obtain very good results with his pupils now as a professional coach. When I expressed my surprise about this fact, another Russian coach remarked, "The explanation is very simple—he does not like people."

References

1. Yerkes, M. and J. D. Dodson. "The Relation of Strength of Stimulus to Rapidity of Habit Formation,." *Journal of Comparative Neurology and Psychology,* No. 18, 1908.

Table 10 A
Stages of Teaching-Learning of Fencing Strokes and Phases of Sensory-Motor Skill Formation

	Stage 1	Stage 2	Stage 3	Stage 4
Name and main task of the stage	Getting acquainted with a new stroke (fencing action). Introduction of the new stroke describing its most important features, ways of execution and application in a bout.	Learning-teaching stage, mastering the basic structure of the movement.	Consolidating of learned skill, efficacious, smooth and precise execution of the stroke, mainly in easy, stable conditions. First attempts to execute the movement in variable situations, but in easy conditions.	Perfecting the skill. Various ways of executing and applying given movement in variable conditions and sometimes in difficult, unforeseen situations.
Exercises and methods applied in a lesson	Coach gives the name, definition of a new stroke, describes the ways of its execution and application in a bout. He demonstrates the new action whole and fast, slowly, divided into component parts, again whole and slow and whole and fast.	The pupil tries to execute new stroke on his own, in front of a mirror, against a wall, with a partner, with the coach. First method of teaching-learning sensory-motor skills. Attempts to master the basic, elementary form of movement.	Numerous repetitions of learned sensory-motor skill in easy conditions – on the spot, slowly; then faster and maneuvering on the piste. To begin with the execution they are slow and foreseen, but gradually coach introduces easily noticed changes. Attempts to introduce simple reaction. Method used: first, second and third attempts of third method in easy conditions.	The choice of way of execution of fencing action adapted to "opponents" (coach's, partners) movements, speed, weapon actions, distance. Variable execution of a given stroke. Application of fencing action as foreseen, unforeseen and partly foreseen actions. Execution an application of action in condition resembling bout and in training bouts and in competitions. Shaping and perfecting technical, technical-tactical and tactical capabilities. Method used: first, second, third, fourth, fifth, sixth and overlearning method.

Table 10 A (continued)
Stages of Teaching-Learning of Fencing Strokes and Phases of Sensory-Motor Skill Formation

	Stage 1	Stage 2	Stage 3	Stage 4
Level of motor coordination		First level of motor coordination – movement in space.	First and second level of motor coordination – movement in space and time. Increase of speed, accent on precision and appropriate choice of rhythm and movement.	First, second, and – most important – third level of motor coordination. Movement in space, time and choice of moment; Versatile execution of well chosen stroke and application in changing situations.
Set of motor coordination abilities		Motor educability and motor control.	Motor educability, motor control and first, easy attempts at motor adaptability.	Motor educability, motor control and – above all – motor adaptability with lightning speed motor improvisation.
Significance of visual, tactile and kinesthetic stimuli	The pupil watches the demonstration and listens to coach's verbal explanations. Important: High level of attention and accuracy of visual perception.	Great importance of visual, visual-tactile and tactile stimuli. Gradually the pupil takes advantage of kinesthetic sense and sense of balance. Visual perception still very important.	In executing sensory-motor skill gradually less impact on visual control, increase of importance of kinesthetic control of movements. Visual perception gradually shifts from how to execute a given stroke to when and what action to apply.	Execution of chosen action based on intrinsic stimuli (kinesthetic sense and sense of balance). Visual perception and attention are directed on assessment of tactical situation – distance, opponent's movements etc. and choice of an appropriate action.
Formation of sensory-motor skill (sensory-motor habit pattern).	Forming a mental picture of action (imagination). Desire to learn a new action (motivation).	Gradual mastering of learned movement in typical, basic form; non variable. Unnecessary movements and contractions of antagonistic muscles occur. Basic motor program of learned stroke forms in CNS	Movement becomes automated (state of secondary unconsciousness). Vision, attention and perception directed not so much on executing an action as on what and when to do – when and how to apply a learned action. The mere execution of a chosen stroke is automated.	Shaping and perfecting variability and plasticity of motor skill. Various applications and various ways of executing a given stroke. Perfecting the basic motor programme in the brain and variability of executory factors.

10. Directing the Process of Training, Taking Competition and the Athlete's Personality Dimensions as a Model

"Time and quality of work will provide better results than selection based on any champion profile; we don't select champions, they select themselves by work, passion, and determination to achieve the highest results."

--Janusz Bednarski

In the early days of modern competitive sport, training was very simple. Athletes trained two or three times a week and hoped for the best. Any improvement in technique or motor abilities (quite often accidental) led to improvement of results.

With the increasing role and frequency of competitions, the intensity and frequency of practice also increased and the first attempts to program, direct and control the process of training were gradually introduced.

To begin with, the control of training was very simple and took the form of comparing training—its intensity, frequency, contents—with the results achieved in competitions (Fig. 10.1)

This simple comparison between the character and amount of training, and competitive results, gave a little information, but not nearly enough to adequately improve and control training. It was difficult to assess the precise correlation between the contents and intensity of training and the athlete's results in competitions. It was particularly difficult to elucidate the hidden factors which led to better or poorer results. Among other things, it was quickly noticed that the same amount and intensity of training produced quite different results among various athletes.

The next step was to look for a way to take the athlete himself into consideration. This led to the analysis of the relationship between: a) the process of training (choice of exercises and the way of conducting them, frequency and intensity of training); b) the form of the athlete (his capacity for effort; his speed, endurance and strength; his techniical and tactical abilities; etc.); c) results obtained in competition (Fig. 10.2).

This was a big step forward: it enabled the coach to prepare more detailed plans to control and conduct training. Many factors came to light, revealing the component parts of an athlete's form as they directly or indirectly influenced competition results. Many tests were introduced to evaluate competitors' physiological state, level of motor possibilities, psychomotor abilities, technique, and tactics.

Not long ago, a "championship model" (model champion, "champion profile") began to be widely used as a basis for diagnosis and prognosis of future achievement, selection of candidates, programming, and directing and controlling the process of training.

At the base of this conception of a model champion was some very simple reasoning: if we know what a champion is like, how he developed throughout the years of training, what his chief characteristics are (body build, weight, height, speed of reaction, etc.), all we have to do is to find the "proper" young person (one that fits the profile), make a detailed plan of training and try to achieve all of the characteristics of the ideal model. Control of training would then consist of comparing, at each stage of training, the young athlete with the model champion.

It seemed so logical and obvious—especially in "simple" sports (one motor skill, one dominant motor quality)—that this conception became very popular. Soon it became "fashionable" to construct various model champions for various disciplines of sport, including the most detailed characteristics—even down to the arch of the foot.

Of course, it has been much easier to construct model champions in simple sports (track-and-field events, swimming, rowing, etc.) than in more complicated sports (fencing, tennis, team games, etc.). Nevertheless, even in these very complicated sports in which so many different factors affect the results in competition, attempts were made to construct champion profiles. Some Soviet authors went so far as to prepare an amazingly detailed model of a champion in fencing, giving all parameters separately for foilists, sabreurs, epeeists, and women foilists. What is more, they gave detailed figures of various parameters which the representatives of various weapons should achieve each year in a four-year training plan.

Those parameters included the speeds of various kinds of reaction (simple reaction, choice reaction, change of reaction).

However, in differentiating between fencers with different weapons, they failed to notice the importance of the stimuli to which fencers react. It is well known that the fastest reaction is to mixed stimuli (epee), less fast to tactile stimuli (foil), and slowest to visual stimuli (sabre). There were many other drawbacks to this model which I shall discuss later on.

The "champion profile" has a certain value in the preliminary selection, planning, conducting, and controlling of the processes of training in some sports—especially when there is one main factor, or very few factors, playing an important role (for example, various manifestations of speed in sprints, a high capacity of the pulmonary and cardiovascular systems in long distance running, etc.), or when one factor seems indispensable (e.g., height in basketball).

Personally, I have had great doubt, for many years, about the over-estimation of the champion profile in sport, particularly in the more complicated sports. True, among the best athletes, one can find certain common psychological factors which greatly influence their performance—like resistance to stress, optimal levels of motivation and arousal, a high quality of certain psychological processes (attention, perception, thinking, etc.)—but there is great diversity in functional and physical qualities. John M. Silva finds further that even attempts to construct an ideal champion profile, based on psychological traits, is sterile and not of very much use: "The trait approach is seen as an exercise in futility or a searching for the ideal profile that may not truly exist at any competitive level."[1]

My chief objection to the over-estimated practical value of the model of champion is the fact that the "ideal profile" is made up of the mean values of various parameters of outstanding athletes, while extreme data have a great influence on mean values. Such a "model" athlete may not exist in reality.

Especially doubtful is the value of the "champion profile" in primary selection of future champions and consequent control of training. Although we may notice certain common traits among top athletes, novice athletes are very dissimilar. So, looking for the traits specific to great champions in very young, future athletes may be of no avail. Let us imagine that Demosthenes wanted to enter a school for public speakers: if the principle of model champion was applied, he would have been chucked out at once.

In this way, I think, many potential champions have been deprived of the opportunity to cultivate their chosen sport. I know several fencers of international standard who were initially rejected but, through persistence, managed to start training and eventually achieved excellent results.

So I think that the "champion profile" as a base for selection, programming and control of training has to play a lesser role than admitted by the majority of contemporary authors. In control of training, it may only help the coach in a very general way, indicating only the direction of action.

Below, I present some additional arguments against too rigid an application of an ideal champion profile in the control of training:

- Many components of an athlete's form influence the results of competition; and not only does each of them develop at a different pace for an individual athlete, but the speed of their development differs between various athletes.

- Detailed monitoring of the progress of various competitors based on the conception of the "champion profile" (various tests, examinations, controls, etc.) may be misleading: Some young people develop well in advance of their physiological age and some lag behind. Children and youth who are delayed in their physiological development may achieve very high results later on—this is especially true for girls.

- We may divide people into sympathicotonic types and vagotonic types with respect to the function of the autonomic nervous system. The former achieve top athletic form very quickly but keep it for a short time, while the latter acquire peak form very slowly, but can keep it for a long time.

- We may divide people into sympathicotonic types and parasympathicotonic types with respect to the function of the hormonal system. The former quickly achieve peak form, but lose it quickly, while the latter, taking longer to gain form, also keep it longer.

- Among top athletes there are competitors, some of whom achieve the peak of form once or twice a year, some every two years—and there are some exceptional athletes who achieve top performance practically throughout the whole year.

- Many factors influence results in competition. All are important separately and even more in their interrelationship—yet there are competitors who achieve outstanding results mainly due to one factor: speed, or good technique, or good tactics, or good motor coordination, etc. Even in such a simple event as the hundred meter sprint, one may distinguish several factors which determine the result: simple reaction to auditory stimulus, execution of start, acceleration of speed, maintenance of top speed, and anaerobic endurance. All these factors play a different role among top sprinters. One can imagine how much more complicated it is in sports like fencing or tennis.

In fencing and other complicated sports (where the number of factors influencing the results is difficult to even estimate), although there are certain similar traits among top athletes, the conception of an ideal model of champion cannot be upheld. By conducting training both in the club and with the national squad, careful observation and analysis of innumerable international competitions, including Olympic Games and World Championships, and various tests and research work, I have drawn the following conclusions:

1. In fencing, one ideal champion profile does not exist. World class results are achieved by various types of fencers: fencers of differing ages; fencers of different schools; tall and short, lean and plump; athletes of various temperaments (apart from melancholics); very offensive and rather defensive types; fencers with different techniques; fencers applying foreseen actions and fencers relying on lightning-speed improvisation; competitors with very good

simple reaction and competitors with fast choice reaction; extraverts and introverts; etc.

2. The top fencers win, not because they have no weak points, not because their assets are ideally balanced, and not because they fit an ideal champion's profile, but because they manage to develop their potential possibilities—their strong points—to the highest degree.

3. In fencing, so many factors (inherited and acquired) play an important part in determining results that a low level or even lack of one factor may be compensated for by another, for example:

   - A certain lack of mobility of nervous processes, typical for a phlegmatic type, may be compensated by good tactics, careful observation of the opponent, and foreseen second intention actions;

   - Even such an important factor as speed of movement may be compensated by fast reaction;

   - Relatively poor coordination of movement may be compensated by great speed and mobility, etc.

The most important thing is speed of reaction—fencers with fast simple reaction base their tactics on premeditated, fast, and energetic actions, while their colleagues with good choice reaction apply more complicated tactics (e.g., "open-eyes" attacks).

Thus, we must admit that the "champion profile" is of little practical use in fencing as a main element of directing and controlling training. Training and its control must take into account the concrete individual traits of a given athlete. This means that in selection, developing physical fitness, teaching technique and tactics, developing psychological processes, building up an individual style of fencing, and preparing for competitions, the coach must take into account the following:

Table 10-A:

Number and percentage of successful actions in the individual final, men's foil, World Championships, Melbourne, 1979.

Type of action	Number of hits scored	Percentage of total hits
Attacks	63	48
Parry-Ripostes	40	33
Counterattacks	24	21
Total	127	100

Table 10-B:

Efficacy of offensive and defensive actions of finalists, men's foil, World Championships, Melbourne, 1979.

Competitor	A/a	R/r	C/c	Hits	IO	ID	1.
Romankov (USSR)	11/8	10/3	4/2	25/13	2.2	1.75	2
Jolyot (France)	7/9	7/5	7/3	21/17	0.87	1.55	3
Dal Zotto (Italy)	19/8	5/5	4/6	14/19	0.90	1.12	4
Behr (W. Germany)	5/7	7/9	6/2	18/18	0.45	1.85	5
Flament (France)	15/9	7/7	2/7	19/23	1.07	1.44	6
Cervi (Italy)	6/13	1/5	4/5	11/23	0.60	0.38	7

A: hits scored by attacks
a: hits received by opponent's attacks
R: hits scored by ripostes
r: hits received by opponent's ripostes
C: hits scored by counter- attacks
c: hits received by opponent's counter-attacks
IO - index of efficacy of offensive actions (hits scored by attacks of all kinds and counter-time, divided by the total of bits received by opponents' ripostes and counterattacks)

$$IO = \frac{\Sigma A}{\Sigma r + \Sigma c} \qquad ID = \frac{\Sigma R + \Sigma C}{\Sigma a}$$

- Careful observation of competitions (visual observation, film, video); analysis of technique, tactics, and the range and efficacy of various fencing actions; practical differentiation of various tactical-psychological types of fencers; recognition of modern trends of development in fencing as a whole and of each different weapon.

- The level of transfer of skills and abilities from practice to training bouts and, above all, from training bouts to bouts in competition.

- Individual characteristics of a given fencer, dimensions of his personality, traits of temperament, his individual style of fencing, the range and efficacy of his fencing actions, his favorite strokes, his ways of solving tactical problems in a bout, the level of his perception, the correctness and speed of his reactions, his self-control and resistance to stress, the level of his specific fitness, the range of his technical repertoire, etc.

- Recognition of the strong points and potential possibilities of each individual pupil—as well as his weak points. The coach and pupil should develop, in the first place, the strong points; they should work on perfecting the actions and abilities which bring the pupil success and which are consistent with the modern style of fencing. Weak points should be considered mainly when they interfere with the possibility of displaying his assets. For example: An active, offensive fencer should perfect and, in competition, mainly rely on offensive actions. He should, however, learn defensive actions to increase the efficacy of his attacks, as the psychological and technical base of an offensive style of fencing is confidence in unforeseen defensive actions.

- Apart from the coach's own observations, he should take into consideration the pupil's self-assessment (the pupil's own assessment of his specific fitness, his technique, his favorite actions, etc.).

Every fencer should be treated by the coach in a different way. The fencing master should avoid trying to push the pupil into an artificial "champion profile," but should help him to develop his specific, individual style of fencing: his specific reactions, technique and tactics. Speaking generally, in training and its control, the coach must take into account: what is actually happening in competition; what actions are used by top fencers; what actions are used by a given pupil; what the pupil's individual characteristics are.

The general trends of development of modern fencing can be assessed by careful observation and analysis of competitions (the means of maneuvering on the piste; the range and efficacy of fencing strokes; the various means of preparing an attack; the areas of target most frequently hit; the methods of judging; the influence of the rules on tactics; new elements in technique and tactics; etc.). For example, many observations of sabre in the fifties and sixties showed that touches were scored as a result of: attacks of various kinds – 50%; parry-ripostes – 30%; counter-attacks – 20%. That was a very general picture of sabre fencing in that period. In training and its control, a coach would have been wise to take this into account, along with the individual characteristics of each given fencer, which often differs from the average considerably.

Table 10-A shows hits scored by attacks, ripostes, and counter-attacks by the fencers in the final of individual men's foil at the 1979 World Championships in Melbourne.

Table 10-B shows the individual differences in the successful application of various strokes by competitors in this final.

Even a superficial glimpse at Table 10-B shows the great diversity of actions displayed by the finalists. In the limited framework of this chapter, it is quite impossible to present dozens of similar tables compiled over a period of many years. Tables 1 and 2 give only a tiny example.

Careful analysis of the range and efficacy of various actions in national and international competitions has allowed me to make objective observations of the development of fencing generally, and the style of fencing of individual competitors. These observations demonstrate, among other things:

- Major changes in fencing in recent years,
- An increased differentiation between different weapons,

- A marked influence of new rules on technique, tactics, etc.

The general conclusions from these observations are that planning, directing, and control of training ought to be based on objective observation of competitions, on the competitor's individual characteristics, and the manner in which he utilizes his skills and abilities in competition. To put it shortly, training ought to be modeled on competitions and the pupil's performance in them.

In programming and directing the process of training, and developing the individual style of fencing for each pupil, the coach must take into account:

- Objective observation and analysis of competition;
- The pupil's performance in competition (his style, range, and efficacy of various fencing actions);
- The ways in which he solves tactical problems;
- The individual characteristics of the pupil.

In order to ascertain the pupil's main and most frequently used ways of making decisions in a bout, we may use the following procedure:

A fencer, for a certain period (e.g., a fortnight), notes, during every training bout, the following successful actions:

- Foreseen first intention attacks,
- Foreseen second intention attacks,
- Attacks with unknown final,
- Attacks with change of decision.

This record, combined with the results of various objective tests, will allow us to make the right choice of exercises in lessons.

The individual characteristics of a fencer, the level of his specific fitness, and his technical abilities, can be assessed by: the coach's observations; questionnaires; psychological laboratory tests; fitness and technical trials; etc.

All these—especially analysis of the pupil's performance and behavior in competition—give a thinking coach plenty of information, e.g.:

- The repertoire of strokes he actually uses in competition (compared to the amount of motor skills learned in a lesson)?
- Can he change easily from one action to another?
- Can he keep up high concentration for a long period of time?
- Does he rely mainly on simple or choice reaction, or both?
- Can he easily shift attention from narrow to wide and vice versa, from external to internal and vice versa?
- What is his optimal level of arousal?
- What is his main attitude toward training and competitions (ego-involvement or task-involvement?)
- What are the main components of his achieving motivation (motive of success, rivalry, aggressive attitude, emphasis on extreme effort, motive of avoiding failure, emphasis on self-efficacy, independence)?

In later chapters, I describe in more detail how to deal with a given competitor after finding out the answers to these and many more questions. In this chapter, I have only endeavored to stress the usefulness and importance of a model of competition, combined with individualization of training and tactics, as a main guideline for programming, conducting, directing and controlling the fencer's training.

Too rigid selection may lead to rejection of really talented people. Attempts to squash everybody into an abstract, universal, stereotyped model of champion may be harmful. Programs that are based on competition and individualization allow the best athletes to rise to the top in due time and for all to find enjoyment and their right place in fencing.

This is my firm conviction and the results of my pupils over many years appear to confirm it, as well as various tests and research work conducted in the Fencing Department of the Academy of Physical Education, Katowice.[2]

References

1. Silva, J.M.:"Personality and Sport Performance: Controversy and Challenge." in: Silva, J.M., Weinberg, R.S. (eds) *Psychological Foundation of Sport*, Human Kinetics Publishers, Champaign ,1984 Vef. 1,140,
2. Czajkowski, Z.: "Directing the Process of Training Taking Competition as a Model." *The Swordsman*, Spring 2001 Vef. 2 , 146.

The Professor In The Classroom
II: Practice

11. Periods and Stages of Training

"It's never too late or too early
to start planning for the future."
--The Athlete's Guide to Career Planning

INTRODUCTION

The whole process of training may be considered from the point of view of a content structure or of a time structure.

Content structure denotes the object and components of training, which, of course, are strictly interrelated.

The main components of training are:

- Energy fitness (strength, endurance, and partly speed);

- Coordination abilities (partly speed, speed of reaction, and many other abilities which may be divided into motor educability, motor control, and motor adaptability);

- Technique and technical capabilities;

- Technical-tactical capabilities;

- Tactical capabilities;

- Socio-psychological preparation (educational influence, developing an athlete's personality, the appropriate motivation and arousal, self-efficacy and self-confidence, resistance to stress, achievement motivation, etc.);

- Basic knowledge of theory and methodology of fencing.

The time structure of a fencer's training consists of:

1. Dividing the yearly training macro-cycle into training periods:

    - Preparatory period;
    - Main (competition) period;
    - Transitional period;

2. Dividing many-years-long athletic activity into training stages:

    - Introductory stage,
    - Basic stage,
    - Competitive stage, and
    - Champion stage—
    - and, sometimes, veteran stage.

In this chapter, we shall discuss the time structure of a fencer's training:

I. The training cycles and periods, and

II. The stages of a fencer's training.

Fig. 11.1.

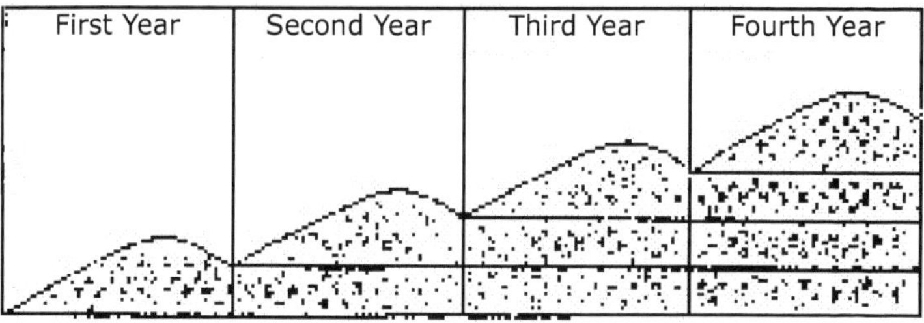

Increase of general fitness (energy and coordination abilities) and fencer's technical-tactical abilities in a theoretical (ideal) four years of consecutive training cycles. During each year the fencer's form undergoes changes in the preparatory, main, and transition training periods, but each preparatory training period starts at a higher functional level than the corresponding period of the previous year.

TRAINING CYCLES AND PERIODS

> *"National squad gymnasts ought to be constantly in fighting form, without reference to peaks and lows of form, nor to fashionable biorhythms. Contemporary sport requires a constant state of high readiness. Training periods have disappeared—preparatory period, competition period, period of rest. We have come to the point that, on any day, a gymnast should be able to efficiently perform his program."*
>
> --L. Akayev

Note: *Below, I present the commonly-held views concerning annual training cycles. Many coaches and authors uphold them. I myself have certain objections to strict and literal adherence to such a division of training cycles and periods. In reality, the concept of training cycles and periods ("periodization") ought to be viewed with a certain reserve. In fencing practice, especially, this concept requires certain modifications in accordance with what happens in contemporary competitive sport: an increased number of important competitions, which take place practically all year round, many of which give points for qualification to bigger events. As a result, all of the athlete's abilities and capabilities are really important and necessary throughout the whole year.*

Here, however, is the classic view of periodized training.

A necessary condition for efficacy of training is the periodic change of the contents and structure of training, following regular cycles.

The principle of training and the principle of periodization of training foresee repetition of these cycles on an increasingly higher level: better cultivated abilities, better developed sensory-motor skills (motor habit patterns), better athletic form, and better results in competitions.

A big ("macro") training cycle (e.g., a year's duration) should be planned and carried out, taking into consideration the influence of the training process on fitness and athletic form. By "athletic form," we mean a state of optimal preparedness for achieving good results in competitions.

In a year's training cycle, we distinguish three phases: a) the phase of achieving athletic form, b) the phase of stabilization and development of athletic form, and c) the phase of temporary decline of athletic form. These phases repeat themselves many times over a long period of time, on an increasingly higher level.

It is important to realize that these phases occur not for any formal, administrative or planning reasons, but as a result of physiologically and methodologically justified changes in the structure and content of training in the various periods of the training cycle. A training cycle, as a rule, is divided into training periods corresponding to the above-mentioned phases, thus: a) preparatory period, b) main, or competition, period, and c) transitional period.

The preparatory period corresponds to the phase of gradual acquisition of athletic form; the main period, to the maintenance and further development of athletic form; and the transitional period, to the temporary lowering of athletic form.

The preparatory period ends, then, when the competitor has achieved athletic form. In this sense, the period also includes preliminary preparation for competitions. The aim of this period is to prepare the fencer—with regard to general and specific fitness, and to technique—for the main period.

During the main period, competitions are most important: the fencer prepares for competitions and participates in them. During the preparatory period, then, competitions play an auxiliary role, while in the main period, competitions play the major role.

The transitional period forms the starting point of a new cycle, secures active rest, and retains a level of athletic form needed to begin a new cycle of training at a higher level than in the preparatory period of the previous cycle (see Fig. 11.1).

In a fencer's training, one can distinguish the following, strongly interrelated, constituent parts:

- Development of general and specific fitness;
- Technical, technical-tactical, and tactical preparation;
- Development of various types of reaction;
- Educational and psychological preparation;
- Theoretical preparation.

In the various periods of training, the meaning and mutual relationship of the constituent parts—including also various elements of technical-tactical preparation—undergo changes. Emphasis on the various components of training should vary noticeably during the different training periods, thus influencing the suitability of an exercise, its higher level, and greater success.

Preparatory Period

The main aim of this period, as already stated, is the acquisition of athletic form by the fencer—thorough preparation for the main period.

Thus the primary tasks of the preparatory period can be briefly and generally expressed as follows:

1. An increase of the general functional-motor fitness of the fencer; development of specific fitness abilities (speed, strength, endurance, flexibility, and power) and neuromuscular coordination.

2. Learning, perfecting and enriching fencing technique, embracing both the footwork and blade movements—to begin with, in easy conditions, without maximum speed or elements of surprise; repeating and improving basic strokes, teaching new fencing actions and new varieties and combinations of known fencing actions.

3. Imparting indispensable information and knowledge regarding the technique, tactics, and methodology of fencing to the pupil.

4. Preparing (at the very beginning of the period) individual training plans for top competitors and collective plans for various training groups of the club; specifying the main training tasks for particular pupils and training groups for the whole year (a training cycle); planning the achievements and results which should be aimed for in the main competitions of the year; introducing active collaboration and cooperation between the club's main coach, other fencing masters of the club (school, etc.), the pupils, and the club's committee, as well as the national fencing organization and the national coaches.

If we plan one training cycle for a year, the preparatory period is rather long, lasting several months, and divided into two parts:

I. The main task of the first part is to raise the level of the competitor's functional and adaptive possibilities. In this part, comparatively little fencing is done: fencing exercises consist mainly of footwork and lessons of a technical direction. In the first part of the preparatory period, the emphasis is put on

   - General physical fitness, achieved mainly by non-fencing exercises, and

   - Work on basic fencing technique, carried out in easy conditions.

II. The main tasks of the second part of the preparatory period are:

   - Further development of physical fitness;

   - Cultivation of fencing-specific motor abilities through general, auxiliary, and fencing exercises;

- Perfection and development of fencing techniques, including the shaping of a fencer's simple and choice reactions;
- Gradual introduction of maximum speed;
- Choice of time, and tactics; and
- The gradual introduction of training bouts, loose play, and competitions (the top class fencers treating them as a form of training for higher-level competitions).

In the second part, the emphasis is put on

- Fencing-specific physical fitness and
- Work on technique, reaction, and tactics—in conditions gradually resembling those of a bout.

Additionally, in the second part, the structure and content of training undergo considerable changes—the main aim being the acquisition of basic athletic form. Hence, the training is strongly connected with fencing exercises—both auxiliary and actual, and various fencing exercises become the main means of training.

In these fencing exercises, the emphasis is put on

- Correct technique;

Fig. 11.2

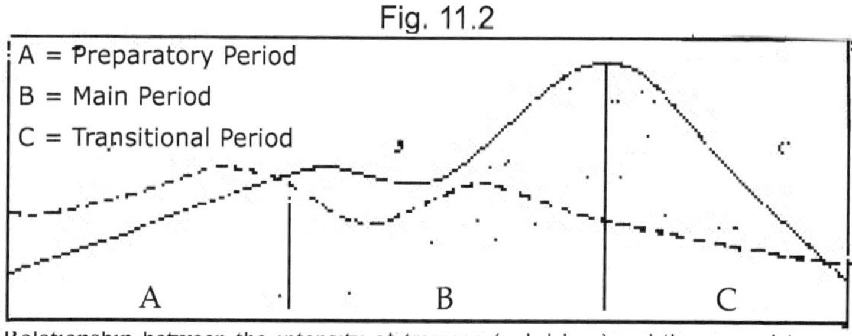

Relationship between the intensity of training (solid line) and the general training load (dotted line).

- Acquisition of new strokes, combined with reaction and tactics;
- And, towards the end of this part, the ability to apply fencing actions under fighting conditions.

Nevertheless, in this second part of the preparatory period, non-fencing exercises do not lose their significance: they are merely applied to a lesser degree, and their choice must now accurately correspond to the specific needs of fencing and the individual characteristics of fencers of a given group, class, or club. The amount and frequency of non-fencing exercises (general P.E. exercises, light athletic exercises, swimming, games, etc.) ought to be decreased in favor of facilitating the acquisition, consolidation, and perfection of the sensory-motor skills (motor-habit patterns) of fencing technique. The variety—though, not the amount—of non-fencing exercises can be increased.

If, during the year, two training cycles are planned, the corresponding preparatory periods of both cycles are noticeably shorter; then, the tasks of the second part of the preparatory period should also be realized at the beginning of the main period (especially during the first of the two cycles).

Main (Competition) Period

The chief tasks of the main, or competition, period can be summarized as follows:

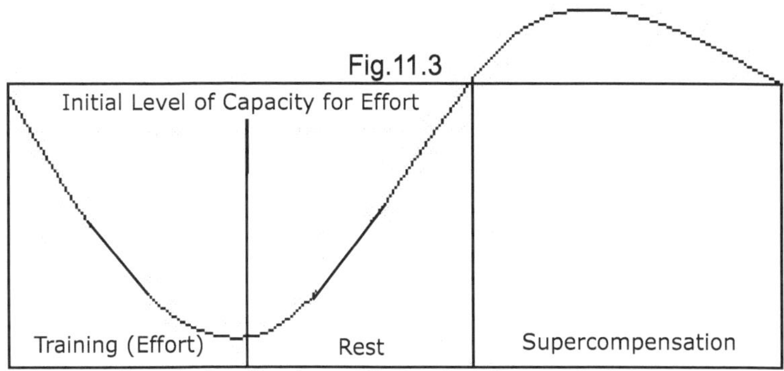

Capacity for effort (curved line) under influence of training

Fig. 11.4

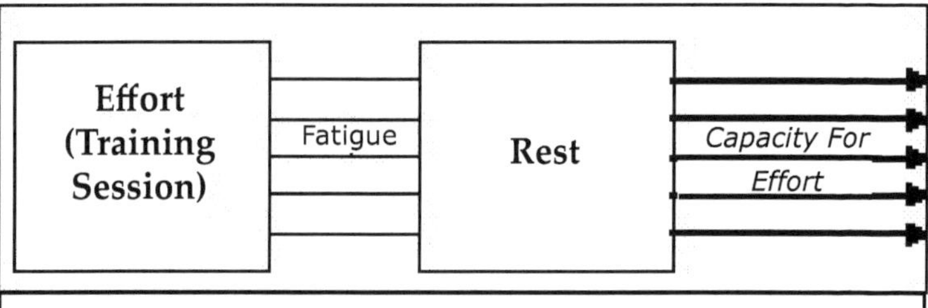

Training consists of effort (training session) and rest, resulting in increased capacity for effort—high athletic form.

1. Further development of specific functional-motor fitness (specific energy abilities and specific coordination abilities) very strongly connected with fencing.

2. Further development of fencing technique, reaction (more exactly, technical-tactical capabilities based on various types of motor responses), and tactics, with strong emphasis on their practical application.

3. Psychological preparation, with emphasis on developing the proper contents, direction, and level of motivation (including chosen aspects of achievement motivation) and building up a fencer's psychological endurance.

4. Direct preparation for—and participation in—competitions.

5. Maintenance—and the further development of—athletic form, the peak of which ought to be reached at the most important competition.

In the main period, more emphasis is given to timing (tempo), the development of different varieties of reaction, and tactics—with the aim of wielding these elements (along with the proper psychological preparation) into one unified process.

During this period, there ensues the perfection of known actions (including those learned in the preparatory period) and their application in various and constantly changing conditions: varying speed, distance, manner of execution, and tactical application.

In the main period, one plans less teaching (less new actions, less new sensory-motor skills) and more perfecting. The exceptionally important factor of this period is participation in competitions—which should be considered as one of the most important methods (and aims) of a fencer's training.

In order to achieve the optimal form for the year's most important event, a fencer should, in the main period, participate in many competitions. Although it is important to use the whole gamut of various forms and methods of training, there is no substitute for taking part in competitions. It is only in competitions that a fencer can show his real worth, and only in competitions that he may achieve real practical experience, thus unifying the effect of all other methods, forms, and means of training.

Frequent participation in competitions, however, must not serve as an excuse for lessening the frequency and intensity of training between competitions. One must try to keep a rational proportion between training and competitions.

One must bear in mind that the intensity of training (high speed, full concentration, very difficult tasks, frequent and fast changes of decision, etc.) does not parallel the general load of training. The relationship between intensity of training and general load (amount) of training is shown in Fig. 11.2.

Some people still maintain that, with numerous competitions in the main training period, the state of high athletic form can be kept up by less frequent and less strenuous training. This view is incorrect. The tendency of modern high performance sport is to combine, harmoniously, frequent participation in competitions with hard training. Experience has shown that those fencers, who frequently take part in competitions and train hard between them, attain systematically good results.

For a few days before an important competition, the time and the amount of fencing exercises ought to be diminished in order to avoid fatigue and preserve freshness and "blade hunger." To provide active rest and not to diminish, too much, the general load of training, more non-fencing exercises and games might be added.

In planning training sessions and competitions—especially in the main training period—the coach must take into account the relationship between:

Fig. 11.5
Training Cycles

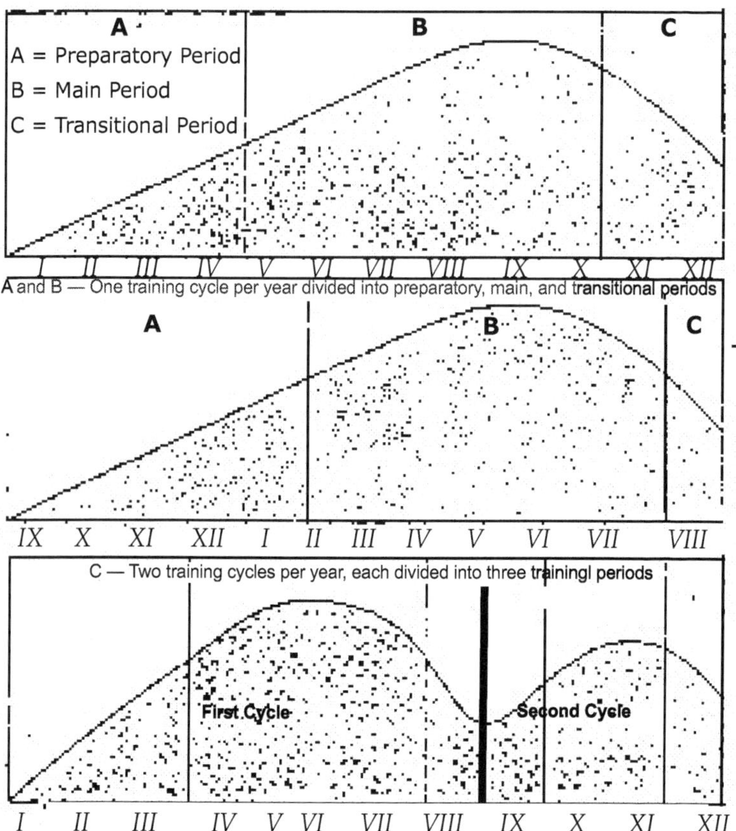

The curve represents the fencer's form(functional capacity, standard of technique, tactics, etc.)

1. Effort (training exercises),

2. Fatigue (as a result of effort, the capacity for work is lowered),

3. Regeneration (as a result of rest, signs of fatigue subside and an athlete's organism attains its normal functional level and capacity for effort),

4. Super-compensation (after a certain amount of rest, the organism not only returns to normal, but temporarily attains a higher functional level and higher capacity for effort; see Fig. 11.3.)

Training consists of alternating effort and rest: the effort and ensuing fatigue act as a powerful stimulus for functional development and increased capacity for effort (see Fig. 11.4). Training sessions must be frequent enough to take advantage of the higher capacity for effort occurring in the super-compensation phase.

Sometimes the training sessions may be so frequent that the fatigue never really subsides and the super-compensation phase is not reached and, consequently, the capacity for effort is temporarily below normal level. In such cases, a longer period of rest may then bring about a particularly high level of capacity for effort.

Non-fencing exercises—especially games like soccer and basketball, as well as various forms of modified indoor competitive games—serve several purposes in the main period: an increase of the general load of training; an increase of general fitness; the cultivation of functional-motor abilities and certain psychomotor abilities; an attractive kind of active rest and relaxation after the high nervous tension of fencing exercises. When conducted outdoors, they give the fencers healthy contact with fresh air, sunshine, water, snow, etc.

In the main period, one uses a wide variety of fencing exercises: warm-up and footwork exercises; work on one's own; work in pairs; varieties of collective exercises; line exercises; individual lessons; loose play and other kinds of training bouts; participation in competitions. The most important exercises of this period are: footwork, individual lessons, training bouts, and competitions.

High intensity, individual lessons ought to be of a mixed type (with more emphasis on perfecting than teaching new actions and abilities): shaping reactions and developing technique, orientation, speed, tactics, etc., while alternating the application of technical-tactical and tactical capabilities.

A great amount of attention should be given to the further development of a fencer's technical-tactical capabilities—a fencer's "combat skills"—which are manifestations of several varieties of a fencer's motor response, such as: fast simple reaction to visual stimuli; fast simple reaction to tactical stimuli; the ability to assess distance correctly; orientation in time and space; the ability to direct the cut or thrust into the opening line; the ability to discriminate between real and false actions; the ability to change one's decision while executing a foreseen action; etc.

Equally great importance should be attached to exercises of tactical direction which develop a pupil's various tactical capabilities and psychomotor abilities, like: power of observation; orientation in the external and psychological situation of a bout; passive and active choice of time ("surprise," "timing," "à propos"); correlating choice of time and a suitable fencing action; understanding the opponent's intentions; drawing conclusions from the external signs of the opponent's actions; applying second intention actions, etc.

In lessons of a versatile (all-round, synthetic) direction, the pupil applies, alternately, lightning-speed improvisation and preconceived actions—actions as a response to the opponent's initiative and actions executed on one's own initiative.

Apart from ultimate, real actions, sufficient time and attention should be given to preparatory actions.

In the main period, lessons of technical-tactical and tactical direction and those of only a tactical direction should become progressively faster, more difficult, more complex, and less technically concrete (the pupil—in constantly changing situations and faced with unexpected actions—must choose his own tactical solutions and technical means of executing them; not relying on specific instructions from the coach).

One must remember, however, that such lessons should still be under the complete control of the fencing master, who points out all mistakes regarding choice of time, tactics, and the execution of an action. From time to time, a lesson should include loose play or a short training bout with the coach.

Transitional Period

Some people believe that this period is not really necessary. They claim that the transitional period, having no concrete training tasks, has a bad influence on the athlete: making him lazy, taking the edge off his keenness, and making him less persevering in his sporting activities.

Above all, this period serves the purpose of securing for the fencer much needed psychological relaxation and rest after difficult and exhausting fencing exercises and competitions, which put a great strain on the nervous system.

Also, a fencer who trains mainly in the salle, in a mask and not very hygienic clothes, must, for health reasons, have a short period during the year for indulging in fresh air and sunshine.

As already stated, the transitional period should ensure a certain (temporarily lowered) level of athletic form and general fitness, so that the following preparatory period can begin at a higher functional and technical level than the corresponding period of the previous training cycle.

Thus, in the transitional period:

1. Fencers do not participate in competitions.

2. The intensity, frequency, and general load of training is markedly lowered.

3. The fencing lessons may be either limited to a few short lessons of a corrective direction or stopped altogether.

4. Other activities and sports are introduced (walks, excursions, swimming, skiing, etc.).

Active rest, new forms of motor activity, the lessening of nervous tension, psychological relaxation, and the lowering of effort, in the transitional period, not only prevent the occurrence of weariness, fatigue, and over-training, but also serve as necessary conditions for achieving a higher athletic form and, consequently, better results in the next training cycle.

Division of the Year into Training Periods

When the training cycle corresponds to one year, then the preparatory period should last 5 to 7 months; the main period, 3 to 4 months; and the transitional period, 1 to 2 months.

There are, of course, many ways of arranging training periods (see Fig. 11.5).

If, for example, the training year begins in Autumn (September), then the main period begins in late spring and early summer, and the transition period at the height of summer (end of July-August).

Below is an example of a training year divided into two training macro-cycles:

	First Cycle:
Preparatory Period	January, February and part of March.
Main Period	Part of March, April, to July.
Transitional Period	August.

	Second Cycle:
Preparatory Period	September.
Main Period	October, November, & half of December.
Transitional Period	Second half of December.

Observations on the Theory of Training Cycles

Above, I have presented the problem of dividing a year into training cycles in a classical way that was very popular in the 1950's and 1960's in Poland and other countries, and which still has many adherents. I think that the development of sport and sport science—along with other factors, like an increase in the number of international competitions—has caused the problem to be regarded with certain reservations. This does not mean, of course, that we reject the idea of training cycles and periods completely.

Here are some remarks about the theory and practice of dividing the year into training periods:

Such an organization of training, rigidly adhering to the conception of a preparatory period (fitness exercises), main period (technique, tactics, and competitions), and transitional period (active rest) is more applicable to branches of sport in which energy fitness plays the most important part. In fencing, it ought to be treated with a certain caution.

In the next section, I describe a multi-year course of athletic training, divided it into the following stages: introductory, basic, competitive, champion, and veteran. Here I may comment briefly on the applicability of periodization to each stage:

Organizing training, taking into account training cycles, is relatively easy in the second—basic—stage of training and may be recommended for that stage.

In the first—introductory—stage, when the pupil develops his functional and adaptive abilities and learns basic technique and tactics, there is more learning than competing, hence these training periods cannot be so well marked.

In the competitive and, especially, champion stages, there are so many competitions—and many of them are extremely important because they affect national and FIE ranking lists and constitute qualification to big events like European Championships, World Championships, and the Olympic Games—that strict adherence to the aforementioned training periods is not quite possible.

1. In many sports—including fencing, gymnastics, tennis, and others—competitions take place all year round; so, in practice, we must accentuate various aspects of training (energy fitness, coordination, technique, technical-tactical abilities, tactics, psychomotor abilities, preparation and participation in competitions, etc.), not strictly according to training periods.

2. In contemporary competitive fencing, top fencers must be like great pianists or violin players. They must practice and perform, practically all year long—changing, of course, the emphasis on particular aspects of training, depending on the dates of competitions.

3. Just the same, the transitional period ought to always be retained, to ensure psychological and physical rest (the rest, of course, ought to be active—changing the varieties of motor activities: walks, contact with nature, etc.).

4. Finally, I think that my description of training periods and my doubts about their usefulness will help an

intelligent, inquisitive coach to draw reasonable and useful conclusions—one ought to use all that seems sound, useful and practical in these theories. I should also add that though I think that strict application of these training periods, especially in the later stages of training (see below) is impractical, the general remarks on cycles and my advice on lessons, exercises, etc., are fully justified and valid.

STAGES OF A FENCER'S TRAINING

"A diversity of the views of specialists on the methodology of training is necessary."
--A. M. Yakimov

The entire process of training that comprises a fencer's career may be divided into four stages: 1) introductory stage, 2) basic stage, 3) competitive stage, and 4) champion stage (we may also include a fifth "veteran" stage: a top-class competitor who, after leaving fully engaged athletic activity, trains a little bit and takes part in minor competitions, purely for health, recreation, and joy).

The first and second stages are practically accessible to everyone. A good coach, skillfully using the proper methods, can produce an average competitor even out of an "anti-talent." To reach the third stage, pupils need a certain amount of talent and good motivation and training. The fourth stage is attainable by highly talented competitors, training systematically and with passion, with an optimal level of motivation and certain necessary dimensions of personality. Between the third and fourth stages, there is a distinct dialectic difference—a remarkable change in training, abilities, and results, which is not so much quantitative as qualitative.

Before I discuss my conception of a fencer's stages of training, I want to stress that I entirely disagree with the conception which is advocated mainly by sports scientists—influenced by sports in which the main emphasis and factor is energy (physical) fitness—who merely identify the process of training with shaping physical fitness. This is very one-sided, as athletic training is a very rich, versatile, many-sided, pedagogical process, including the shaping of energy fitness, motor coordination, technique, technical-tactical and tactical capabilities, psychomotor abilities, the education of the competitor, and the development of his personality.

Such narrow-minded authors divide a long-term process of training—for them, mainly shaping physical fitness—into four stages, which are completely different from my conception. For them, the stages are: (1) shaping "all-round" (general) fitness, (2) shaping semi-specific fitness, (3) shaping specific fitness, and (4) teaching technique and tactics.

Some authors even advise that, in the first stage, not only should one exclusively apply all-round fitness exercises, but that these exercises should be as remote as possible from the chosen branch of sport. With a certain exaggeration and sense of humor, one could conclude that the fencer ought to start with ski-jumping, the skier with swimming, and the marksman with rock climbing.

The above-mentioned classification does not take into consideration the many-sidedness, complexity, and specificity of the training process in modern, highly-competitive sport, because:

1. In this latter classification, the very names of the stages are the result of the already-mentioned identification (and limitation) of the process of training mainly with developing "physical fitness"—with a distinct underestimation of the role and importance of technique, tactics, and psychological processes which are inseparably connected to motor activity.

2. This classification overestimates, one-sidedly, the importance of all-round fitness—mainly energy abilities—in all stages of training. In reality, a high level of—and paying due attention to—all-round fitness is important and necessary in the first stage of training, as a factor of increasing the functional and adaptive possibilities of the organisms of young athletes. However, as empirical observation shows—and as I have proven by many tests—the higher the stage of training, the less important the level of all-round fitness and the lower its influence on results in competition; contrary to what many authors and coaches believe (see Chapter 12).

3. When discussing, drawing conclusions, and giving advice based on this traditional classification of training stages that takes into account only physical fitness, sensory-motor skills and responses, technical-tactical and tactical abilities, psychomotor abilities, etc.—which, after all, play such an important role in nearly

all branches of sport, especially in combat sports and team games—are neglected and underestimated. This outdated classification does not take into account the very important principle of specificity of training and very essential qualities of contemporary, competitive sport (see below).

4. Recommending that, in the first stage, training ought to be limited to only all-round fitness, "prohibiting" the application of specific fitness and technique exercises, is absurd. In branches of sport with many sensory-motor skills, rich technique, and a great importance of tactics and cognitive processes, exercises connected with a given branch of sport—apart from a certain amount of general fitness exercises—ought to be introduced in the first stage of training.

All of this shows that there is a need to adopt an new, more rational, view of the stages of training.

I also disagree with the entirely opposite conception, according to which the coach tries, even in the first stage, to achieve the highest results possible in competition. The following is a presentation of my ideas of a more comprehensive and rational means of conducting the process of training in consecutive training stages.

My Conception of the Stages of Training

I – Introductory Stage

The main object of this first—introductory—stage of training ought to be to prepare a young athlete (a child or youth) for the next stages of training. I repeat, once more, with emphasis: the object of the first stage is not to produce a very young champion, but to train in such a way that the young fencer enjoys the sport and has a chance to become a real champion in the further stages. This takes place by developing energy and coordination abilities, technique and tactics, psychomotor abilities (including perception, speed of reaction, various qualities of attention), the right direction and level of motivation; developing the child's knowledge and love of the sport; educating his personality; and giving him sport enjoyment.

From this main aim—preparing for the next stages of training—distinct tasks follow: developing all-round, semi-specific, and specific fitness; developing various coordination abilities (motor educability, motor control, motor adaptability); increasing the functional possibilities of various organs, systems, and the organism as a whole; increasing adaptive abilities; acquiring basic technique and tactics; gaining the necessary, basic knowledge about a given branch of sport (in our case, fencing); stimulating the right contents, direction, and level of motivation; sustaining the right level of arousal; providing sport enjoyment; stimulating self-esteem and self confidence; developing team and task cohesiveness.

The introductory stage influences and determines the pupil's further athletic activity, forming physiological, technical, psychological, and social bases for the continuation of training in the next stages. In this respect, one has to stress the large, unique role of the coach as a source of inspiration and motivation, whose general conduct, views, behavior, empathy, energy, and enthusiasm ought to encourage pupils to imitate him.

The first stage ought to last two or three years, during which one should conduct three group lessons a week—lasting one and a half to two hours. To begin with, exercises developing all-round, functional-motor fitness (energy and coordination abilities) should comprise approximately forty percent of the training time; semi-specific and specific fitness, thirty percent; and technique and tactics, thirty percent. At the end of the introductory stage, one may increase the time devoted to technique.

Fitness exercises should concentrate on both energy abilities and coordination abilities. One should introduce a lot of various games and activities which not only develop the level of fitness and physiological function, but also increases arousal, interest, and sport enjoyment, and develop adaptive abilities, teaching many different basic sensory-motor skills.

As regards coordination abilities, one should, to begin with, emphasize the development of motor educability (the ability to learn new motor skills), then motor control (the ability to precisely direct movement), and then motor adaptability (the ability to execute and apply various motor skills—and various forms of motor skills—in various and changing conditions).

Teaching technique, we start, naturally, from the on-guard position, then movements on the strip, lunge, fleche, and ways of holding, directing and controlling the weapon, then basic thrusts and cuts, next parries, ripostes, etc.—gradually introducing exercises resembling bouts, and bouts themselves.

When conducting fencing exercises—technique and elementary tactics—we develop at the same time, whether we want it or not—as a "positive by-product"—specific energy and coordination abilities: fencing speed, fencing strength, fencing power, fencing endurance, etc.

When teaching basic fencing actions, we want the pupils, at the beginning, to acquire the basic structure of the movement. We then gradually introduce variability of execution (different speeds; different rhythms; different distances; various kinds of lunge, fleche, etc.). At first, the pupils should execute various actions slowly and in very easy conditions, then more quickly and in more difficult conditions. We then introduce exercises resembling bout situations. Finally, the pupils take part in training bouts and, after gaining some experience and skill, take part in competitions.

When teaching technique, we initially apply invariable exercises (the action executed always in the same manner) and then, gradually, use variable exercises (many different ways of executing lunge, fleche, parry, etc.). We use massed (block) exercises (many times repeating the same stroke) and then we apply distributed (random) exercises (interchanging various strokes—e.g., parry four, riposte, stop-hit, etc.). We should strive, relatively early, to introduce variable and random exercises, which are much more effective and realistic. When the pupil attains a certain level of technical capability, we try, as often as possible, to combine variable and random exercises—from time to time, however, coming back to easier forms of conducting exercises.

Planning yearly training programs in the first stage, the coach should underline training tasks (learning certain skills and abilities), rather than result tasks (achieving certain competitive goals or rankings). In the beginning, the coach should not stress rivalry too much, but rather learning, cooperation, and task cohesion.

A very important point is motivation. One should cultivate interest (cognitive aspect) and love (emotional aspect) of the chosen discipline of sport (fencing), as well as sport enjoyment—drawing pleasure from lively motor activity, exercises, bouts, and also cooperation with the coach and colleagues.

In teaching fencing actions (the sensory-motor skills of a fencer's technique)—apart from the basic, most frequently used methods—the coach should, from time to time, introduce task methods and creative methods (problem-solving methods). With children it is rather difficult, but when ably applied, it gives excellent results in the form of the development of self-efficacy, self-confidence, initiative, and the understanding of the essence of fencing exercises and competition. From the very beginning, cooperative and friendly leadership styles ought to be applied—developing the pupil's independence, self-efficacy, initiative, and sense of responsibility for the effectiveness of training and for their own attitudes and behavior (see Chapter 9).

Because children, generally, experience difficulty in sustaining a high level of concentration of attention for a long time, exercises ought to be conducted in a very interesting, lively, and colorful manner; frequently changing the contents, tasks, and methods (my research has shown that children, after fifteen minutes of intensive footwork exercises—when they have to react to a coach's signals—stop practicing with full concentration and joy, and their reaction times become markedly lowered). However, while taking care to ensure a joyful and pleasant mood during exercises, the coach should not allow the lesson to cease to be an educational, organized training unit—the children doing whatever they like and the coach losing control.

I believe that the basic forms of training in the introductory stage ought to be conducted exceptionally, conscientiously, colorfully, and with variation. The main form ought to be group lessons, containing different small forms enriched by short individual lessons—which at the beginning, ought to be assessment lessons and, later on, also perfecting and mixed lessons (see Chapter 13:).

Sergey Paramonov of Kiev maintains that giving individual lessons in the first stage of training does not positively influence the formation of sensory-motor skills among young children.[1] I am of a completely different opinion. Even a very short individual lesson, given by an experienced coach, may facilitate the understanding of the structure and role of a given motor skill, and the way that it is executed and, later, applied in a bout. Such short individual (very often, assessment) lessons—of course, keeping collective lessons as the main form of practice—not only help learning, but have additional assets: they increase the joy of training and the pupil's motivation; they allow the discovery of errors; they facilitate words of encouragement and verbal instruction regarding further exercises, conducted alone or with a partner; they lead to knowing the pupil better and establishing empathy.

Although competitions are not so important in the first stage, just the same—thinking of the future—young children ought to be gradually prepared for and introduced to training bouts and, later on, to competitions (youth events).

Very gradually, but relatively early, exercises resembling bouting conditions, as well as loose play and other training bouts, ought to be introduced. It is important not to overdo it because the motor skills (fencing actions) are not yet firmly established, not completely automatized, and too big an emphasis on bouting may lead to serious technical faults which are very difficult to eradicate.

Careful and cautious introduction of training bouts is necessary for the following reasons:

1. Without the first attempts, the children will not learn how to fight;

2. The first training bouts, the first loose play, increase the level of emotions, arousal, motivation, and interest;

3. They constitute the irreplaceable school of practical competitive experience;

4. They help the development of a high level of perception, various qualities of attention;

5. They teach a sense of surprise (timing);

6. They force young fencers to try to apply the appropriate, correctly chosen actions in different tactical situations;

7. They constitute a practical school of tactical capabilities.

Of course—especially in the first stage—the time devoted to exercises ought to definitely be greater than the time allocated to training bouts. Also, too-early and too-frequent participation in competitions may have bad consequences: spoiling technique, inducing errors of execution and application, leading to very one-sided tactics (only relying on one or two favorite strokes).

A coach's advice on tactics offers priceless help for the pupil, but only a fencer's own practical experience, gained in bouts, facilitates the acquisition of technical-tactical and tactical capabilities (according to the saying that knowledge may be transferred, but one must gain experience, oneself).

In the first stage, as far as technique is concerned, the main task is very good mastery of basic fencing actions and the gradual introduction of their application, first in changing situations in a lesson, then in a training bout, then in competition. So the pupil, relying on his technique, gradually acquires technical-tactical capabilities (assessment of distance, assessment of the threatened line of target, choice of appropriate parry, etc.) and tactical abilities (preparatory actions, simple examples of second intention, sense of timing); this is promoted by specially chosen exercises of technical-tactical and tactical direction, by participation in loose play, and by the first, minor, competitions for fencers of a given age-group. There is, of course, a cyclical correlation, as newly acquired capabilities allow better and more efficient participation in loose play and competitions.

Some coaches introduce loose play far too early and, equally too early, send their young pupils to competitions. To justify this error, they say that, after all, competition is the most important part of fencing and the children will learn to fight only, or mainly, in competition. Every extreme may, and often, leads to the absurd. Perhaps it is tactless of me, but I think that such views and attitudes from coaches are a sign of ignorance and laziness. A child learns technical-tactical and tactical capabilities in loose play and competitions only after having acquired basic technique relatively well. As Raoul Clèry aptly remarked, "A fencer may apply only those tactics which his technique allows."[2]

In recent years, the emphasis on competitions has markedly increased, as has their number. One can even notice a certain exaggeration, an imbalance between training and competition. One should remember that a great pianist or violin player shows his skill by taking part in various concerts and festivals, but increases his skill by judicious practice. The same is valid for fencing. Competition is a very important factor, not only as rivalry and an opportunity to show one's skills, but also as a very important and indispensable factor of a fencer's education—yet it is not a substitute for practice, and vice versa. Over the last few years, quite a lot of coaches—under the pressure of various competitions, eliminations, ranking lists, and qualifications, and also striving to achieve early successes—have been introducing training bouts for children too early and have been sending the children too early and too frequently to competitions.

Application of too early and too frequent training bouts, as well as too frequent and early competitions for children, sometimes results from the coach's lack of knowledge or, simply, laziness. It is much easier to say to children, "Take the electric boxes and play," than to program and conduct group lessons containing warming up, interesting and versatile footwork, pair exercises, line exercises, individual lessons, and loose play, interspersed with verbal explanations and, perhaps, interesting anecdotes from the history of fencing.

It must be stressed with emphasis that too early and too frequent loose play and competitions for children, although often bringing early successes, really do more harm than good. Participation in loose play and competitions is only beneficial when a fencer has learned well the basic motor skills (basic fencing strokes) and technical-tactical capabilities. Otherwise, he may acquire faulty motor habits and not be able to concentrate on tactics because, without good acquisition of motor skills, he has to think, in a bout, not on what action to apply, but on how to execute it. As a result, in a bout and especially in competition (a higher level of arousal, the desire to win, the fear of defeat), he may commit numerous technical errors and make many thoughtless decisions. Technical errors, especially fixed during a competition, are very difficult to eradicate. Even when, with the great effort of the coach and pupil, they seem to be eradicated, they usually reappear as a, so-called, dominant reaction in difficult, stressful situations, when the fencer's level of arousal is very high.

Although, in the introductory stage, the athletes are still very young and the majority of exercises are conducted in a collective form, the coach ought to gradually introduce the principle of individualization, whose full name is the principle of an individual approach, collectivity, and the leading role of a coach.

Individualization implies that the coach, in training, while developing the pupil's personality, should take into account an athlete's dimensions of personality, traits of temperament, emotional stability and instability, body build, etc.

Collectivity means that the coach should train and educate in, and through, a team—underlining the importance of team and task cohesion.

The leading role of a coach is perhaps self-explanatory, but it ought to be added and stressed that it consists not only in teaching, advising, and explaining, but also in setting a good example. We teach and educate, not only by what we say, show, and instruct, but by what we are.

In order to recognize the personality dimensions and traits of temperament of young pupils, laboratory test are not, to begin with, necessary. For an experienced coach, it is quite sufficient to carefully watch a pupil's behavior and attitudes during exercises, games, etc. Playing soccer or basketball (with the aim of developing all-round fitness) may supply plenty of information to an experienced coach about a pupil's activity, level of arousal, achievement motivation, initiative, inhibitions, speed of reaction, emotional stability or instability, extroversion or introversion, liveliness, etc.

II – Basic Stage

The main tasks of the basic stage are:

- Increasing the level of semi-specific and specific fitness—including both energy and coordination abilities;
- Markedly widening technical, technical-tactical, and tactical abilities;
- Forming an individual style of fencing;
- Developing psychomotor abilities (perception, various qualities of attention, accuracy and speed of reaction);
- Gaining the basis of "fencing thinking";
- Taking part in competitions;

- Achieving a certain planned level of performance.

In this stage, the general role of training markedly increases—four to five lessons (meaning training sessions, comprising group exercises and individual lessons) a week, for two to three hours each. This stage lasts from three to four years.

The time devoted to all-round (general) fitness exercises decreases, and that of semi-specific and specific fitness exercises increases. So the percentage of time devoted to various kinds of exercises is:

- 15 – 20% all-round fitness;
- 25 – 30% semi-specific and specific fitness;
- 50 – 60%, fencing exercises.

(We realize, of course, that "pure" fencing exercises of technical and tactical direction produce, whether you want it or not, a very valuable "by-product," further developing fencing-specific fitness: a fencer's speed, a fencer's strength, a fencer's power, a fencer's coordination).

Semi-specific and specific fitness, and strictly fencing exercises, develop, of course, psychomotor abilities—the psychological processes strictly connected with a fencer's performance: perception, attention, speed of reaction, operative thinking, etc.

In this stage, the fencers should achieve the second phase of technical, technical-tactical, and tactical capabilities—the association phase. The best ones, at the end of this basic (second) stage, reach the third phase—purposeful and versatile activity.

Exact mastery of basic fencing actions ceases to be the main task of the competitors: they have to learn many new fencing actions and—most importantly—be able to apply them in conditions resembling competitions, in training bouts, and in competitions.

Now comes a very important and, unfortunately, often neglected aspect of training: knowledge of theory. The unity of cognition and activity, the principle of unity of theory and practice, I consider to be extremely important and useful. Mere knowledge, without practical abilities, is of course not enough; but vice versa: practical activity, without theoretical knowledge—without understanding why and what we are doing—is equally bad or even worse. Teaching fencing without verbal explanations, without theory, without proper terminology is, to me, like Pavlov's experiments with the dogs or like teaching monkeys various tricks in the circus—based not on motor skills, but on conditioned reflexes. In fact, I think that such "monkey training" is not only inefficient, but humiliating to human beings.

After being acquainted with elementary terminology in the first stage of training, now the fencer ought to know, very well and precisely, full terminology, including: a) the basic classification of fencing actions and b) the tactical classification of fencing actions (the classification based on various ways of choosing and executing a given fencing action in a bout). This is extremely important because:

1. It raises the pedagogical value of training,

2. It makes verbal contact with the coach, and between the pupils, much easier,

3. It greatly helps the understanding of the essence of fencing, including the principles of training and tactics;

4. Further, as I have mentioned many times, knowledge of terminology leads to accurate and fast perception and quick assessment of the situation, because—I dare to repeat once more—to look is not the same as to see and to see is not the same as to perceive; we perceive well and truly, on a higher conceptual-functional level, only those things which we know well, understand well, can explain and give a name to.

The fencers also ought to learn a basic knowledge of tactics, the importance and variety of preparatory actions, various properties of attention, external and internal attention, wide and narrow attention, the role of motivation and arousal on our motor activities, etc. They ought to understand—and take advantage of, in competition—that one basic fencing stroke may be applied in a bout in many different manners, and fulfill many tactical roles. For example, a direct thrust may be used as:

- Direct attack,
- Direct riposte,
- Direct counter-riposte,
- Feint of attack,
- Stop-hit,
- Stop-hit with opposition,
- Remise,
- Feint of stop-hit.

Counter-time may not only be applied in many different manners, using different strokes, but its tactical application may be quite different: it may be applied

- As a foreseen, second intention action,
- As one possible ending to an attack with unknown destination, or
- As a switch-over reaction—change of intention during a foreseen action (see Chapter 2).

In the basic period, when teaching and perfecting technique—that is, sensory-motor skills (motor habit patterns)—important changes are introduced (the beginning of this might take place, on a small scale, in the introductory period). These changes have two aspects:

1. There is much greater emphasis on the variability of different actions. Many coaches teach only one way of performing a lunge, fleche, parry, etc., whereas the logic of a bout, the changing tactical situations, and common sense all dictate that exact execution of a chosen action ought to depend on the circumstances.

For example: the lunge may be an acceleration lunge, explosive lunge, waiting lunge, or gliding lunge; we may take a parry, far from our body, close to our body, or very close to our body; we may use a removing parry, beat parry, opposition parry, or flying parry; we may parry in place, while retreating, after retreat, with evasion; etc.

2. In the second stage of training, we must increasingly emphasize the development of certain "deviations" from basic, "classical" forms of executing certain strokes, adapting the execution to the individual traits of a given fencer: body build, height, length of limbs, temperament, natural inclinations, etc.—paying great attention to distinguishing between a correct, right, and reasonable individual style and simply bad technique. There may be certain differences in on-guard positions, the distance between the feet, the position of the trunk, the position of the armed hand, ways of maneuvering on the piste, etc.

The mild degree of individualization of training (for example, different treatment of extroverts and introverts, of girls and boys) practiced in the introductory stage, becomes more important in the basic stage. Now the coach helps the pupil create an individual style of fencing and to adopt dominant tactical features (see Chapter 7).

One should remember that, while working with a fencer to develop an individual style of fencing and preferred tactics, one should take into consideration the given competitor's strong and weak dimensions of personality, and his inborn predispositions. The chosen, encouraged style of fencing ought to be based on the competitor's strong points, at the same time trying to diminish the negative side of his weak points. For example: a fencer of choleric temperament, highly extroverted, with a strongly developed motive of success, very active and full of initiative, should base his tactics and style of fencing on great mobility, active ways of conducting a bout, courage, and frequent use of fast and energetic offensive actions. But here, this fencer must remember that the psychological and tactical basis of the successful application of *offensive* actions is confidence and prowess in applying unexpected *defensive* actions. Offensive fencers, going aggressively forwards, just about ready to launch an attack, must be ready and able to parry an unexpected action from the opponent.

In this stage, young fencers must be taught—as already mentioned—terminology and tactics, since this greatly facilitates: (a) perception; (b) understanding of tactics in a bout; (c) understanding the opponent's actions and intentions; (d) correct choice of one's own actions. The fencer must realize—a very important rule—that to fight efficiently, to achieve good results, he must understand his—and his opponent's—actions, thoughts, intentions, and feelings.

Gradually, during this stage, more importance is attached to a broad range of psychological preparation: developing the pupil's personality; an active approach to training, competing, and life itself; shaping resistance to difficult and extreme situations; developing the right kind of motivation (stressing the importance of intrinsic motivation and task involvement); inducing self-efficacy and self-confidence; and—of course—developing and perfecting the psychological processes connected with motor activity (exercises and competing). The best ways to achieve all of this—apart from the coach's personal influence and example—are very special exercises, demanding a high level of attention (and its divisibility and mobility), speed and accuracy of perception, speed and accuracy of reaction, and choice of action; all of this in a "time shortage" (because of the very short distance between fencers, reactions, decision making, and execution must be very fast—much faster than, for example, in tennis where the flight of the tennis ball often lasts 400 milliseconds and the tennis player has "plenty of time" to notice the ball, run to it, and execute the appropriate stroke).

Much more important and frequent now is participation in competitions of various kinds and levels, and—in the process of training—training bouts of various kinds: loose play; bouts with the hits counted; bouts with certain technical-tactical tasks (for example: in epee, counting hits only to the leg or arm; giving two points for riposte; counting only direct attack and parry-riposte; etc.).

Very important, and often underestimated, is close contact and cooperation—exchange of thoughts, opinions, and doubts—between the master and pupil, especially after competitions, or during and after individual lessons. The coach, preparing yearly training programs—which include training tasks and result tasks—should discuss these matters with the pupils. While exchanging thoughts, giving verbal explanations, and assigning tasks, the coach ought to take into account the age, maturity, and experience of the pupil.

From among the small forms of exercises applied in a collective lesson (group lesson), line exercises (queue exercises, stream exercises) become more important. Pupils at this stage have already acquired a high level of basic fencing strokes and, in line exercises, they can perfect them, paying special attention to speed, accuracy, change of rhythm, and reaction. Line exercises do not serve the purpose of learning, but perfecting. Their great assets are: cooperation, team spirit, and, at the same time, rivalry (for example, seeing who can be faster); as far as physiological effort is concerned, they resemble conditions of a bout in which explosive energy (fast, energetic execution of attacks) is alternated with periods of relative rest (waiting for the next turn of action).

Equally important—and very often underestimated—are exercises in pairs, which develop the pupil's understanding of fencing, power of observation and perception, ability to notice the "opponent's" (partner's) mistakes, various qualities of attention, and, above all, self-efficacy.

It is extremely important to teach and perfect fast and accurate sensory-motor responses, which form the basis of technical-tactical capabilities. This is done mainly by means of exercises of unforeseen and partly foreseen actions. At the same time, we should shape the pupil's perceptiveness, fast operative thinking and—connected with it—the ability to quickly assess the tactical situation and choose the appropriate tactics. This is especially important in all of the not infrequent cases where a young fencer with very good motor coordination and very fast reaction, who does very well in lessons, becomes helpless in competition bouts: he cannot choose the right action, does not understand the opponent's intention, and cannot notice his own errors of perception, thinking, and execution. This is very often connected with too high a level of arousal and motivation—and the master must notice it and take the proper steps—(see Chapter 6).

Concerning transfer of skills and conquering successive thresholds of difficulty, the main task in the basic stage of training is to begin with overcoming the second threshold of difficulty: transfer of skills, abilities, and capabilities from exercises to training bouts; and then overcoming the third threshold: transfer of skills, abilities, and capabilities from training bouts to bouts in competition.

One should avoid—and this is very important!—"double-lane traffic," the essence of which is that a fencer, in individual lessons and other forms of exercises, learns and perfects certain strokes, actions, and capabilities which he does not use in competition; and, in competition, he uses actions which he does not perfect in practice. This is very bad. As I often mention: in fencing, we may consider that only those skills, capabilities, and psychomotor abilities that a given fencer applies effectively in competition are really acquired.

III – Competitive Stage

For many fencers, this is the stage of their highest achievements, as only very few really reach the next stage—the champion stage—and great results on an international scale. Fencers who do not reach the champion stage do take part, in the third stage, in some national and international competitions, but not of the highest importance, or in Junior categories.

In the third stage, the accent is on: further development of semi-specific and specific fitness; various coordination abilities, with special emphasis on motor adaptability with lightning-speed motor improvisation; widening the repertoire of motor skills (fencing actions) and capabilities; perfection and variation (variable execution and application of the same action) of already-acquired skills and capabilities.

In this stage, the application of the principle of individualization—which began to be applied in the previous stages—becomes more and more important. The coach strives to individualize, more, the exercises, tactics, and style of fencing of each pupil, taking into account the pupil's dimensions of personality, his traits of temperament, body build, fitness predispositions, level of performance, experience, tactical inclinations, general motivation, and achievement motivation (ego-involvement, task-involvement, motive of success, motive of avoidance of failure, etc.).

In training, the importance of training bouts increases. One should not, however, overdo it, as every extreme—as stated above—may, and often does, lead to the absurd. Many coaches—including national squad coaches—justly appreciating the great value of training bouts as extremely important in tactical preparation, introduce too many training bouts too often, especially before important competitions, and especially during various training camps. Not infrequently, several successive training sessions consist solely of training bouts, which is a very one-sided and bad practice.

When practice bouts counting hits are very often repeated (to the exclusion of other kinds of exercises), it is obvious that each competitor wants to win and, to obtain victory, applies only his well-known favorite strokes, which might become "reflex-compulsory" actions; he does not try to introduce new abilities and actions. His chief motive is not to learn, but to win. In such a way, his repertoire of actions becomes "ossified," and what is more, such a restricted repertoire of actions is easily deciphered, and finding appropriate counter-actions does not constitute a serious difficulty for the opponent.

The other extreme is seen when many sessions and hours are devoted to training bouts without counting the hits—loose play. To begin with, the fencers usually fence with eagerness and even enthusiasm, introducing new solutions, new actions, and newly acquired capabilities. But, pretty soon—without pressure to score a hit, without counting victories—such loose play becomes boring and monotonous; fencers lower their concentration of attention and interest, lose eagerness and enthusiasm—in fact, they "learn" dissipation of attention, and lose speed.

In this third, competitive stage, there is, of course, plenty of perfecting already-known motor skills (fencing actions) and capabilities, but one should not neglect introducing new actions and new capabilities. Learning new strokes facilitates the attainment of higher levels of motor coordination, especially motor educability (which is, of course, good for motor adaptability); it increases the pleasant emotions and interest of fencers and—of course—prevents ossification of the repertoire of strokes. The more actions one learns and uses in competition, the more difficult it is for the opponent; and the easier it is to deal with various kinds of opponents.

In this stage, the general load of training increases considerably: the minimum (perhaps, optimum) being everyday group lessons, lasting from two and a half to four hours, comprising various forms and kinds of exercises, including individual lessons and training bouts. Also, there ought to be more frequent participation in competitions.

In many countries, special training camps for the national squad are organized, lasting from a few days to two weeks. If conducted properly, and not too frequently, they are an excellent form of practice: cooperation of the country's leading coaches and fencers; intense and miscellaneous training; contact with nature, sunshine, water, and snow; an opportunity for active rest and excursions—and the mere change of conditions also acts positively on motivation and creates a pleasant atmosphere. During training camps, one may conduct exercises twice or three times daily. However, if such training camps are too frequent, they have certain negative aspects: too-frequent separation from one's coach, club, school, university, family, etc.

In the competitive stage, the coach should promote the pupil's self-efficacy, independence, and initiative. In pair exercises, for example—apart from elementary technical drills—exercises demanding high perception and concentration, initiative, fencing cleverness, and independence ought to be introduced. To give a few examples: pupils must think up and practice a minimum of ten various kinds of defense against an opponent's attack starting with an action on the blade; they must think up as many varieties of counter-time as possible; they must practice a given stroke in different tactical applications (different intention, varied distance, different reaction by the opponent, etc.).

In the third stage, as already mentioned, the fencer must demonstrate much more initiative, self-efficacy, and responsibility; co-operating with the coach in preparing a yearly training plan (including training and competition tasks); discussing the lessons and competitions, sometimes proposing new exercises, etc.

In technical and tactical preparation, the fencer, of course, should attain the, so-called, autonomous phase of the application of technique and tactics. That is to say, he should perform many-sided, versatile, purposeful activity with the emphasis on which stroke to apply and when, and not simply how to execute a given stroke. (In the beginning, a basketball player devotes eighty to ninety percent of his attention to how to dribble the ball, and there is not much attention left to perceive the situation of the game. A very young fencer, in the first stage of training—in a training bout, and even more in competition—pays more attention to how to execute lunge, fleche, parry, than to what action to use and when to apply it.) As far as transfer of skill is concerned, the fencer, in the third stage, ought to master well the third "threshold of difficulty": ably and efficaciously transferring motor-skills, responses, and capabilities from training bouts and training competitions to bigger competitions—which, perhaps, constitutes the most salient sign of progress and of the efficacy of training.

A fencer's behavior during competitions, added to his obtained results, constitutes a real test of his pre-dispositions, talents, level of preparedness, psychological traits, as well as of the coach's work and the quality of the training process.

To properly judge the progress and level of an athlete—and to appropriately and correctly make plans for the future—it is not enough to assess the results of competitions. It is also necessary to evaluate the pupil's style of fighting, range and efficacy of applied fencing actions, good points and shortcomings, and his ability to deal with difficult situations. It is also advisable to periodically conduct specially chosen tests of semi-specific and specific fitness, level of coordination, speed of motor responses, speed and accuracy of applied actions, as well as psychological tests which inform us about such important items as: dimensions of personality, emotional stability and instability, type of temperament, simpathicotonic or vagotonic tendencies, etc.

IV – Champion Stage

Only very few extremely talented and well-trained competitors reach the fourth stage. They are those athletes who have achieved, in previous stages (especially the third one), outstanding results, and have distinguished themselves by certain traits of personality: the right set of achievement motivation; perseverance in achieving tasks and goals; diligence, courage and self-confidence; independence and responsibility.

In the champion stage, it is "obligatory" to think prospectively, constantly gaining new capabilities and widening one's possibilities. The fencer who reaches this stage not only takes advantage of his talents and acquired skills and capabilities, but actively and consciously tries to raise their level—trying, at the same time, to eliminate, or at least minimize, his weak points of functional-motor fitness, technique, tactics, and psychological preparation.

The coach's role undergoes (ought to undergo) a fundamental change. To superficial observers, it might seem that his role as a teacher decreases. He becomes an advisor, a guide for the pupil (who ought to, himself, define his own goals and tasks in the training program and co-direct the entire process of training, including preparations for important competitions and, to a large degree, the contents of individual lessons). This is a very difficult task because, while applying an extreme variety of the cooperative and friendly leadership styles, the coach must still play a leading role and positively influence the pupil. This "new" style of leadership and cooperation demands reciprocal respect and empathy on both the coach's and competitor's sides. The coach's changed style of leadership—which may seem to some as a decrease of his role—means, contrary to what some might think, a higher responsibility and more difficult task: developing, to a higher degree, the pupil's initiative, conscious effort, self-confidence, and creative cooperation—all of which markedly increases the chances for great success in competition (and in life!).

Coaches of the dictatorial style of leadership mostly do not understand this change of role. They try to compensate for their lack of profound knowledge and educational capabilities (and, sometimes, simply because of laziness) by a cascade of strict orders, negative reinforcements, punishments, and a domineering attitude. During competitions, such coaches "wildly" encourage their competitors, shouting commands and an avalanche of advice. They behave in such a way, completely oblivious to the fact that: 1) an avalanche of advice and orders only increases the pupil's arousal, spoils his concentration, and does not help on the piste, at all; 2) such behavior absolutely cannot compensate for a lack of rational training and the appropriate treatment of pupils.

Each competition ought to be understood and treated appropriately. Small competitions, like club or area tournaments—while very important for beginners—are, for a high-class fencer, merely a kind of training competition; national classification tournaments—a higher level of competition—play the role of training, verification of athletic form, and fulfillment of planned training tasks—plus, usually, collection of points for bigger competitions. Obviously, at World Cups, University Games, continental championships, World Championships, and, of course, the Olympic Games, the fencer should try to achieve the highest results possible.

Each participation in a competition ought to be the object of thorough analysis, both by the master and the pupil. Both should analyze the good points, the progress made, the victories, and also the defeats and mistakes. In analyzing the errors, they should define them: errors of perception and reaction (not noticing the opponent's movements in time—late reaction), errors of thinking (bad tactics), and errors of execution (bad technique). They should also try to find the sources of the errors (too-high arousal, not enough training, inadequate methods of training, etc.) and ways to remedy them.

In the champion stage, new elements of training ought to appear: analysis of participation in competitions and realization of tasks in group lessons and, especially, individual lessons; introduction of new tasks in training bouts (e.g., an increase of speed of simple attack, perfection of second intention actions, defense against the opponent's action on the blade, change of intention in foreseen actions, etc.); application, in competition, of actions, acquired and perfected in training, and their successive assessment. This, of course, requires—not only from the coach, but also from the competitor—a profound knowledge of theory, tactics, and methodology of training—one of the most important tasks for a competitor in the champion stage.

Contrary to the views and practices of many coaches, it is necessary not only to perfect known actions and capabilities, but, equally, to widen the repertoire of actions and capabilities, to increase the fencer's technical and tactical versatility. The latter, of course, has to be done carefully and reasonably—one must not try to teach tactics and ways of choosing certain actions "contrary to nature": the teaching of new strokes and abilities ought to agree with a given fencer's body build, personality, temperament, style of fencing, and tactical inclinations.

In developing functional-motor fitness, one has to emphasize energy abilities—semi-specific and specific—with motor and physiological characteristics which strictly correspond to fencing (see Chapter 12). All-round, physical fitness exercises ought to be practiced in rather small amounts as in this stage they fulfill the role of active rest, psychological relaxation, and prevention of overstraining certain systems and organs most active in fencing. In this stage, all-round fitness exercises practically have no influence on the results in competitions. Aerobic fitness, however, does help to speed up the process of restitution after strenuous effort.

When it comes to transfer of skills, the most important, of course, is the fourth threshold of difficulty: transfer of abilities, skills, responses, and capabilities, from less important competitions to big ones (plus, obviously, transfer of skills from lessons to loose play, and from loose play to any competition, does not loose its importance).

Generally speaking, one may say that, in the champion stage, the role of the competitor in the process of co-directing his training—especially in pre-competition periods—becomes very significantly more prominent. The importance of cognitive processes, motivation, self-confidence and self-efficacy come to the fore. One should realize that, all things being equal (physical fitness, technique, tactics, etc.), the winner of a bout is the one who is more courageous, more sure of himself, more full of initiative, with optimal arousal and resistance to stressful situations.

The importance of the coach as a "training technologist" decreases, but he markedly increases his role as an educator, advisor, inspirer, and moral tutor.

FINAL REMARKS

"The dust of the past is not always worthy of respect."
--Claude Débussy

The traditional classification of training stages is very one-sided because it takes into account only the shaping of various kinds of functional-motor fitness—mainly energy abilities—and disregards other extremely important component parts of training: sensory-motor skills and responses, technical-tactical abilities, tactics, psychological traits and processes. Some authors advise, in the first stage of training, emphasis on only all-round fitness, with exercises as far as possible from the chosen branch of sport. In many branches of sport, the idea of excluding specific technical-tactical exercises from the first stage of training is not to be accepted. Perhaps such views might be valid in certain branches of sport where the most decisive elements determining the results in competition are energy (physical) abilities—but I am not convinced even of that. For example: even the highest development of energy abilities will not help a pole-vaulter achieve great results without the appropriate acquisition of a very difficult and complex motor skill; in rowing—as is well known—strength, endurance, and speed are very important, but results of oarsmen depend also, to a large degree, on well-acquired technique of rowing (sensory-motor skills). It is particularly faulty (not to say absurd) to conduct, in the first stage of training, only all-round fitness exercises as distant as possible from a chosen branch of sport.

In the first stage—apart from necessary all-round fitness exercises (to develop motor and adaptation possibilities of a young organism, to prepare a good basis for specific fitness, to give children fun and enjoyment)—one should give appropriate time and attention to semi-specific and specific fitness exercises, plus—very important—to teaching technique and tactics. In certain sports, we should even start with technique. For example, in tennis, we should teach young boys and girls first how to hold the racket, the elementary strokes, and how to move on the court, and then develop the speed and power of the strokes, and the speed and endurance of movement on the court. Contrary to the stubbornly repeated myth, my advice is logical, in accordance with physiological and sociological knowledge and common sense, and brings good results.

Exercises developing aerobic capacity, applied to young children before puberty, are far less efficacious than the same exercises applied in adolescence. A child's improvement in athletic preparedness and competition results, very often is due to an increase of skill (motor skills and technical-tactical capabilities) and, simply, the development of his body (height, weight, strength). But, of course, as we shall see in another chapter, a child's results in competition depends much more on the level of all-round physical fitness, than those of adolescents and adults (see Chapter 12). Similarly, exercises developing anaerobic capacity and strength exercises are much more effective for adults than for children.

Only capabilities, depending mostly on the functions of the nervous and muscular systems—sensory-motor skills and responses—and on coordination abilities and coordination of the receptory system, nervous system, and motor system, improve markedly under the influence of exercises, and not merely age or maturation.

The old, traditional classification of training stages does not take into consideration the very important principle of specificity of training. It is obvious that each motor activity and each sport has different physiological, bio-mechanical, and psychological demands (see Chapter 2, Table 2-A).

My proposed classification of stages is valid for fencing, and may turn out to be valid for other branches of sport in which technique, tactics, and psychomotor abilities play an important part. One thing is sure, the above-proposed description of training stages is strictly connected with PRACTICE—which is "a queen of truth"—and is verified by PRACTICE. I am strongly convinced that the only real, "pitiless" test of the truth of a theory is PRACTICE. Theory is created by the needs of practice, it serves practice, and is verified by practice.

I should like to finish this chapter by stating that progress in any branch of human activity—including scientific and athletic activities—enters the future only by a search for a new path.

References

1. Paramonov, S.W.: *Podgotovka shpadzhista*, „Zdorovya", Kiev 1986,
2. Cléry, R.: *L'Escrime*, Presse Universitaire de France, Paris 1973,
3. Czajkowski, Z.: Nauczanie techniki sportowej, second edition, RCMSKFiS, Warszawa, in press

12. Energy Skills, Energy Abilities, Sensory Motor Skills, and Competition Results at Different Stages of Training

"It is easier to completely destroy a thousand cities than to abolish a myth."
--Ignacy Paderewski

"What a strange century in which it is easier to split an atom than abolish a myth."
--Albert Einstein

ENERGY ABILITIES AND SENSORY-MOTOR SKILLS

"It is important to distinguish between the changes in the central nervous system which are assumed to occur when skill acquisition takes place and other physiological changes—such as increased strength and endurance—which also may occur under conditions of practice. Both types of change may contribute to the level of performance reached in any particular skill. But when an individual is training, he should know the effect of his methods on the internal neural process and on the cardiovascular and muscular systems, and not assume that the methods beneficial to one necessarily aid the others."
--Barbara Knapp

In a fencer's training process, simply speaking, we develop functional-motor fitness—which includes energy abilities and co-ordination abilities—and sensory-motor skills, closely connected to technique, tactics, and psychomotor abilities.

A sensory-motor skill may be defined as a learned cognitive-motor activity, which allows for previously established tasks to be achieved exactly, accurately, fluently, efficiently, adroitly, without undue loss of time and energy, and very often in a state of non-consciousness.

We distinguish closed (intrinsic), intermediate, and open (extrinsic) motor skills. Closed motor skills are performed with little attention paid to external situations (e.g., gymnastics, jumps, dancing, etc.), while the performance of open motor skills closely involves taking into account external stimuli: the environment and changes occurring in it, the opponent's movement, etc. (e.g., in fencing, tennis, team games, car driving, etc.).

Recently, Richard Schmidt has introduced a slightly different classification of motor skills, dividing them into: motor types (track-and-field events, swimming, rowing, cycling, weight-lifting, etc.), cognitive types (playing chess, playing cards, etc.) and cognitive-motor types (fencing, tennis, soccer, volleyball, badminton, baseball, etc.).[1] The given examples explain the essence of the meaning of these terms. Distinguishing open and closed motor skills, and also skills of motor and cognitive-motor types, is extremely important, since it is obvious that training methods ought to correspond to the type of motor skill (and yet, quite often, coaches of a sport with open skills, and of cognitive-motor type, teach the motor skills as if they were closed and of a motor type).

Learning and performing motor skills is strongly connected to coordination abilities. There are many of them, such as speed and accuracy of reaction, orientation in time and space, accuracy and proper rhythm of movement, change of speed and direction, coordination between the movement of the arms and legs, keeping of balance, etc. All of the very numerous coordination abilities may be divided into three main groups: motor educability, motor control, and motor adaptability.

The most typical energy abilities are strength and endurance. A mixed ability—connected both with energy fitness and coordination—is speed and its various features.

The performance of motor skills depends on coordination abilities and energy abilities, in a very specific way, different for each activity.

Sensory-motor skills, and the various capabilities associated with them, play an immense part in human life: everyday-life activities, productive work, artistic activity, transportation (e.g. driving), recreation and sport.

Energy abilities depend on the physiological processes of cells, tissues, organs, systems, and the entire human organism— constituting an interrelated entity. Motor coordination abilities—and thus, motor skills—depend mainly on receptors and the locomotory system, and are co-coordinated and directed by the nervous system.

Though energy abilities—and, especially, coordination abilities—are connected with motor skills, and influence, to a large degree, their learning and application in life and sport, there occur striking differences, especially between energy abilities and motor skills. This, of course, demands from the coach: a) a thorough understanding of the physiological bases of—and differences between—energy abilities and motor skills, and b) different, appropriate methods of developing energy abilities, and teaching and perfecting motor skills. Although it is so obvious and important, many coaches and even sport scientists, strangely enough, do not appreciate the importance of these differences.

Of course, it happens very often that an exercise, originally meant to teach and perfect a motor skill, happens to develop, at the same time, in a specific way, a given energy ability or set of abilities (for example, when a fencer learns direct attack with lunge—his main aim—he simultaneously develops fencing speed and power.). Generally, however, one should choose different exercises—and different forms and methods of conducting them—when developing a given energy ability and when teaching and perfecting a given motor skill.

When choosing exercises, and the methods of conducting them, the coach must be well-aware which exercises and methods develop energy fitness, as well as what kind of energy fitness they develop; which exercises develop various aspects of motor coordination, and which exercises and methods are necessary to teach and perfect motor skills and—strictly connected with them—technical-tactical and tactical capabilities.

The coach should also be aware of the fact that, in all branches of sport, motor skills are important and, in some sports, their meaning is decisive (see Chapter 2, Table 2-A).

The importance of general, all-round, energy fitness is very often largely overestimated: its value in many sports, especially in the competitive and champion stage, is not significant (see previous chapter and below).

Table 12—A1
Salient Characterisitcs of Energy Abilities

They are inborn predispositions.
They develop as a natural process of maturation and, also, under the influence of exercises; without exercises, the level of energy fitness markedly decreases.
Their number is limited.
Fitness abilities are shaped and developed.
The importance of verbal explanation, demonstration, terminology, instruction is negligible.
Perceptive and cognitive processes have little influence.
Physical fitness is determined by the physiological processes of the entire organism.
In adult age, the level of energy abilities markedly diminishes.
Intelligence does not play an important part.
Body build, weight, length of extremities, inborn "physical" predispositions, etc. are very significant.
Very important: the significance of various types of energy abilities undergoes considerable changes according to the years of athletic activity and stage of training.

Table 12—A2
Salient Characteristics of Motor Skills

They are acquired, learned.
Motor skills are very durable, once learned—for example, cycling or swimming—they do not disappear, even after a long interval without training.
The number is practically unlimited.
Motor skills are learned.
Verbal explanation, terminology, demonstration, visualisation (mental images), etc. are very important.
Motor skills depend, to a very high degree, on speed and level of perception, various qualities of attention, imagination, and thinking (especially open motor skills of the cognitive-motor type).
Motor skills depend, mainly, on cooperation of the nervous system, receptors, and locomotory system.
Preservation of—and even learning and perfecting—motor skills is possible even in quite advanced age.
In learning and perfecting sensory-motor skills, and applying them in competition—especially open skills of cognitive motor type—the role of intelligence is very marked.
Much less significance of somatic build and effort capacity.
The importance of the quality of motor skills steadily rises with the years of athletic activity and stage of training, until a quite adult age.

So, appreciating the importance of energy fitness and its relationship to motor skills, we must realize that physical fitness abilities and sensory-motor skills are, in many respects, very different. The following points emphasize the differences between energy fitness and motor skills, stressing their characteristic features:

1. We teach motor skills (demonstrations, verbal instructions, explanations, etc.); we shape and develop energy abilities. (We may influence the performance of a movement by demonstrations, verbal explanations, or manual guidance, but no demonstrations or verbal explanations will influence the oxygen processes in mitochondria).

2. The level and improvement of energy abilities depend on the physiological functions of the entire organism; learning motor skills depends on cooperation of the nervous system, receptors, and locomotor system.

3. The number of energy abilities is limited; the number of possible sensory-motor skills is practically limitless.

4. In shaping and developing energy abilities, the role of cognitive, mental, and decision-making processes is negligible; whereas, in teaching-learning motor skills, technical-tactical and tactical capabilities, the role of these processes is essential.

5. Different qualities of attention (level of concentration; range, selectivity, divisibility, shifting of attention) play a very important role in teaching-learning motor skills. Their role in the process of shaping energy abilities is incomparably smaller.

6. Both physical abilities and sensory-motor skills improve under the influence of the appropriate exercises, but, in these respects too, substantial differences occur.

7. A person who has acquired a certain sensory-motor skill—for example, swimming or cycling—will be able

to perform it, even after a long spell of time without training. Yet even a short break in training causes a fast and marked decrease in the level of energy fitness.

- Energy abilities develop under the influence of exercises and, also, the influence of biological development (ontogenesis), but with the increase of age, their level markedly lowers. Motor skills may be perfected and learned in an advanced age. (A certain difficulty experienced by some old people when trying to learn a new motor skill is due not so much to a lowering of motor educability and other coordination abilities, but is the result of a lowering of qualities of attention and perception. Just the same, as mentioned before, even very old people can, effectively, use motor skills which had been well acquired before. Welford "found evidence that older people can maintain an established skill to an age considerably beyond that at which they can, without undue difficulty, learn a new skill."[2]

- Many centuries ago, when the average life-span of a man was 36-40 years, fencing masters, leading a very active life, gave lessons—and even took part in duels—to the age of 80 and more!)

8. In shaping energy abilities and in teaching-learning motor skills, different, appropriate methods ought to be applied (it seems so obvious, yet I have found in several textbooks advice to apply certain methods, typical for the development of physical fitness, in teaching motor skills).

9. The importance, role, and inter-correlation of energy fitness abilities and sensory-motor skills, differ remarkably in various branches of sport (again, see Chapter 2, Table 2-A).

10. Very important and very often underestimated: the importance of various kinds of energy fitness (all-round fitness, semi-specific fitness, specific fitness) differs considerably in different stages of training (for example: all-round, general fitness is quite important in the first, introductory, stage of training, but in the fourth, champion, stage, its significance is minimal; see below).

11. The quality of sensory-motor skills, speed of learning, durability and accuracy of movements, and—especially—speed and accuracy of choosing the appropriate actions in a bout, depend on many coordination abilities.

The salient features of, and differences between, energy fitness abilities and sensory-motor skills are presented on Tables 12-A1 and 12-A2.

THE INFLUENCE OF GENERAL, SEMI-SPECIFIC AND SPECIFIC FITNESS, AND PSYCHOMOTOR ABILITIES ON FENCERS' RESULTS IN COMPETITION, IN DIFFERENT STAGES OF TRAINING

"The fatigue encountered in swimming and running is mainly in the effector mechanism so that hard physical training can make a great difference to performance in the longer events. In fencing and the racket games on the other hand the receptor and translation mechanisms are as important as the effector. Many tennis players would acknowledge that they can play tennis all day provided they are a little more skilled than their opponents even though they take a great deal of physical exercise in the process."

--Barbara Knapp

Before we tackle the main theme of this subchapter, the principle of specificity of training ought to be, once more, stressed. The coach must remember a very simple rule: what is good for one branch of sport may not be so good for another. As happens very often, the obvious things are not easily noticed and the obvious conclusions are not put into practice.

Concerning transfer of skill, we may differentiate positive transfer (the exercises develop the right physical abilities, coordination skills for a given branch of sport, and are applied in competition), neutral transfer (the exercises do not influence athletes' skill or results in competition, positively nor negatively), negative transfer (the exercises have a negative influence on performance in a given branch of sport).

Many coaches overestimate the value of energy (physical) fitness in fencing—especially all-round, general fitness—and apply, for example, long-distance running, which produces a long-distance runner's endurance and is rather useless in fencing; or they apply a lot of weight-lifting exercises, developing the size, strength, and power of muscles, but spoiling the subtle and accurate wielding of a weapon. As Albert Einstein wittily and cleverly remarked, "After working with a pick-axe, one does not play violin," (see Chapter 1).

Many coaches not only overestimate the value of basic fitness in a fencer's training, but also disregard the fundamental necessity of changing the structure of training and the choice of exercises in different training stages: taking into account an athlete's age, experience, technical skills, etc. (see the previous chapter and below).

Different kinds of energy fitness (all-round, semi-specific, and specific fitness)—like other component parts of the training process—change markedly in their significance, and influence on competition results, in different stages of training.

This ought to be obvious when one considers elementary knowledge of physiology, psychology, sport science, the effects of different exercises on the human organism, etc.; and it is confirmed by empirical evidence and by research and various tests. As the head of the Fencing Department at the Academy of Physical Education in Katowice, I have conducted numerous tests to find out the most important factors in training, in different stages of a fencer's career.[3]

Before I describe, in short, one typical set of tests showing the changing importance of various kinds of energy (physical) fitness, and other factors, on a fencer's results in different stages of training, I am going to review—in a very short, concise and simplified manner—the meaning of all-round, semi-specific, and specific fitness:

1. All-round (general, basic) fitness—state of muscles and other organs, motor performance, specific movements, and physiological processes, not connected with, nor resembling, a given branch of sport (e.g., for a fencer: running, jumping, swimming, cycling, certain gymnastic exercises, etc.);

2. Semi-specific fitness—motor performance, forms of movements, and physiological processes, not exactly the same as in a chosen branch of sport, but similar and helpful for the development of specific fitness—positive transfer of skills (e.g., for a fencer: lunge or fleche from a squat-down position; catching a tennis ball or bean bag with a lunge or fleche; somersault then fleche; sitting crossed-legged, then jumping to on-guard position as fast as possible on a given signal; etc.);

3. Specific fitness—movement and physiological processes, used exactly as in a chosen branch of sport (e.g., for a fencer: movement and physiological effort used in proper fencing exercises and bouting).

Now I will describe one set of tests which I conducted a few years ago with sixty leading sabreurs from Silesia (Poland). These tests gave a mass of information and led to many conclusions. I shall discuss only a few of the most important and valid ones. I will depict the tests in a very short manner, without giving hundreds of figures, detailed statistical analyses, etc.

Sixty fencers were divided into four groups, according to their age (and, of course, length of training):

1. 13 years old and younger (introductory stage of training);

2. 14 through 17 years old (basic stage of training, beginning of competitive stage);

3. 18 to 20 years old (competitive stage);

4. Older than 20 (competitive and champion stages).

The numerous and various tests included assessment of:

- All-round (basic, general) fitness.

- Semi-specific and specific energy fitness, and the most elementary technical skills.

- Chosen psychomotor abilities (speed and accuracy of sensory-motor responses, visual-motor coordination, concentration of attention, etc.).

In each age group (stage of training), I prepared a ranking list based on competition results for one year.

All-round energy fitness was assessed by a set of tests containing: a 40-meter shuttle run, starting from a standing position; running

Fig. 12.1
The Interrelationship between Various Kinds of Physical Fitness, Psychomotor Abilities, Basic Technical Capabilities, and Competition Results of Fencers of Different Ages

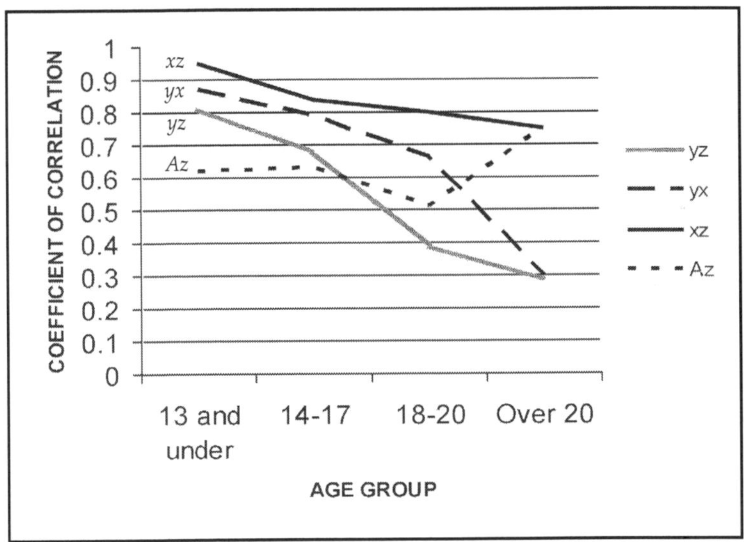

yz – coefficient of correlation between all-round fitness and competition results (high early, declines sharply).
yx – coefficient of correlation between general and specific fitness (high early, declines sharply).
xz – coefficient of correlation between specific fitness and results in competition (highest early, declines slowly).
Az – coefficient of correlation between psychomotor abilities and results in competition (modest early, increases sharply ages 18-20 and after).

Fig. 12.2
The Correlation Between Various Types of Energy Fitness, Psychomotor Abilities, And Results in Competition, Depending on Age and Training Stage

	COEFFICIENT OF CORRELATION			
Age Group	yz	yx	xz	Az
13 and under	0.81	0.87	0.95	0.62
14-17	0.68	0.79	0.84	0.63
18-20	0.39	0.66	0.80	0.51
Over 20	0.29	0.30	0.75	0.75

yz – coefficient of correlation between all-round fitness and competition results.

yx – coefficient of correlation between general and specific fitness.

xz – coefficient of correlation between specific fitness and results in competition.

Az – coefficient of correlation between psychomotor abilities and results in competition.

4m, ten times (back and forth); an "envelope" run; bending over (flexibility); sit-ups; standing long-jumps; push-ups with hand-clapping; and throwing a 3kg medicine ball.

The test of semi-specific and specific physical fitness, plus basic technical capabilities, contained: catching a tennis ball with fleche twenty times; speed of fencing steps, advances and retreats, 4m, five times, as fast as possible; specific speed: execution, five times, of cut to head with fleche; speed and accuracy of fencing actions: execution, five times, of a compound action—four-beat and cut to head with lunge, return to on-guard position, and attack with feint to head, cut to flank with fleche; speed of reaction and movement: fifteen times, attempt to hit a falling glove with a thrust with lunge; psychomotor abilities: speed of various types of reaction and various aspects of space-time orientation measured on a special apparatus.

Special ranking lists for each age group were made. Analysing the ranking lists of various tests, and the ranking lists of results in competitions, using various statistical methods, we drew many interesting conclusions (see Figure 13.1 and Table 13-B).

The most important results of these tests indicate that:

1. The correlation coefficient between all-round energy fitness and a fencer's results in competitions diminishes markedly with the age and training experience of the fencer—from 0.81 (in the youngest group) through 0.68 and 0.39, to 0.29 (in the senior group). It shows that all-round fitness is important, really, only at a very young age, in the first stage of training. Later on, its significance diminishes. Among senior fencers—competitive and champion stages—all-round fitness does not improve competition results; it only provides active rest, psychological relaxation, prevention of traumas, and facilitation of after-effort recovery.

2. Very young fencers, in competition, have to rely mostly on all-round, basic energy fitness (strength, endurance, speed, power, mobility) because their technique and tactics, fencing experience, perception, and speed and accuracy of reaction are still rather poor.

3. The correlation between all-round (physical) fitness, on one side, and semi-specific and specific fitness, and basic technical skills, on the other side, also gradually diminishes: 0.87, 0.79, 0.66, 0.30. It again shows that the value and significance of all-round fitness in the later stages of training is greatly overrated.

4. The correlation between semi-specific and specific fitness, and basic motor skills, on one side, and the results of competition, on the other, diminishes very little over time and is always, in all stages of fencing—and all ages of fencers—very important: 0.95, 0.84, 0.80, 0.75.

5. The coefficient of correlation of psychomotor abilities and results in competition, constantly increases: 0.62, 0.63, 0.51, 0.75. It means that in all stages of training, and with fencers of different ages, one should pay a lot of attention to the development of specific psychomotor abilities strictly connected with a fencer's motor activity: speed and accuracy of perception, speed and accuracy of reaction, visual-motor coordination, etc. (The coefficient of correlation, 0.51, in the 18-20 age group, is due to a well-trained and talented fencer who showed excellent results on reaction meters, and in other psychological tests, but whose too-high level of motivation and arousal considerably lowered his results in competition—he was ranked number 15 in his group. This, of course, demonstrates that, in spite of excellent psychomotor abilities, a fencer's results can be seriously affected by his level of arousal (see Chapter 6).

Then the final and obvious conclusion may be summarized as follows:

In a fencer's training, one should take into account the principle of specificity (and individualization, of course) to ensure successive transfers of skill from exercises to training bouts, and from training bouts to competitions. In choosing exercises, and the methods of conducting them, one should pay attention, above all, to those factors which markedly influence the level of performance, efficacy of actions, and results in competitions, taking into consideration various tasks of different training stages.

References

1. Schmidt R.A. *Motor Control and Learning.* Second Edition. Champaign, 1988. Human Kinetics.
   __________ *Motor Learning and Performance—from Principles to Practice.* Champaign, 1991. Human Kinetics.
2. Knapp B.: Skill in Sport. London, 1970. Routledge and K. Paul.
3. Czajkowski Z.: Z badań nad czynnikami wpływającymi na wynik sportowy w szermierce. Katowice, 1991. Podstawowe problemy badawcze w naukach kultury fizycznej.

13. Modern Concepts of the Individual Lesson (Part 1)

"The development of technique requires regular practice, attention and concentration, and constant correction. A fencer is like an opera singer who needs lessons on a regular basis to improve or maintain his or her high standard of performance. Lessons have different purposes aiming at the different aspects of the development of technique, tactics or training."
--Michel Alaux, *Modern Fencing*

THE INDIVIDUAL LESSON: ESSENCE, SIGNIFICANCE, VARIETIES AND DIRECTIONS

"There cannot be any comparison between one who repeats a given chapter a hundred times and another who repeats it a hundred times and one."
--Talmud

Introduction

"A man, engaged in work which he loves, is never fully satisfied—constantly he tries to learn and to develop."
--Anna Koptieyeva, *Ivan Ivanovich*

Within the general system of high competitive sport, a coach must have his own views and methods—in a way, his own school. As Ozolin puts it, "A great coach walks his own path." The fencing coach takes advantage of his knowledge and practical abilities in the whole process of a fencer's education—in teaching, training, educational influence—applying various forms and methods of conducting exercises. Within this process, the individual lesson is a highly characteristic, specific and valid form of fencing exercise, known and developed for many hundreds of years.

Especially during the individual lesson, the fencing master plays the roles, simultaneously or in turn, of teacher, educator, friend, helpful advisor and adversary. Thus, he must retain and develop a high level of energy fitness, coordination abilities, technical and tactical capabilities, as well as pedagogical and didactical skills. A fencing master's movements ought to be correct, precise and realistic, often unusually fast, and they ought to compel pupils' imitation. From this arises the necessity for the fencing master to increase not only his own knowledge but, equally, his motor fitness and practical capabilities.

In the long history of fencing, the individual lesson has been known for many centuries. It underwent many changes corresponding to the development of weapons, ways of fighting, role and importance of fencing, transformation of habits (for example, fighting in duels, knights' tournaments, battles, physical education, competitive sport) and progress of our knowledge. Nowadays, in high competitive sport, the individual lesson, and other forms of training, we try to take advantage of, and apply, new advances in knowledge, practical experience, the development of sport science and basic sciences like psychology, pedagogy, didactics, etc., and also a coach's pedagogical intuition, common sense and empirical experience.

In a fencer's training, two basic forms are used: the collective lesson (group lesson) and individual lesson. ("Just in case," let me remind you that "form," as used here, means the organization in time and space of teacher (coach) and pupils (athletes). "Method" means a way, based on experience or scientific research, of achieving a certain goal.)Within the collective lesson, many different basic forms (small forms or sub-forms) are used. In these forms (and other, still smaller forms within the collective lesson), one applies different methods of conducting exercises. One method for example, consists of repetition of a chosen stroke; see Chapter 14. This form may be applied in such different sub-forms as exercises on one's own, exercises in front of a mirror, exercises with a mannequin (dummy), exercises in pairs, and queue exercises (exercises in a line). Within one sub-form (for example, pair exercises) one may use different methods: repetition of a chosen stroke; responding, with a predetermined action, to the opponent's (practice partner's) pre-announced movements; etc.

In coaching, we apply—or ought to apply—different methods, depending on the goal which we want to achieve,. So, while we apply one set of appropriate methods for shaping and developing energy abilities—strength, endurance, speed (continuous method, interrupted method, etc.), other methods ought to be used in shaping and developing coordination abilities. In doing so, we must take into consideration the very different importance of different abilities in the various disciplines of sport. Further, we have to differentiate between improvement of motor educability, motor control (directing movement) and motor adaptability, including the specific aspect of lightning speed improvisation.

Still more different methods must be applied in teaching-learning and perfecting sensory-motor skills and capabilities: technique, technical-tactical abilities, tactics, and psychomotor processes. This diversification of methods requires that we not only choose different methods depending on the branch of sport and type of sensory-motor skill—but, equally, we have to consider the stage of teaching-learning the motor skill. The fourth stage of teaching-learning a motor-skill—the perfection of a skill—is very different in branches of sport based on closed motor skills compared to those based on open motor skills. In teaching-learning open (extrinsic) motor skills, we apply different methods in the second stage, teaching a motor skill, and in the fourth stage, increasing the lability of the motor skill (see chapter: Periods and Stages of Training).

Generally speaking, the methods used in training may be divided into:

1. Verbal methods (lectures, discussions, verbal explanations, analysis of training and competitions, correction of errors, talking with competitors, praising, etc.);

2. Demonstrative methods (demonstrations, film, video, slides, diagrams, drawings, etc.);

3. Visualisation and mental methods (cognitive analysis of exercises, visualising ways of executing and applying actions, concentration of attention, self-motivation, etc.);

4. Practical methods (exercises, training bouts, competitions).

As I have already mentioned—and it has to be strongly emphasized—we use different methods while shaping energy abilities ("physical fitness"), different methods to develop various coordination capabilities, and still different methods when teaching and perfecting technique and tactics (technical capabilities, technical-tactical capabilities, tactical capabilities, psychomotor abilities—psychological processes strictly connected with motor activity). As the main topic of this chapter is the fencing lesson, we shall concentrate mainly on methods used in teaching-learning a fencer's sensory-motor skills and capabilities. One has to remember, however, that certain exercises—meant mainly to teach strokes, motor-skills and capabilities—develop, at the same time, energy fitness, coordination abilities and psychomotor abilities (perception, attention, etc.). When a fencer, in a lesson, practises a compound attack with advance lunge then, apart from learning technical execution of this fencing action, he additionally perfects his mobility on the strip, feeling of surprise ("timing"), perception, concentration, mobility and shifting of attention, strength of leg muscles, speed of muscle contraction, coordination of arm and leg movement, and speed of reaction and movement. Just the same, generally in specially chosen exercises, we try to focus attention on one or a few chosen elements.

In teaching and perfecting a fencer's technique (in teaching sensory-motor skills), one may—using various criteria of classification—distinguish the following methods:

1.
   a. *Whole* method;
   b. *Part* method;
   c. *Mixed* method.

2.
   a. *Reproductive* method (from strictly imitative methods to demonstrations accompanied by precise descriptions and advice);
   b. *Task* method;
   c. *Creative* or *Problem-solving* method.[1]

3. *Whole—Part—Whole* method (not to be confused with mixed method. The essence is

that the pupils, after a few explanations, engage in a whole sporting activity, like trying to play basketball or fencing, getting the general idea of the game. Then the coach chooses one motor skill and the pupils learn it, using the above-mentioned methods.)

Choosing the appropriate method is very important in all stages of teaching-learning motor skills—and, of course, various methods are interrelated. For example, the coach describes a new stroke, giving its name and definition, explaining the way of applying it in a bout (verbal method). Then there is a demonstration (demonstrative method). Under the influence of verbal instruction and demonstration, pupils form a mental picture of the stroke—visualization method—and then they attempt to execute the stroke, themselves (practical method).

In fencing, in teaching and, especially, in perfecting fencing actions (the sensory-motor skills of a fencer's technique), it is important to know, to understand, to distinguish and to choose the appropriate method and skillfully apply it in individual lessons. The methods used in fencing lessons will be described in detail in Chapters 14 and 15. To make these methods more understandable and to underline their meaning, I will recount briefly the stages of teaching-learning a fencing action (sensory-motor skill) and then the essence, varieties and directions of an individual lesson will be described.

The teaching (basic teaching and perfecting) of a fencing action may be divided into four strictly interconnected stages:

1. *Introducing* the action—getting acquainted with a sensory-motor skill – the coach gives the name of the stroke which will be taught, its definition, and its application in a bout. He then gives a demonstration—first fast and in its entirety; then slowly, breaking it into its component parts; then again slowly, as a whole; and then again as a whole at full speed. This stage of teaching-learning a fencing action corresponds to the first phase of developing motor skills, which is the formation of a mental picture of the stroke. Demonstration

and verbal explanations ought to elicit, among pupils, a desire to learn the action—acquisition of a motor skill.

2. *Teaching* the action—mastering the basic structure of a sensory-motor skill – taking into account the coach's verbal explanations and demonstrations, as well as a mental picture of the movement, pupils try to execute a given stroke. To begin with, it is slightly clumsy and there is usually too much muscle contraction and unnecessary additional movements. In this stage of learning, the pupils rely mostly on visual control, watching the weapon arm and body movements carefully.

3. *Fixing* the action—automatization of a sensory-motor skill – unnecessary muscle contractions and movements gradually disappear. The action is executed more precisely with the appropriate rhythm and amplitude, with ease and while keeping the correct cadence; the importance of visual control diminishes and the execution of the movement is based more on intrinsic stimuli—sense of balance and kinesthetics. Gradually, the action is executed better and better, but mainly in stable, unchanging conditions. Slowly, the coach introduces conditions somewhat resembling those in a bout which imposes the task of choice of action and a certain lability of its execution. In the second stage, as far as motor coordination is concerned, most important is motor educability (ability to learn new strokes). In the third stage, more important is motor control (directing the movement) plus the first, very easy and simple, trials of motor adaptation.

4. *Perfecting* the action—developing the plasticity of a sensory-motor skill—acquiring the capability to quickly choose the appropriate action and its variable application in constantly changing and often unpredictable situations in a bout. Here, particularly important is speed and accuracy of perception as well as motor responses, concentration, divisibility and shifting of

> attention. Visual control is focused on the assessment of the tactical situation and not on how to execute the stroke. The chosen movements are executed "automatically"—in a state of non-con-sciousness"—based on kinesthetic stimuli.

(Many physiological processes taking place in our organs are completely unconscious (we do not realize how the muscles contract, how the level of sugar in our blood changes, and so on). When we are learning a new stroke—for example, a fencing action—we do it with full concentration, consciously and under visual control. When the motor skill is well-acquired, its execution is automatic and in a state of "non-consciousness").

As far as motor coordination is concerned, most important is motor adaptability, including its particular aspect: lightning-like speed, motor improvisation. In this stage, technical capabilities (correct execution of a movement) and technical-tactical capabilities (automatic execution/application of a stroke based on acquired motor responses) are strictly connected with (1) psychomotor abilities—psychological processes connected with motor activities (perception, various qualities of attention, choice of action and its execution indices)—and (2) coordination abilities, including motor adaptation (speed and accuracy of movement, its appropriate rhythm and range, orientation in time and space, plasticity of movement, uniting component parts into one sequence of movement and—above all—the appropriate choice of an action).

It is obvious that in the various stages of teaching-learning fencing actions—thus in various phases of the formation and perfection of a sensory-motor skill—the coach has to apply different methods.

One has to realize that in the process of teaching-learning sensory-motor skills, especially in the second stage of learning, the occurrence of certain errors is inevitable: faulty execution of a stroke, unnecessary movements, too much contraction of muscles, inappropriate rhythm, lack of fluency, clumsy connection of the component parts of a movement, etc. These are mostly errors of performance. In the fourth stage, there may—and usually do—appear errors of application: incorrect choice of action, late reaction and also technical mistakes—bad execution of movement. One should not be afraid of errors; one should notice them early enough and try to correct them to prevent their fixation—the automatization of a bad sensory-motor skill. Noticing the mistakes, understanding their essence and causes, and the ways of eliminating them, are very important in teaching technique and tactics and I have described them in detail elsewhere.[2]

Some fencing coaches teach sensory-motor skills (fencing actions) as if they were closed motor skills, paying attention only to ways of execution and form of movement. One may teach this way only in the second stage: repetition of a chosen stroke with emphasis on correctness and accuracy of movement. In the next stages, especially in the fourth stage—perfecting the action (and developing the plasticity of the sensory-motor skill)—one has to necessarily teach and perfect the actions while making into consideration the obvious fact that fencing actions are open (external) sensory-motor skills of the cognitive motor type.

A sensory-motor skill (a fencing action) in the fourth stage of teaching-learning is "impregnated" with various technical-tactical capabilities, insuring not only its execution, but, equally—and above all—its application in a bout in changeable, often unpredictable situations—and while facing an active opponent. These technical-tactical capabilities, strictly connected with perfect acquisition of motor skills, are based on specific manifestations of learned motor responses (to be distinguished from conditioned reflexes), like: assessment of distance and choice of appropriate footwork, identifying the threatened area of target, differentiating between real and false actions, directing the thrust or cut into the opening area of the opponent's target, "sentiment du fer"—orientation by feeling of the blade, ability to change intention while executing a preconceived action, ability to prolong or stop the action if, and when, necessary, etc.[3] What is said above is not only valid for fencing, but for all branches of sport with open sensory motor skills of cognitive motor type with an important value of tactics, psychomotor processes and a very specific set of coordination capabilities (of course, in other sports, the technical-tactical capabilities are quite different).

In the individual lesson, and in all small forms of group lesson in the whole process of training, the fencing master ought to apply the appropriate leadership style—the best one being a cooperative and friendly style—and ably apply the principles of training, including methods of teaching-learning (didactic methods).[4] Particularly important—and unfortunately very often neglected—are principles of specialization and specificity of training, the principle of individualization (to be more precise: the principle of individualization, team cooperation and the leading role of a coach), moderation, the positive transfer of skill, as well as the principle of unity of theory and practice, and cognition and activity.[5]

THE ESSENCE, VARIETIES AND DIRECTIONS OF A LESSON

> *"Come, Monsieur, salute. Your body straight. Lean slightly on the left thigh. The legs not so widely separated. Your feet together. Your wrist in a line with your hip. The point of your sword facing your shoulder. The arm not quite so stiff. The left hand about the height of the eye. The left shoulder more squared. The head erect. The bold look. Advance. The body firm. Engage my sword in quart and keep on. One, two. Recover. Again with firm foot. A leap back. When you make a pass, Monsieur, the sword should be thrust out and the body kept well back. One, two. Come, engage my sword in tierce, and keep on. Advance. The body firm. Advance. Start from there. One, two. Recover. Again. A leap back. Parry, Monsieur, parry."*
>
> --Moliere, The Citizen Turn'd Gentleman

Fighting with various kinds of weapons is as old as humanity. From the very beginnings of fencing, in various epochs, in different countries and using different weapons, fencing masters have been teaching the art of yielding weapons. Many ancient legends, fairy tales, poems and songs contain scenes of fighting with different cutting and thrusting weapons. For many centuries, descriptions of various methods of teaching fencing have been known.[6] Moliere, in his wonderful comedy, *The Citizen Turn'd Gentleman* (1671), gave a capital picture of fencing lessons as they were conducted in the second half of the 17th Century (incidentally, the Fencing Master's role in the first performances of The Citizen Turn'd Gentleman was played by a real professional fencing master).

Moliere's Fencing Master gives only commands and verbal instruction, although some coaches of that time had been trying to introduce more modern and rational methods. One such master was Vernesson Sieur de Lyancourt, whose style of teaching fencing could be justifiably called a school of common sense and rationalism.[7] It may seem strange and paradoxical that even today one can see fencing coaches who conduct fencing lessons in nearly such a way as the Fencing Master did with Moliere's Mr Jourdain. When I talk about old-fashioned methods of conducting a fencing lesson, I mean such methods as constantly giving verbal orders and unrealistic, artificial movements, including catching the pupil's blade and fixing the point on the coach's plastron. De Lyancourt's lessons were very realistic. His practice resembled the actual conditions of real combat. He ridiculed the habit of some fencing masters of helping their pupils too much and in an artificial manner. Among other things, de Lyancourt wrote, "Have you ever seen, in real combat, somebody who would be foolish enough to catch your sword and direct it against his own breast?"

Before I describe, in detail, modern rational methods of conducting exercises in a fencing lesson, I will try to present the essence and significance of the individual lesson, with its varieties and directions.

In the first, introductory stage of training, the main forms of conducting exercises are group lessons (collective lessons). Within the group lessons, the coach, from time to time, gives short individual lessons—assessment lessons (see below). In the next successive stages of training, the individual lesson becomes more and more important; one should, however remember that the individual lesson, important as it is, only fulfills its tasks, and is efficacious, if:

a. it is conducted rationally, and

b. it is supplemented with other forms of training, including exercises on one's own, line exercises, pair work, loose play (training bouts), etc.

Exercises in pairs are particularly efficacious and useful because they teach fencers a many-sided and comprehensive understanding of fencing, high level and accuracy of perception, independence and initiative, power of observation, and inquisitive attitudes.

The individual lesson should not lead to pupils developing passive attitudes. On the contrary, it ought to shape creative and active attitudes. All that the pupil learns in a lesson ought to find its application, first in loose play, and then in competition—a positive and rational transfer of skills.

The individual lesson, as a form of training, is only applied in fencing and is virtually unknown in other disciplines of sport.

The exceptional and peculiar value of the individual lesson lies in the direct and close contact of teacher and pupil—coach and competitor. The fencing master, using verbal explanations and instructions, and by his attitude, movements, knowledge and capabilities, creates conditions for executing and applying a given action and/or various tactical solutions. The pupil—sometimes not even fully consciously—learns certain strokes, rhythm of movement, feeling of surprise (tempo, l' à propos), choice of appropriate action, the ability to guess and foresee the opponent's intentions, etc.

The coach, by his movements and the creation of various tactical situations, in a way, makes the pupil choose an appropriate action and develops the fencer's speed of reaction, speed of movement, various qualities of attention and power of observation. The fencing master perfects the competitor's technique, technical-tactical capabilities, tactics, his psychomotor abilities and teaches and improves all aspects of the pupil's coordination—motor educability, motor control (precise directing of movements) and motor adaptability (choosing and applying appropriate actions in the changing and often unpredictable situations of a fencing bout).

In a lesson, the fencing master makes possible the acquisition of knowledge and capabilities in a very practical manner—in realistic situations, with weapon in hand. To make the lesson effective and "real," the fencing master's movements must be "real"—realistic, very often the same as those applied in a bout. The pupil, in a lesson, ought to see those situations which occur in competition and, in competition, he must perceive those situations which occur—and which he practiced—in a lesson. Several centuries ago, progressive teachers of fencing were aware of this and described it in their books.[8] In an individual lesson, the fencing coach directly influences his pupils and, applying the principle of individualization, chooses the appropriate way of conducting the lesson and the proper methods, taking into account the fencer's dimensions of personality, traits of his temperament, body build, achievement motivation, tactical inclinations, etc.

While conducting an individual lesson, the coach constantly moves from easy situations to difficult ones, and vice versa, from simple to complicated, and vice versa, from slow to fast, and vice versa, from helping to hindering, and vice versa, and from playing the role of teacher and friend to the role of opponent, and vice versa. The lessons ought to be interesting, stimulating, colorful, versatile, and changeable, with the application of appropriate exercises and methods; they ought to increase the pupil's interest in fencing and love of it.

Very important are empathy, friendly relations, and emotional attachment between the master and his pupil, and a mutual confidence in each other. As I keep saying, "A pupil will reach as far as his coach believes in him and shows it." I cannot resist the following illustration:

At the 1964 Olympic Games in Tokyo, just before the final of the Men's Foil, I warmed up my pupil Egon Franke. After the lesson, I told him, smiling, "You are in such good form that I cannot accept anything but gold." He took it to heart. Facing the excellent French foilist Jean-Claude Magnan, he raced out to a 3 – 0 lead. Magnan, however, equalized at 4 – 4. Finally my pupil, with a very courageous direct attack scored the decisive hit and won Olympic gold.

Structure of the Lesson.

An individual lesson consists of three parts:

Introductory Part—functions as a physical and psychological warm-up before the main part of the lesson. It establishes close contact between the master and pupil, reciprocal understanding, respect and empathy. The introductory part facilitates the pupil's gradual increase of level of arousal, optimal level and direction of motivation, increase of speed and accuracy of perception and reaction. The pupil assesses the distance, repeats easy and well-known actions paying special attention to basic strokes, gains a feeling of self-confidence, enjoys efficacious and easy execution of known actions, gradually increases speed of movement; he gets ready for the main part of the lesson.

Main Part—The exercises of the main part depend on the training period, stage of fencing education, experience and the level of skills as well as on the main aims of the lesson and its variety. They might be:

- Repetition and perfection of known actions and abilities;

- Teaching/learning new fencing strokes;
- Shaping of specific sensory-motor responses as a base of technical-tactical capabilities;
- Shaping and perfecting of accuracy and speed of perception, concentration and other aspects of attention, speed and accuracy of choice of action, and tactical capabilities.

Very important is the development and perfection of the feeling of surprise ("timing, tempo")—the ability to recognize, in a fraction of a second, the situation appropriate to the application of a given action (for example, a surprising direct attack, stop-hit, or other action suitable to a given situation). At the same time, various fencing exercises shape and perfect, as a desirable side-effect, fencing-specific strength, power, speed, endurance, as well as coordination capabilities.

Final Part—relaxed execution of well-known and rather easy actions and capabilities; the final instruction; practice with the fencer's non-dominant hand; assessment of the pupil's performance; directions and motivational remarks. If, after the individual lesson, a fencer is going to fence, the third part ought to be much shorter or all together omitted.

Varieties of Lessons

Depending on the main tasks, we distinguish the following varieties of an individual lesson: assessment lesson, teaching lesson, perfecting lesson, mixed lesson, warming up lesson, corrective lesson, demonstration lesson, and methodological lesson.

•*Assessment Lesson* – applied mainly in the first (introductory) stage of a fencer's training. In this stage of training, with beginners—children—the main form of conducting exercises is the group or collective lesson. From time to time, however, as a part of the collective lesson, the fencing master chooses a few pupils and conducts short individual lessons (it is advisable that the other pupils watch them). The main tasks of these short individual lessons are: assessment of skills learned in group lessons; assessment of level of understanding the exercises and knowledge of fencing terminology; correction of errors and mistakes; advice regarding further practice; motivating the pupil to further efforts. In higher stages of fencing training, the assessment lessons are applied in certain circumstances—for example, after a long interval or pause in training (when the pupil was absent or sick) or when the coach meets a new pupil (a new member of the club or a situation in the training camp of the national squad, etc.).

• *Teaching Lesson*—a lesson in which mostly new actions and capabilities are taught. In other words, the main task of a teaching lesson is the introduction and teaching-learning of a new fencing action or capability. Sometimes, the new element in training may be uniting the basic fencing strokes into one fluent compound action—putting together single motor skills into a sequence of movements, forming a compound action. For example, the pupil already knows direct thrust, disengagement, binding, and elementary footwork and now he begins to learn and smoothly execute, as one tactical unit, attack with advance-lunge, four-beat and thrust with disengagement. Also the coach gives some new information.

• *Perfecting Lesson*— the fencing master practices, with his pupil, actions which the pupil already knows, though has not yet acquired very well, or actions which are both well known and executed. Here the main task is fixing and perfecting sensory-motor skills (fencing actions) and technical, tactical and technical-tactical capabilities. For example, the pupil already knows direct attack with lunge, executed and practiced with the first method. Now, he practices direct attack with full speed on a given signal (for example, the coach's step forward) or he tries to hit with a direct attack, maneuvering on the piste as in a competition, trying to surprise his "opponent"; or he uses a given stroke—e.g., disengagement as an attack, riposte, derobe or redouble.

• *Mixed Lesson*—contains the repetition and fixing of known actions and capabilities, their perfection and the introduction of new fencing actions and capabilities. Thus, a mixed lesson contains: fixing and perfecting known actions, teaching-learning new actions or capabilities, and verification and assessment.

• *Warm-up Lesson* – conducted during competition, shortly before the competitor begins fencing. Its main task is direct preparation for competition. A competitor repeats basic strokes; the lesson should increase his self-confidence and help him gain his own optimal level of arousal. It is a great art of an experienced fencing master to be able to influence a competitor's mood, increase his self-confidence, calm him if he is too nervous, or stimulate him if he is too calm. If many of a coach's pupils take part in a given competition, it is difficult to conduct many individual lessons. In such a case, he may conduct collective exercises, line (queue) exercises or fencers may conduct appropriate exercises in pairs. Both individual and collective exercises should be followed by bouts.

• *Corrective Lesson*—applied after many bouts or after a sequence of competitions. Its aim is the calm improvement of form of movements and elimination of technical errors. Besides, in corrective lessons, one may apply more exercises with the fencer's non-dominant hand in order to prevent scoliosis, to improve coordination of movements and assure rest to fencer's dominant side.

• *Demonstration Lesson*—usually conducted during coaching courses and methodological conferences. The lesson is conducted by an experienced master and should serve as an illustration, example and model of a given variety of lesson and various ways of conducting exercises. The coach conducting the lesson explains the lesson's development, variety, direction and the methods applied, as well as ways of executing a given stroke, its application in a bout, ways of noticing and eliminating errors, and ways of determining the causes of mistakes. Such a lesson is a very valuable way to illustrate a point exposed in a lecture.

• *Methodological Lesson*—given by an experienced fencing master to a younger coach or instructor, the aim of which is explanation, demonstration and practical application of various methods of teaching and perfecting fencing actions and specific technical, tactical and technical-tactical fencing capabilities. It also teaches ways to improve speed and accuracy of perception, various qualities of attention and various types of motor responses. In such a lesson, the pupil learns, not only how to execute and apply various actions and abilities, but also, above all, how to teach and perfect them.

The above classification is based on the basic aim of the lesson—to assess, to teach, to perfect, to prepare for a bout. Taking into consideration another criterion of classification, namely the content of the exercises, we may distinguish the following directions of a lesson.

• *Technical Direction*—teaching, fixing, or perfecting appropriate, correct, efficacious ways of executing a fencing action (sensory-motor skill)—fluency of movement, appropriate rhythm, appropriate speed, necessary range of movement, good coordination of movements of the armed hand and legs.

• *Technical-Tactical Direction*—teaching, fixing, or perfecting a fencer's technical-tactical capabilities, based on acquired specific sensory motor responses, for example: choice of appropriate footwork, according to the distance between two fencers; choice between parry and counter-attack; choice of appropriate parry; change of intention as a result of the opponent's unexpected movement; differentiating between opponent's false and real actions, etc.

• *Tactical Direction*— teaching, fixing, or perfecting tactical capabilities, both regarding preparatory actions (reconnoitering opponent's movements intentions, misleading the opponent, drawing specific actions from the opponent) and real, ultimate actions (application of attacks and other strokes as foreseen actions—first and second intention—as unforeseen actions, and partly foreseen actions—actions with unknown destination and with change of intention).

• *Versatile (all-around) Direction*—many-sided, versatile, all-around teaching, fixing, or perfecting of technique, sensory-motor responses, tactics, concentration, range, shifting and lability of attention, quality of perception and feeling of surprise (timing).

Taking into account these two classification of lessons—variety of a lesson (its main task) and direction of a lesson (content)—one may apply different combinations, for example: a teaching lesson with a technical direction (teaching technique); perfecting lesson with a technical-tactical direction (perfecting already known technical-tactical capabilities); perfecting lesson with a tactical direction (perfecting already known chosen tactical capabilities—for example, the ability to apply second-intention actions, using counter-time or counter-riposte), etc.

Summing up, we may state generally that in individual lessons, one teaches and perfects sensory motor skills (components of a fencer's technique), and thus concrete fencing actions (thrusts, cuts, attacks, parries, ripostes, stop-hits, etc.) and the ability to apply them in a bout—technical-tactical and tactical capabilities. In realizing these tasks, one also shapes and perfects psychological processes very closely connected to motor activities—perception, various qualities of attention, decision taking (choice of tactics and concrete actions).

More important details about the individual lesson—methods, choice of exercises, ways of conducting exercises, etc.—are described in the next two chapters.

References

1. Czajkowski, Z. *Trening szermierza,* vol. I-II, AWF, Katowice 1988.
2. Czajkowski, Z. "Metoda prób i błędów," *Sport Wyczynowy* No. 11-12/1998.
   __________. "Błędy w nauczaniu, uczeniu się i stosowaniu nawyków czuciowo-ruchowych," *Sport Wyczynowy* No. 7-8/1999.
3. Czajkowski, Z. "Teoria i metodyka współczesnej szermierki," *Sport i Turystyka,* Warszawa 1968.
   ____________. *Taktyka i psychologia w szermierce,* AWF, Katowice 1984.
4. Czajkowski, Z.: *Zdolności przywódcze trenera i style kierowania,* Rocznik Naukowy Idô, vol. III, Rzeszów 2000.
5. Czajkowski, Z.: *Nauczanie techniki sportowej,* second edition, RCMSKFiS, Warszawa 2004.
6. Czajkowski, Z.: *Rozwój szermierki w Europie od czasów średniowiecza do przełomu XIX i XX wieku,* Dissertation, AWF, Katowice 1984.
7. Czajkowski, Z.: "We can still learn a lot from Vernesson de Lyancourt." *Człowiek i Ruch – Human Movement,* No. 2/2002.
8. Czajkowski, Z.: "Modern Conception of the Individual Lesson." *The Swordsmaster* Summer 2002, Fall 2002.

14. Modern Conceptions of the Individual Lesson (Part 2)

"In an individual lesson, the coach is, at the same time, a teacher and an opponent. His explanations and actions should always take these two directions into account. All of a coach's actions in an individual lesson should resemble, as closely as possible, the conditions of an actual bout."
--Constantine Bulotchko

THE BASIC METHODS USED IN THE INDIVIDUAL LESSON

"Leggendo le vostre pagine mi e parso spesso di rivedervi sulla pedana con la vostra bella guardia equilibrata, col vostro attaco corretto, il bel portamonto del ferro, la sciabola in mano; tutte cose che potete bene insegnare perché sapete con esattezza eseguire."

"While reading your book, I often saw you on the piste again before my eyes—your well-balanced en garde, correct attacks, control of the weapon, sabre in hand--all the things you could teach so well because you knew how to execute them so precisely."
--Nedo Nadi, introduction to Leon Bertrand's *Cut and Thrust*

The main object of this chapter is, as the title implies, a description of the basic methods used in the individual lesson. It is obvious that the choice of exercises and methods used in a lesson depend on the variety and content of the lesson (see the previous chapter). It is worth remembering that the methods and their importance are only secondary to the task—the objective—you wish to achieve. So, we use one set of methods when we try to teach a given stroke, different methods when we try to develop speed, and still other methods when we teach the application of various actions in a bout.

A very important task of a lesson is, of course, teaching technique—teaching correct, efficacious execution of many fencing strokes (sensory-motor skills). Technique is very important in fencing. As the famous master, de Bazancourt, puts it,

> *"Technique donne confidence. Confidence est l'étai principal, l'appui important de la defence et de l'attaque. Avec une bonne technique, un tireur d'un âge au-dessus de la moyenne est a l'egalité avec un jeune et athlétique tireur de vingt-cing ans. Ce que recommende l'étude de la technique."*
>
> "Technique gives confidence. Confidence is the main support for defense and attack. With good technique, a fencer past middle age is on even terms with a young and athletic competitor of twenty-five--which recommends the study of technique."

But one must remember and draw practical conclusions from the fact that in fencing, unlike acrobatics or figure-skating, technique is not everything. We must not only teach technique—how to execute various fencing actions—but also how to apply them in the changing conditions of a bout, taking into account our opponent's movements. In other words, the coach must teach, not only technique, important as it is, but also technical-tactical capabilities, tactics, speed and accuracy of perception, various qualities of attention, speed and accuracy of various kinds of reactions and other psychomotor abilities, i.e., psychological processes, closely connected with motor activities.

It is worth stressing that all methods used in an individual lesson may be—and ought to be—applied also in pair exercises. As mentioned above, the first task is to define the objective and then to choose the appropriate methods. I strongly emphasize this point because, judging by certain textbooks of theory of training, one would think that methods are primary and of supreme importance. Methods are secondary to the goals you wish to achieve.

In the individual lesson and pair exercises the following methods are used:

1. Repetition of a chosen stroke;
2. Execution, by the pupil, of a given stroke as a response to the coach's previously announced movement;

3. Choosing an action from previously announced actions;

4. Choosing an action from previously unannounced action;

5. "Rivalry" (contradictory tasks);

6. Training bout with the master.

1. *Repetition of a chosen stroke.* The pupil executes, many times in succession, a given stroke—e.g., direct thrust with fleche, cut to head with lunge, quarte binding with advance and disengagement, thrust with lunge, etc.—with an emphasis on accuracy of movement, appropriate rhythm, coordination of the movement of the hand and legs, and accurate fixing of the point or cut. He practices as if the given action was a closed motor skill (this is exceptional, used only in this method). Here, the movements are executed in the first level of coordination—movement in space (speed, timing, etc., are not important). The important coordination factors are motor educability and control of movement (motor control). The coach does not execute any preliminary movements. There is no surprise, no change of situation, no choice of action. The fencer concentrates on the mere form of the movement and begins its execution when it is convenient for him. The fencing master only corrects possible mistakes and gives necessary advice. The pupil tries to gradually rely less on visual control and to base the execution of the stroke on kinesthetic stimuli (receptors in the muscles, tendons, and joints) and sense of balance.

This method is applied in teaching new strokes (sensory-motor skills) and in the introductory part of a lesson with a fencer who already knows the stroke well.

After having learned the basic structure of the movement and the correct execution of a stroke, one may—using the same method—begin shaping the speed of execution (the second level of motor coordination—movement in space and time).

In this form of lesson, in accordance with the principles of accessibility and graduation of difficulty, the pupil begins the execution of a given stroke in its simplest form. For example: first, direct thrust on the spot—extension of the armed hand and fixing the point; then the same, executed with an advance; then direct thrust with lunge—with initial emphasis on accuracy of movement, and then also on speed of execution.

Furthermore, the pupil practices a given action on the fencing master's instruction—but not immediately following the coach's words. First, the pupil chooses the correct and appropriate distance, then he concentrates his thoughts on the most important details of the movement, and only then, having acquired a state of readiness, concentration of attention, and optimal level of arousal, does he execute the chosen stroke.

When the pupil repeats a given action many times, he must, at any cost, avoid rhythmic execution as it leads to a lowering of attention. Between executions of a given action, one should apply pauses of different lengths of time. During each pause, the pupil ought to relax his muscles, concentrate his attention, and take care to conceal the beginning of his movement, thus avoiding betrayal, by some unnecessary gesture, of the onset of the action. This pause—letting the pupil take time to relax, consider his next movement, focus his concentration, and prepare himself for the next execution-—is only recommended in the first method. In other methods, which are more complicated and realistic, the pupil, even after successful execution of a stroke, must be fully concentrated and ready to deal with an unexpected action by his "opponent" (coach).

It is advisable not to repeat one action for a very long period of time (massed exercises), but to execute various, sometimes very different, actions (random exercises). It is more difficult, but closer to the conditions of a real bout and, besides, forces the pupil to program the movement before each successive exercise (a different action demands a different, appropriate motor program).

If the pupil commits a mistake when executing the given movement, the fencing master should not point it out the first time, but should give the pupil a chance to notice the mistake himself (intrinsic feedback). If, however, the pupil does not notice, or repeats, the mistake, the coach should tell him about it, trying to find out its cause and ways to remove it (extrinsic feedback).

2. *Execution of a given stroke as a response to the coach's pre-announced movement.* The essence of this method is that in the lesson the pupil performs a previously announced action in response to the coach's foreseen and pre-announced movement, according to the simple motor response model: known stimulus, known reaction.

This method should be applied relatively early—in the first, introductory, stage of training, when the pupil has already acquired and fixed the basic structure of a given movement. The pupil is not only learning and perfecting the execution of a fencing stroke, but also learning and perfecting its application in conditions—although, relatively easy ones—somewhat resembling those of a bout. In the training of fencers of all classes, and in all stages of the training process, this method is frequently used in order to shape and perfect simple reaction and those technical-tactical abilities which are based on it: foreseen actions, executed in response to some predicted, foreseen movement by the opponent—for example, an advance, some movement of the weapon, signs of lowering of attention, a careless shortening of distance, or an unwitting betrayal of intention.

The essence of this method relies on the fact that the pupil knows what movement his "opponent" (coach) will do and he knows with which movement to respond. For example, the fencing master announces, "On my step forward, you will make a direct attack with lunge," or, "On my point-in-line, you will execute four-beat, direct thrust with lunge," or, "On my movement with bent arm, you will execute a stop-cut to forearm," or, "On my attempt to bind your blade, you will derobe," etc.

In this method also, one should gradually increase the level of difficulty. So, the coach should begin with slow, easy movements (but this does not mean artificial and unreal movements, nor does it mean with rhythmic execution).

Consider the following example: the master announces that on his attempt to change the engagement, the pupil should execute counter-disengagement—thrust. To begin with, the coach executes the change of engagement slowly and the fencer performs counter-disengagement on the spot. Then, the coach's movement is slightly faster and executed from a slightly longer distance so the pupil has to execute counter-disengagement faster and with an advance. Next, the coach's movement is still faster and executed from an even longer distance and the pupil has to perform his movement—counter-disengagement—faster and with a lunge. All of it, of course, is previously announced and foreseen; there is no choice of action. It is a simple motor response.

The discussed method, based on a model of simple motor response, facilitates learning certain technical-tactical abilities and, besides, the pupil gains elementary, basic knowledge about tactics and practical abilities. In the example above, the pupil realizes in practice that a thrust with counter-disengagement (as a derobe or attack by counter-disengagement) may be applied—in contrast with direct thrust, disengagement, or cut-over—only as a reply to the circular movement of the opponent's weapon (i.e., on change of engagement, circular binding, or circular parry).

Using this method, the fencer learns and perfects a sensory-motor skill as a whole, which includes:

a. The preparatory period (concentration of attention, high level of perception, looking for an expected stimulus—a movement announced by the coach—preparing the motor program of the expected response);

b. The latent or central period of motor response (perceiving and recognizing the stimulus, taking decision to execute a certain movement, sending the executive impulses from the brain to the muscles); and

c. The final or executive period (execution of the foreseen action).

This point is extremely important to understand because, looking from the outside, we see only the movement (the final period of motor response) and, very often, we do not appreciate the processes and abilities which occur just before the execution of the action. It must be understood well that the efficacy of the preparatory and latent periods determines the quality of the action and its early beginning (speed of reaction).

A coach must insist that the pupils understand that a very well executed and fast movement, when started too late (slow reaction) is a "bad" movement. So, for example, if the coach announces, "On my step forward, you execute direct attack with lunge," he must insist that the attack hit him just before he finishes the advance. Too late a start of the attack, in such a case, would make possible a successful parry by an opponent (see Chapter 5).

Teaching and perfecting technical-tactical capabilities based on speed of simple motor response is particularly important:

- For competitors who have very fast simple reactions (such as Witold Woyda, double gold medalist in foil, Olympic Games, Munich, 1972)

- For fencers who are "warrior" types—who base their tactics on lively mobility, speed of reaction and speed of movement, foreseen first intention actions, feeling of surprise ("tempo," "timing"), and applying "cutting-through" tactics (see Chapter 8).[1]

3. *Choosing an action from previously announced actions.* This method is frequently used with higher class fencers. It is based on a model of choice reaction or differential reaction and—much more rarely—on intuitive reaction. The coach announces which of the two, three or four actions he may execute, but he does not say which exact action (from those previously announced) he will apply at any given moment. The pupil's task is to recognize the coach's movement and to execute, as soon as possible, the appropriately chosen counter-action. In other words, "the pupil knows all the answers, but he does not know which question will be asked." For example, a fencing master, teaching basic defense to an epeeist, announces, "I am going to apply one of the following actions: I will attack, either in the inside line, outside line, or low line. On my attack to high inside line, take counter-sixth parry—riposte. On my attack to high outside line, either parry six--riposte or stop-hit with opposition in sixth. Against my attack in low line, stop-hit to the forearm,"

The coach begins with the previous method, announcing several times which action he is going to use, to make it easier and increase the pupil's confidence. Only then does he proceed to use the third method. He uses, at random, the previously announced actions, without telling the pupil which will be next, and the pupil must choose the right counter-action. The coach starts with slow movements and then progressively increases the speed, trying to take his pupil by surprise. He starts from immobility (which is easier for the pupil) and then, maneuvering on the piste (which is more realistic and more difficult). As the pupil's capabilities increase, the choice of actions becomes more difficult and more numerous—thus four, five, or more possibilities, plus an increase of speed and a constant change of distance—which demands an increase in the pupil's speed of response (a shorter latent period of reaction and faster execution of a chosen stroke), high divisibility of attention, and motor adaptability (movements of the armed hand ought to be coordinated with the movements of the legs according to the distance).

This method shapes and perfects more complicated and difficult technical-tactical capabilities and certain psychological processes: a high level of concentration; a high level of attention—its selectivity, range, divisibility, and flexibility; mobility of nervous processes; operative thinking; etc. Most important, perhaps, is perception on a higher conceptual-functional level. As I keep saying, to look is not the same as to see, and to see is not the same as to perceive. We perceive, really, only what we know and understand well.

We may distinguish two levels of perception: 1. lower level, sensory-motor perception; 2. higher level, conceptual-functional perception. When we listen to a foreign language which we do not understand or look at a written language (say Arabic) that we cannot read, we perceive on a lower level. When we understand the language or know the Arabic alphabet, we perceive on a higher level. In other words, we perceive on a conceptual-functional level only such facts, objects, situations, etc., which we know well, understand, can describe, explain, and name. When someone who does not know fencing looks at two fencers on the strip, he sees various movements, but has no idea what they are about (sensory-motor perception). For somebody who knows fencing well, everything is clear: he recognises preparatory actions, he sees the attacks, parries, ripostes, etc., and he even guesses the fencers' intentions, feints and real actions. This is conceptual-functional perception. This is why a coach should teach proper terminology from the very beginning and develop, among his pupils, the ability to perceive on a higher level.

This third method may be applied in three different varieties:

a. The coach's initiative. In this variety, the initiative belongs to the coach—he starts the movement. For example, the coach announces that he will execute, arbitrarily, advance, point-in-line, or direct attack. The pupil must recognize the "opponent's" movements, and respond, accordingly: on the coach's advance, direct attack; on the coach's point-in-line, beat-attack; on the coach's attack, parry-riposte. As another example, the coach may announce that he will execute, at random, one of the following actions: an attempt to take the pupil's blade, an attack in low line, or an attack with a very fast return to on-guard position. The pupil must recognize the coach's action and react accordingly: derobe; stop-hit from above; parry, riposte with fleche.

b. The pupil's initiative. Here, the initiative belongs to the pupil—he starts the movement. For example, the pupil executes a preparatory movement—a reconnoitering step forward (though not yet an attack—just a simple advance). The fencing master has announced that, on the pupil's advance, he will either remain motionless, make a direct attack with lunge, or will begin a compound attack with a bent arm. The fencer, after recognizing the coach's movement, must execute a direct attack with lunge, parry-riposte, or stop-hit.

c. Attack with unknown destination ("Open-eyes Attack"). The essence of the attack with unknown destination is that the pupil begins an attack with a certain movement—feint or action against the blade—not knowing how he is going to finish. He chooses the final movement of his attack, depending on what his opponent does (how his opponent reacts). In open-eyes attack, the beginning is foreseen and the final part, unforeseen (see Chapter 2: "Fencing Actions—Terminology, Their Classification and Application in Competition," Table 2-D).

For example: a foilist begins his open-eyes attack by binding the coach's blade and advancing. The coach has previously announced that on the pupil's attempt to bind his blade, he will either try to defend himself with parry four, derobe, or not react. The pupil, executing bind and step-forwards, tries to decipher, by sense of sight and touch, the "opponent's"—the coach's—movements. When the coach tries to parry, the pupil must execute thrust with disengagement; when the coach derobes, the fencer must execute counter-time by a second taking of the blade; if the master does not react, the pupil must finish his attack as a direct thrust with opposition in fourth.

Another example: a sabreur begins an open-eyes attack with a feint to head and advance. The fencing master has previously announced that he will either not react, take fifth parry, or apply stop-cut. The pupil, executing his first movement—feint to head and advance—very carefully watches the coach and, depending on the reaction, finishes his attack with either a cut to head with lunge, a cut to flank with lunge, or by counter-time by parrying the counter-attack.

The essence of the third method with open-eyes attacks is that the fencer, when beginning his attack, does not know which of the coach's previously announced actions will be applied.

To begin with, in all varieties of the third method (and the fourth method; see below), the fencing master creates easy conditions: only two or three possible choices; easily recognizable movement; no maneuvering. As the pupil's technical and technical-tactical abilities, quality of reaction, and other psychomotor abilities (qualities of attention, perception, speed of choosing an action, etc.) improve, the fencing master introduces more difficult conditions: a larger number of possible choices; displacement on the piste; an increase of speed of movement; less recognizable movements; "hidden," not easily noticed beginnings of the coach's movements (the master does not betray his intentions); etc.

4. *Choosing an action from previously unannounced actions.* This method—in its varieties—is applied with higher class competitors with good technique (a large repertoire of strokes and a high level of execution) and a high level of technical-tactical capabilities. The essence of this method relies on the fact that the coach, playing the role of opponent, executes various, previously unannounced actions and displacements on the piste while the pupil's task is to perceive the actions in a fraction of a second, to recognize the movement and intention of the "opponent," and to choose the appropriate counter-action and execute it. This method has many different applications and varieties, but its essence remains the same: the pupil recognizes the "opponent's" movements and chooses the right defensive, counter-offensive, or offensive action.

For example, in open-eyes attack practiced with the fourth method, the coach does not say at all how he may react to the pupil's first movement. Of course, when teaching and perfecting change of intention during the execution of an action, the coach does not even mention that he may change his action (see below). The same goes for unannounced, surprising actions, executed by the coach just after the pupil has finished his foreseen, preannounced action. It is very important that the coach quite frequently surprises his pupil by a sudden fast attack just after the pupil has finished an exercise: otherwise the pupil, after having finished a foreseen action, often diminishes his attention. In a competition, not every action finishes successfully, so the fencer must be ready (with a high level of attention!) to continue the bout. I have seen even quite experienced fencers, when their attack was not successful (too short or parried) become completely helpless because of habitual lowering of attention after one action. In this respect, the custom of many coaches to bang the pupil's blade after being hit is very stupid because it produces a habit of "extinguishing" attention after finishing an action.

The fourth method is very versatile and we may distinguish five main varieties of it. Its most typical variety, the so-called "mute lesson" ("leçon a la muette") was already known in the 19th Century. (The name "mute lesson" is not very correct because "lesson" refers to a form of practice and not a method. So, it must be understood that the "mute lesson" is one of the varieties of exercises.)

a. *The coach's initiative* (the so-called "mute lesson"). The initiative belongs to the coach. He moves on the piste and, from time to time, executes various actions—not previously announced. The pupil must try to maintain the appropriate distance, watch carefully, and react to the coach's actions. For example: when the coach "carelessly" advances, the competitor executes a simple or compound attack; when the coach extends his arm, the pupil executes an attack with beat or binding; when the coach attacks, the pupil defends himself with the appropriate parry; when the coach applies a compound attack, or attacks with hesitation or a bent arm, the pupil counter-attacks with a stop-hit; etc.

b. *The pupil's initiative.* The pupil, on his own initiative, executes some preliminary movement—for example, a reconnoitering step forward (it is not yet an attack; he is simply approaching the coach). The fencing master—without any preliminary announcement—may execute various movements and actions. The pupil identifies the "opponent's" movement and intentions and chooses the right action—for example: direct attack, if the coach does not react; action on the blade, if the coach puts point-in-line; appropriate parry, if the coach attacks; etc.

c. *Attack with unknown destination* ("Open-eyes Attack"). The pupil, choosing the appropriate situation, executes the first movement of an attack. He begins with a feint or action on the blade and the next movement is executed depending on what the "opponent" does (the pupil foresees and plans only the first part of the movement; the final part of his attack is chosen, taking into consideration the coach's action). This method differs from the method of choosing from among pre-announced actions (the third method) by the fact that the fencing master does not, at all, announce which actions he might choose.

Examples of this variety of method 4:

- An epeeist begins his open-eyes attack by a feint of thrust in low line with an advance, not knowing what his "opponent"—the coach—will do. If the coach does not react, the fencer finishes his attack by direct thrust to the thigh with a lunge; if the coach takes a parry, the pupil executes a thrust with disengagement, hitting the forearm in high line; if the "opponent" stop-hits, the fencer applies counter-time with thrust in opposition in the line of six; if the coach retreats, the fencer continues his attack with fleche; etc.

- Or, a sabreur begins his attack with a feint of cut to head and a step forwards. If the coach does not react, he finishes with a cut to head, if the coach reacts with parry five, he makes a cut to flank with lunge; if the coach counter-attacks, he executes counter-time, etc.

d. *Change of intention while executing a foreseen action ("surprise during the action").* The pupil executes a given foreseen action—first or second intention—and hits many times in succession. His intention is to hit his opponent with a pre-programmed, foreseen action. The coach allows himself to be hit many times. After many actions conducted according to the plan, the coach unexpectedly changes his action and executes an unforeseen stroke. In such a case, the pupil must change his original intention and finish his attack with a different movement, in accordance with the new situation. For example: a sabreur executes, many times in succession, an attack—feint of cut to chest, cut to flank. The coach takes parry four and the pupil hits his flank. After many successful attacks by the pupil, the coach, instead of taking the expected parry four, executes a stop-cut to head. Then the pupil, in a fraction of a second, has to change his intention and apply counter-time, parrying quinte and hitting with a riposte. Or, if the coach does not react at all, the pupil has to finish the attack with a cut to the chest. The unexpected and unannounced action of a coach, in such exercises, might be called "surprise during the action."

e. *An unexpected action by the coach after the pupil's action ("surprise after the action").* In this variety of the method, the coach allows his pupil to hit him many times, in succession, with a given action. From time to time, however, just after his pupil has hit him, the coach takes the fencer by surprise by applying an unannounced action, mostly by some variety of attack. The pupil must, at once, assess the situation and execute an appropriate action—e.g., a parry or counter-attack. This is very important and very often underestimated by many coaches. This variety—"surprise after the action"—is very valuable and practical as it prevents the "automatic" exclusion of attention by the pupil after the completion of an action. It shapes the maintaining of concentration—its shifting (flexibility)—the speed and accuracy of sensory-motor responses in the fast and often changing circumstances of a bout.

5. *Rivalry (contradictory methods)*. This is a very good method and, I think, too rarely used. The reasons that it is so infrequently used are: a) it is not appreciated by many coaches and b) though it is a very sad fact, many coaches are not fit enough to use it. The rivalry method requires a high level of specific fitness from the coach, good reaction, speed and great dexterity in the execution of his fencing actions—not only of his arm movements, but, equally important, speed and accuracy of his lunges and fleches. This method ought to be applied with fencers of different classes, keeping in mind that the speed, variety, and difficulty of the exercises ought to correspond to the level of the competitor's skills, abilities, and experience. The contradictory task method makes the rivalry factor prominent, increases emotions, arousal and motivation, makes the training more interesting for the pupils, and, generally, creates more realistic conditions, more like actual competition. Also—and highly important—it facilitates the transfer of skills and abilities from training to loose play and then to competition.

The essence of this method is based on the assumption that the coach and the pupil—in a slightly conventional manner and limited to various degrees—are trying to reproduce certain fragments of a bout and, in doing so, both have opposite tasks—striving to the end that a given fragment of a bout ought to finish with hitting one's opponent.

Contradictory, rivalry tasks may be very different. They may be very simple and limited. For example, the coach has the task of hitting the pupil with a direct attack with lunge—first from immobility and then maneuvering on the piste—and the pupil must defend himself with a given parry. After an accepted number of trials, the roles change: the pupil attacks, the coach defends himself. It is a very simple example and yet the task is very difficult: one variety of attack and one variety of defense.

But contradictory tasks may be still much more complex, difficult and versatile. For example, one of the participants has to score a hit, either by direct attack or by a defined attack with one feint. The defender must defend either with one parry or two.

The contradictory exercises may be still much more complex and more like the conditions of a real bout. For example, the pupil attacks with an advance-lunge, applying any chosen variety of attack—simple, compound, with action on the blade, counter-time—and he may also hit with counter-riposte, remise or redouble. The coach has full freedom of choice of any action he deems expedient. He may, thus, try to hit his attacker with a counter-attack, riposte, derobe, etc. After a given number of trials, the participants switch roles.

6. *Training bout with the master.* This is, in a way, a further development of the fourth method—"the mute lesson"—and the fifth method—contradictory tasks. The pupil and the coach conduct a training bout which, for the coach, is an excellent occasion to assess his pupil's skills, abilities, progress and mistakes, strong and weak points, ways of reacting, level of concentration (focus) and other qualities of attention, mobility, etc. It is immensely important to assess how the pupil transfers, to a bout, those skills and abilities acquired in a lesson. The fencer judges his skills, abilities, ways of conducting a bout, and efficacy on the basis of intrinsic feedback (he assesses his movements, actions and tactics), knowledge of results (does he hit his opponent, are his parries efficient, are his stop-hits in time), and extrinsic feedback (the coach's assessment, remarks and instructions).

Of course, the great majority of training bouts (in various varieties) are conducted by fencers within group lessons (collective lessons), but short bouts with the coach, as a part of the individual lesson, are very valuable. Some years ago, the great Italian master, Giuseppe Mangiarotti—who educated a great number of outstanding epeeists and foilists—always finished each individual lesson with a short bout, even when he was quite old. My first, and most excellent, fencing master, Jan Pieczynski, also used to introduce loose play as part of the individual lesson. Training bouts with a coach, nowadays, are used rather rarely. They require the coach to have high personal fitness, to engage in constant personal exercises ensuring mobility, speed, accuracy of movement and feeling of surprise—"scelta di tempo." I am always surprised when I see fencing coaches who come to the salle and, without even any warm-up or exercises on their own, at once proceed to conduct lessons. One aspect of the training bout with the coach has to be very strongly stressed: we consider the fencer's skills and abilities to be fully learned and acquired only when he can apply them successfully in a bout.

The tasks in a training bout in an individual lesson, like in group lessons, may be very varied. For example: the pupil only defends and the coach only attacks, or vice versa; certain strokes may be excluded from the repertoire of those allowed (in a case, for example, when a foilist uses counter-attack too frequently and has no confidence in his parries, counter-attack may be excluded); certain successful actions are "rewarded" by being counted as two hits (thus, the rewarded actions may be—according to what is established before the bout—direct attack, counter-riposte, counter-time, riposte with fleche, a hit to the foot, compound counter-attack, etc.); the coach, in the bout, may play the role of a given adversary or apply a given defined set of movements and actions typical for certain psycho-tactical types of fencers (defensive type, offensive type, those who use "cutting through" tactics, etc.).

To demonstrate the importance of this method, I will quote from my own experience. One of the greatest sabreurs of all time, Jerzy Pawlowski—many time Olympic Games and World Championship medallist, winner of many international tournaments, and a phenomenally talented fencer—had certain difficulties competing against Horwath, a young, left-handed, Hungarian sabreur. I studied Horwath's bouts very carefully —both in the salle and on film—and then tried to imitate his tactics in lessons with Pawlowski. In 1962, in the match for the team gold medal at the World Championships in Buenos Aires, the last, decisive, bout was between Pawlowski and Horwath. Paw?owski, using the tactics he learned specifically for Horwath, won the bout, securing the gold medal for the Polish team.

While conducting a training bout with a pupil, the coach does not cease to be a teacher: he pays attention to how the pupil fences and notices the pupil's mistakes—errors of perception, reaction, execution, or tactics—and, of course, praises good actions. The coach may convey his remarks verbally or practically, demonstrating certain movements or "punishing" his pupil by hitting him. For example, a fast stop-hit against the forearm when the pupil, a sabreur, exposes it during an attack is sometimes more efficacious and convincing then many verbal instructions.

In the training of high-class fencers, practice bouts constitute a very good method—interesting, lively and efficacious. They are conducted in real—"natural"—conditions, resembling those of bouts in competition. These bouts increase the pupil's emotions and arousal; they facilitate improvement and allow for a many-sided assessment of his skills and abilities. This method teaches fencing as a whole, in its entirety. Isolated exercises teach and perfect only one chosen skill or ability in artificial conditions; in the practice bout, one uses and perfects an unlimited amount of skills and capabilities.

However, in spite of the immense value of training bouts, practiced both in individual and collective lessons, one should not neglect practicing other exercises and using other methods. As I have said before, a fencer, like a great violinist or pianist, improves his abilities, not only in competition (on the stage), but also through assiduous, isolated exercises, concentrating on one chosen detail of the whole.

THE APPLICATION OF THE VARIOUS METHODS

The discussed methods of conducting exercises in the individual lesson can, and must—as I have mentioned—be equally applied in group lessons and, particularly, in pair exercises. The exercises ought to be diverse and changeable, applying various methods of choosing and conducting exercises.

A very wide choice of exercises and methods may be used in the over-learning method. It may emphasize technical abilities, relying on a long chain of very fast movements, which are preannounced with the pupil perfecting speed, accuracy of movement, change of rhythm, the ability to execute and apply various actions. Or it may emphasize technical-tactical capabilities, consisting of a series of unforeseen fencing actions developing the pupil's lightning-like speed improvisation. The over-learning method may, then, be considered as a compound method in which we use the basic methods described, above. Its aim is to make "easy" in a competition, that which, objectively speaking, is quite difficult. When our aim is to improve speed, accuracy, change of rhythm, and many technical abilities, we mainly use a combination of the first method (with an emphasis on speed) and the second method. When our object is to improve technical-tactical capabilities, we mainly use the third, fourth, and fifth methods.

What does it mean to use over-learning to make easy that which is difficult? If, for example, in a very quickly executed chain of actions, the pupil performs an attack by disengagement, riposte by disengagement, counter-riposte by disengagement, derobe by disengagement, redouble by disengagement, etc., as one fluent action, then the application of a single disengagement—in an attack or riposte, etc.—in a competition will seem much easier.

While using the over-learning method with the object of improving technical abilities, the coach announces his actions and tells the pupil what he must do.

Example in epee

Pupil: Attacks with binding—direct thrust with step-lunge

Coach: Parries and ripostes;

Pupil: Counter-ripostes and redoubles, then quickly resumes on-guard position;

Coach: Attacks in low line;

Pupil: Stop-hits;

Pupil: Takes parry eight and ripostes to arm with an immediate remise to trunk and jumps back to on-guard position;

Coach: Attempts to execute counter-time by a secondary taking of the blade;

Pupil: Applies compound counter-attack;

Coach: Goes back, and

Pupil: Attacks by beat disengagement with fleche; etc.

As I have stressed, all of the actions are preconceived and, in order to facilitate the pupil's fast and fluent execution of actions, and concentration on quality of execution, the coach may even shout during the action what the pupil must do next.

In the other variety of over-learning, where the main object is to develop technical-tactical abilities, fast and accurate reaction, good perception, choice of action, and high qualities of attention (level of concentration; range, divisibility, sustenance and shifting of attention, etc.), the coach constantly changes his positions and surprises the pupil with various actions, to which he must react appropriately. In this variety of over-learning, the coach mainly uses the fourth and fifth methods.

FINAL REMARKS AND PRACTICAL ADVICE FOR COACHES

"Mere knowledge without experience does not give the surgeon self-confidence."
--Ambroise Paré, Surgical Canons and Rules, XVI century

The main methods, presented above, applied in the individual lesson and pair exercises, serve, above all, to teach and perfect sensory-motor skills—fencing actions—and the technical, technical-tactical and tactical capabilities, as well as psychomotor abilities, to which they are connected.

The first method—repetition of a given stroke—serves the purpose of introductory teaching of a given movement in the second stage of teaching a motor skill and of increasing the speed of execution in the next stages of teaching and perfecting a motor skill.

In teaching fencing actions (the second stage of teaching and perfecting a motor skill), we apply the mentioned methods: whole method, part method and mixed method, as well as reproductive methods, task methods and problem solving methods. These methods are described in great detail in other texts.[2] All methods of teaching movement have their assets, good points, and certain weaknesses. Therefore, the coach should wisely use different methods according to the main task of the exercise and the pupil's personality and stage of training.

Practice shows, however, that for fencing, the best method of teaching is the mixed method with a large proportion of the whole method. One must keep in mind, moreover, that certain actions—for example, feint attack—should not be taught with the part method. A general rule is as follows: you may use the part method of teaching only when dividing the whole sequence of movements does not change its component parts.

For example, you may teach parry-riposte by disengagement with the part method, dividing it into: 1. fourth parry; 2. lowering the point into the low inside line; 3. elevating the point into high outside line; 4. extending the arm and fixing the point on the target.

After some time, the pupil will be able to execute it as one fluent action. Feint attack, however, must be taught using the whole method because dividing it into two parts (as many coaches do)—extension of arm and then lunge—is simply wrong. The extension of the armed hand alone, without the first stage of lunge or fleche, does not constitute a real threat to the opponent and, equally important, the attacker does not gain distance.

Let me repeat what I have said earlier: extroverts generally like whole methods and inquisitive introverts prefer part methods.

If you consider other criteria of classification of methods (reproductive methods, task methods, problem-solving methods), then basing teaching on reproductive methods (with demonstrations and explanations), intermingled, from time to time, with task and problem-solving methods is most useful. One should avoid using strictly imitation methods without verbal explanations—except when dealing with very young children.

Now, I shall summarize, emphasize, and discuss the most important conclusions derived from the description of basic methods in the individual lesson, the main object of which is—I repeat once more—teaching-learning and perfecting of a fencer's sensory-motor skills and capabilities.

1. Motor skills and capabilities may be considered fully acquired only if a competitor can apply them efficaciously and accurately in competition. This stresses the importance of the principle of transfer of skills. Motor skills and capabilities, acquired in a lesson and other forms of training, are transferred to a training bout and then these motor skills and capabilities are transferred from a training bout to competition (they can be applied in competition).

2. A lesson may only be considered good if an observer, a connoisseur of fencing, can recognize the type of lesson, its directions, main tasks and which methods are used by the coach. As Michael Marx, five-time U.S. Olympic fencer, wittily remarked, "It irritates me to see a fencing coach give a lesson as his master did twenty or thirty years ago or do simply whatever just comes to his head."

3 In an individual lesson, and other forms of exercises with a weapon, a fencer must be appropriately protected (mask, fencing jacket, glove, etc.). Giving a lesson to a pupil who is wearing only a tee-shirt, which is very widely practiced—something that never ceases to astonish me— is a sign of extreme stupidity. Practicing without adequate protection not only may lead to accidental injury, but—much worse—makes the coach apply unrealistic movements (not fully extending his arm; not trying to hit the pupil when he ought to; facilitating the pupil's movements by assuming certain artificial poses and moves; reacting to unconvincing feints by the pupil; etc.). Still worse, the coach's unrealistic actions teach the pupil bad reactions. It is very important that the coach hit a pupil who does not parry in time or exposes his arm in an attack, etc. The coach cannot execute the proper actions if the pupil is not fully protected.

4. Equally absurd are the various mannerisms used or demonstrated with great joy and pride by many fencing masters. I mean, among other silly habits:

- Helping the pupil fix his point by "banging" his blade in the final execution of a thrust,
- The coach artificially exposing head, trunk, flank, or arm to be hit and waiting for it, artificially aiding the pupil's hit,
- Rrequiring the pupil to parry a thrust or cut which does not threaten the pupil at all,
- Demanding a parry against a movement which obviously requires a stop-hit,
- Not keeping the proper distance,
- Demanding that the fencer always immediately return to on-guard position after lunge.

Generally speaking, the way the coach executes a stroke and the choice of exercises should both correspond with the range and efficacy of actions used in competition.[3]

My impression is—especially while watching fencing masters giving warm-up lessons at competitions when many people are watching—that these utterly senseless and even destructive habits (various artificial poses, banging the pupil's blade, very loud verbal comments, showy behavior, etc.) are a form of—though, perhaps not fully conscious—showing off and trying to attract the attention and admiration of other people.

Theatrical poses and banging the pupil's blade may be, in a way, a reaction to, or the result of, an increase of noradrenalin in the coach's blood. But, I think, that instead of trying to impress the onlookers with various poses, etc., the coach should take advantage of his elevated arousal by making faster and longer lunges in a lesson.

As I have mentioned, the famous French fencing master, Vernesson de Lyancourt, in the 17th Century, already criticised silly habits and illogical actions of certain masters. And the German author, Schiller, wrote, "Mit der Dumheit kämpfen die Götter selbst vergeben." ("Against stupidity, the gods themselves battle in vain.")

5. In order to be able to conduct training properly and efficaciously, the coach ought to be fit and his movements ought to be precise, lively, variable, and correct. The coach's personal fitness and his ability to yield the weapon ought to be exemplary, which is, of course, very important, both in conducting lessons and performing demonstrations. Therefore, a good fencing master should take care of his motor fitness and practice footwork and various strokes with the weapon. Such coaches never cease to astonish me, who enter the fencing gym (sometimes they are late), shout at the fencers, and then—without any personal warm-up—proceed to conduct exercises.

6. As I have mentioned several times already, all basic methods applied in the individual lesson can, and should, be used and applied in pair exercises. Pair exercises, frequently under-appreciated, are very useful. They teach self-dependence (self-efficacy), speed and

accuracy of perception, inquisitiveness, resourcefulness, and—so important in fencing and in life—a feeling of independence and responsibility.

7. While taking advantage of knowledge and the results of scientific research, the coach also relies on his personal practical experience, pedagogical intuition, and common sense, maintaining, at the same time, his individual style of behaving and teaching. Although great coaches share some typical traits, there exists no one unique ideal coaching style. The most eminent coaches, trainers of world-class competitors, have very often used different ways and methods of conducting exercises.[4]

8. Exercises may be variable or invariable and blocked or random. Teaching and perfecting only one version of an action (invariable exercises) should be avoided. A lunge, for example, ought to be variable: different lengths, different speeds, different rhythms, and different coordination of the arm and legs.

   Invariable exercises mean execution of a given stroke or fencing action in the same, invariable, basic form. In a bout, however, a fencer should use different actions—lunge, fleche, parry, etc.—variably, according to the tactical situation, distance, the opponent's movements, and his own intentions.

   Once a pupil learns a basic form of a given action, he should proceed to learn and perfect its different variations. For example: depending on various factors of the bout situation, the lunge may be executed as acceleration lunge, explosive lunge, waiting lunge, or gliding lunge; a parry may be executed as a removing parry, beat parry, flying parry, parry with opposition, etc., and may be executed in place, with a step backwards, after a step backwards, etc.; remise may be applied as a direct continuation of an attack or as a stop-hit against riposte, etc. So, it is of great importance to teach pupils variability of execution.

Blocked (or massed) exercises mean repetition, many times, of one stroke. For example: fifteen times parry four, direct riposte or fifteen times derobe, etc. Distributed (or random) exercises mean the interchanging of various strokes. For example: the pupil executes parry four, riposte, parry six, riposte, direct attack with lunge, stop-hit, etc. Massed exercises are only used in the second stage of teaching sensory-motor skills. In the third and fourth stages, random exercises ought to be used because: a) a fencer must prepare a different motor program in his brain before executing a given stroke, b) the situation in random exercises is more like the situation in a bout, and c) they require better motor coordination and sustenance of a high level of concentration.

It is preferable to employ variable exercises (different ways of doing the same motor skill) and random exercises (practicing various motor skills). (Blocked and invariable exercises should be applied only at the beginning of the first—introductory—stage of training.)

9. Some coaches give very long individual lessons. Long individual lessons (45 to 60 minutes) should be practiced rarely. They may contain the teaching of a new stroke and perfecting of already well-acquired actions, in easy, slow conditions. Long lessons, also, should not be applied just before a competition. Perfecting and mixed lessons—conducted very energetically, with emphasis on speed of reaction and movement, and demanding great mobility, divisibility and shifting of attention—ought to be much shorter (15 to 25 minutes).

   I have conducted the following tests: I gave long, 45 minute, individual lessons to a few pupils and then, with each of them, I conducted three short, 15-minute, lessons, with periods of rest between them. After each lesson, each pupil was tested on apparatuses measuring speed of simple reaction, speed of choice reaction, visual-motor coordination, numbers of mistakes, etc.

The results were very clear that: a) after a long lesson, the reaction times and other psychomotor parameters were worse than before the lesson, b) after short lessons, accuracy, speed of reaction, and other parameters were much better.

10. Very important in the individual lesson, as in the entire processes of training, is the application of the principles of individualization and moderation (trying to avoid fatigue and over-training). An assessment of the performance of American athletes at the Olympic Games in Atlanta yields the generally accepted conclusion that the two most important errors committed by some coaches were: a) a lack of individualization of training, and b) a lack of moderation in training, leading to fatigue and over-training.[5]

    Fatigue, over-training, and lowering of motivation is usually caused by coaches who, as a source of success, believe in "murderous effort," excessive training loads, and very exhausting exercises.[6] These coaches, perhaps, took too literally the words of Pope John Paul II, "The most precious gift which a man can offer to God is suffering." To me, far more sensible and applicable are the words of St. Augustine, "Unconstrained curiosity is far better than severe discipline."

11. Introductory training, acquiring a basic repertoire of fencing actions and capabilities, preliminary stages of teaching-learning sensory-motor skills ought to be conducted in easy conditions, with a relatively low level of arousal. Teaching and learning in very difficult conditions, with a very high level of arousal, under psychological pressure might be faster, but the results of such teaching are short-lasting, inaccurate, and less flexible.[7]

12. Apart from the abilities to apply methods appropriate to the tasks, a very important factor influencing efficacy of training is the appropriate choice of exercises. This problem will be discussed in the section of the

following chapter, entiled "Various Ways of Choosing Exercises in a Lesson."

References

1. Czajkowski Z. "Teoria i metodyka współczesnej szermierki." Warszawa 1968. Sport i Turystyka.

   __________. Taktyka i psychologia w szermierce. Katowice 1984. AWF.
2. Czajkowski Z. Trening szermierza, vols. I and II. Katowice 1988. AWF.

   Bulotchko, K.T.: Voprosy trenierskoy tiechniki, mietody dozirowki nagruzki v individualnom urokie, Sbornik statyey, Fizkultura i Sport, Moskva 1968,

   Szabo, L.: *Fencing and the Master,* Corviba Clado, Budapest 1977.
3. Czajkowski Z. "Directing the Process of Training, Taking Competition as a Model." *The Swordsman,* Summer, 2001 (part 1); Fall 2001 (part 2).
4. Czajkowski Z. "Na dwu krańcach dwa przeciwne bogi." *Sport Wyczynowy,* 1997, nr. 3-4

   __________. "Knowledge, Skills, Personality and Work of a Coach." *The Swordmaster,* Spring 2001.
5. Czajkowski Z.: "Przed Sydney – Wnioski z Atlanty." *Sport Wyczynowy,* 2000 nr. 1-2.
6. Czajkowski Z. "Celem ćwiczeń nie jest „dawanie w kość", ale podwyższanie umiejętności ucznia." *Sport Wyczynowy* 1997, nr. 11-12.
7. Czajkowski Z. "Istota i znaczenie pobudzenia w działalności sportowej." *Sport Wyczynowy* 1995, nr. 7-8 and 9-10.

   __________. Motywacja i pobudzenie w działalności sportowej. „Rocznik Naukowy AWF w Gdańsku" 1999, vol. VIII, pp. 5-32.

   __________. Pierwszy etap szkolenia sportowego. Katowice 1995. ZSKF Makroregion Śląski.

15. Modern Concepts of the Individual Lesson (Part 3)

"The secret of individual teaching lies in the master's ability to pass on to his pupil his own technique, precision, smoothness, speed, and sense of blade. His meticulous attention to detail, and his ability to use his pupil's physical possibilities to the best advantage, will either make or mar the subject which is his task to mould and turn into a fencer."

--Roger Crosnier

HOW TO CHOOSE AND CONDUCT EXERCISES IN A LESSON

"Constant repetition of the same exercises makes athletes stupid."

--Janusz Iskra

Introduction

"The popular saying that training, to be effective, ought to be painful, is—from the point of view of physiology—absurd."

--Jan Chmura

In the first chapter on the individual lesson, I outlined the basic information concerning a lesson's essence, structure, varieties and directions.[1] In the next chapter, "Basic Methods Applied in an Individual Lesson," I described the main methods, their varieties, and the ways they ought to be applied in a lesson. The present chapter is devoted to choosing the exercises and the various ways of conducting them (the same principles may also be applied to other forms of training, including pair exercises). The appropriate choice of exercises in a lesson is extremely important because, in practice, it often happens that the coach chooses the exercises without any logical justification, not taking into account many important factors and conditions like: the level of the fencer's abilities, stage of training, strengths and weaknesses, etc. To again quote Michael Marx, "It irritates me to see a fencing coach give a lesson as his master did twenty or thirty years ago or do simply whatever just comes to his head." As I have mentioned before many times, and what never ceases to astonish me, is the fact that many fencing coaches—educated and seemingly intelligent people—when conducting a lesson, commit many errors and perform many silly movements contrary to elementary principles of teaching and to common sense.

As I have stressed before, when choosing the contents and ways of conducting exercises, whether in an individual lesson or a group lesson, one should always take into consideration the athlete's ability level, stage of training, training period, dimensions of personality, and many other factors. In addition, the coach must bear in mind the different criteria of choosing exercises and the different ways of conducting them. This promotes diversity of the training process; it embraces various sides of training and competition, developing technique and tactics, shaping energy abilities, coordination abilities, and psychological processes strictly connected with motor activities (psychomotor abilities). It is also a necessary condition for applying the principle of individualization, which is of the utmost importance when dealing with fencers of higher classes.

Before I describe some selected examples of how to choose and conduct exercises in a lesson, I will try to give a few elementary and basic rules and some practical advice.

1. The object of appropriately chosen and properly conducted fencing exercises is to teach and perfect the execution and application of fencing actions:

    - with strong emphasis on their efficacy,
    - in conditions resembling a bout,
    - or in a bout itself.

—in other words, technical-tactical and tactical capabilities applied in variable, and often unpredicted, circumstances. One should realize and remember that a fencing action—a sensory-motor skill of a fencer's technique—is not merely a movement (execution of a given stroke), but the strict and interdependent connection of speed and accuracy of perception, choice of action, and execution. In other words, a fully understood fencing action embraces all three periods of sensory-motor response: preparatory period, latent period, and executory period. The same action—e.g., lunge, attack, parry, counter-attack, etc.—may, and should, be executed and applied in a variable manner, with different speeds, and changing rhythm, depending on lightning-like speed assessment of the bout situation: distance from the opponent; the opponent's movements, actions, intentions; our movements, etc.

2. In the lesson, the exercises—the choice and methods of conducting them—ought to be connected with the object we want to achieve and both the coach and pupil ought to fully realize this. I underline, once more, that the aim of exercises is not "murderous effort," bringing the pupils to extreme fatigue, but an increase of the competitors' fitness and abilities.[2]

3. A lesson's contents, choice of exercises, applied methods, varieties and directions, as well as the duration and intensity of effort, ought to correspond with

   - a fencer's training stage, level of fitness and abilities,
   - his dimensions of personality: extroversion or introversion, emotional stability or instability,
   - type of nervous system and temperament,
   - prevalence of sympathetic or parasympathetic system,

- intelligence, speed of sensory-motor responses,
- prevalence of simple or compound reactions,
- tactical tendencies, etc.

Each lesson has to have a clear, well-established, main object and, in order to achieve it, appropriately chosen, particular tasks and the methodological means to realize them.

1. To begin with, then, the master must define what he wants to achieve, teach and perfect, and, only then, how to teach it—by means of which exercises and methods. The coach gives a lot of technical and tactical advice but, from time to time, does not give it directly but "leads" his pupil to "discover" the appropriate answers and movements, applying task and problem-solving methods.

2. Fully respecting the primary program of a lesson, the coach—if the necessity arises—creatively introduces improvisation, changing the tasks and introducing new situations into the lesson, or repeating, for a longer time, actions and abilities not yet well-acquired by the pupil.

3. Once more, I have to underline the necessity of using "real," realistic, threatening movements and avoiding artificial, unreal, exaggerated ones. The application of the latter (unreal, artificial movements) not only does not teach the pupil proper reactions, but teaches bad, inadequate choice of actions and/or incorrect, inefficient execution of movements. When the pupil does not execute a parry in the appropriate time, or does not use the appropriate parry, the coach's action should hit him. Equally important is changing the rhythm of the exercises. Rhythm is a very powerful element of surprise in a bout. The coach who executes movements in always the same rhythm "kills" his pupil's sense of

timing, ability to react to surprise, and concentration of attention.

4. In teaching, perfecting, and mixed lessons, of a tactical or versatile direction—apart from teaching and perfecting certain actions and tactical capabilities (preparatory actions, second intention actions, etc.)—the fencing master must, sometimes, play the role of various tactical types or of a concrete opponent with a specific, individual style of fencing and well-defined tactics. In epee fencing, such exercises are particularly recommended, since the biggest differentiation of psychological types of fencers occurs in this weapon (for example: a very mobile, offensive type; a more passive, defensive type; one who uses simple, fast actions; one who uses complicated, compound actions with many binds; a fencer who holds his epee in a low line or who holds it like a fishing-rod; one who relies mostly, in defense, on retreat, or parries, or counter-attacks; etc.).

5. One should not go out of one's way to teach the pupil very long exchanges of strokes, learned "by heart" and executed "mechanically" (although this can occasionally play a legitimate role in the over-learning method), but should change conditions, and create situations so that the sequence of movements and application of strokes is a logical and realistic development of the changing tactical circumstances: changing distance, choosing actions, countering the coach's actions, trying to avoid being hit, trying to hit the "opponent," foreseeing the coach's actions, etc.

6. One ought to shape the fencer's speed and accuracy of perception, his qualities of attention, his active attitudes and determination, and also his strong desire to score a hit (to win a bout and achieve his tasks and objects). In rivalry exercises and situations resembling a bout, the pupil should try to finish each encounter by scoring a hit against his "opponent" (coach). Rivalry

exercises and training bouts with the master are very "real," very useful, and make the lesson more attractive, emotional and colorful. They increase the pupil's fighting attitude and create conditions resembling, closely, those of a competition. One should remember, however, that it is very necessary and useful to mingle very difficult and complicated exercises (which demand great concentration of attention, speed and accuracy of reaction) with simpler exercises (which are much easier, well-known, and increase a pupil's self-efficacy and self-confidence).

7. In choosing the exercises in a lesson, one should also take into account the appropriate proportions of offensive, counter-offensive, and defensive actions; of simple and compound actions; of foreseen, unforeseen, and partly foreseen actions. Further, these proportions should be adapted to the pupil's dimensions of personality and his tactical type.

8. The pupil's active approach, conscious effort, initiative and motivation are crucial to the success of the lesson. The competitor ought to understand well the aim and ways of executing various exercises. This can be verified from time to time by the coach's questions and actions. The understanding of exercises and fencing, in general, is greatly facilitated by the application of proper, precise terminology. We perceive, quickly and accurately, on higher, perceptual-functional level, only what we know well, understand, and are able to name. Unfortunately, many coaches use very primitive jargon or rely only on demonstrations. (Demonstrations are, of course, very important in the first stages of training.) With fencers of a higher class, however, too many demonstrations lead to mental laziness and a lack of concentration. With higher class fencers, one should rely, to a large degree, on verbal explanations, restricting demonstrations principally to dealing with tactical matters and when illustrating an error. The fencing master, merely by the way he conducts ex-

ercises, should develop the pupil's interest (cognitive aspect), love of fencing (emotional aspect), very valuable intrinsic motivation, and qualities of attention. As Yogi Ramacharaka aptly remarked, "Interest increases the level of attention, and a high level of attention increases interest," and, "Concentrated attention penetrates a problem like X-rays through a piece of wood." Concentration and other qualities of attention (range, sustenance, selectivity, divisibility, shifting) are some of the most important factors in successful fencing.

9. The best way of dosing the training loads in a lesson is to mix easy and difficult exercises, slow and fast movements, foreseen and unforeseen actions. In a lesson, therefore, one should constantly mingle periods of increased effort and lesser intensity; the coach should sometimes facilitate the pupil's execution of certain actions and sometimes impede them. It is also advisable to introduce into a lesson short—thirty to sixty second— interludes. Personally, I am in favor of not very long individual lessons—fifteen to twenty-five minutes. Such lessons—as shown by my research and practical experience—considerably shorten pupils' reaction time and increase speed of movement. Very long lessons, on the contrary, increase reaction time and negatively influence the speed of movement as well as pupils' perception and attention.

10. In an individual lesson and the entire process of training, not only are the coach's personal fitness and technical abilities important, but equally important is his educational influence and ability to transfer his knowledge and capabilities. One should remember that a coach is successful, not only because of what he knows, but because of his ability to pass on his knowledge and capabilities to the competitor; this is of decisive value. All great fencing masters—without exception—are excellent pedagogues and teachers.[3] Of utmost importance is a coach's personal example: his punctuality, work ethic, logical consistency in his

activities, ways of wielding a weapon, enthusiasm in conducting exercises, and self-control during competition.

11. The importance of the individual lesson is so high that, very often, a coach's value and qualities are assessed merely on the ways he conducts them. This can be misleading. Of course, the individual lesson is very important, but its real value is high only when: a) it is conducted in a rational manner with proper choice and execution of exercises and using the appropriate methods (the importance of variable and distributed practice has already been stressed in the previous chapter) and b) it is logically supplemented and harmonized with other forms of training (small forms of collective lessons: exercises on one's own, exercises in front of a mirror, group exercises, footwork exercises, pair exercises, line exercises, training bouts, etc.).

Personally, I think that the value of a coach and his efficacy ought to be assessed, not only by the quality of his individual lessons, important as they are, but also by other factors: the coach's leadership style and pedagogical influence, his work in improving the professional level of younger instructors and coaches, and his part in developing the theory, practice and methodology of fencing.

VARIOUS WAYS OF CHOOSING EXERCISES IN A LESSON

"To the question of what a fencer has to practice in an individual lesson, the answer is: everything."
--Zoltan Schenker Ozoray

In his famous play, *The Citizen Turn'd Gentleman*, Molière gives such a simple definition of fencing:

> "Je vous l'ai déjà dit, tout le secret des armes ne consiste qu'en deux choses, à donner, et à ne point recevoir; et comme je vous fis voir l'autre jour par raison démonstrative, il est impossible que vous receviez, si vous saves détourner l'épée de votre ennemi de la ligne de votre corps: ce qui ne dépend seulement que d'un petit mouvement du poignet ou en dedans, ou en dehors."
>
> ("I have already told you, the whole secret of fencing lies in two things only, to give and by no means to receive [hits]; and as made plain to you the other day by demonstrative reason, it is impossible for you to be hit, if you know how to turn the sword of your enemy from the line of your body: this depends solely on a slight movement of the wrist inwards or outwards.")

Although it sounds very simple and easy, applying these principles in a bout is very complex and difficult—it requires good acquisition of many different motor skills, technical-tactical and tactical capabilities, speed and accuracy of reaction and movement, choice of action in a fraction of a second (fencers' movements and reactions are very fast and the distance between both fencers is very short; in tennis, for example, the flight of a ball often lasts four hundred or more milliseconds, so there is much more time to run and hit it than, while fencing, to recognize a threatened line and parry the opponent's blade), constant concentration of attention, observation of the opponent and prediction of his intentions. Therefore, fencing exercises do not end with acquiring technical capabilities (how to execute various and numerous actions)—this is only the beginning! The real difficulty, essence, and charm of fighting with weapons lie in effective application of actions in a bout with an active opponent.

All of fencing—as already mentioned in Chapter 1—is comprised of:

1. On-guard position and displacements (all varieties of steps, lunge, fleche, advance-lunge, advance-fleche, etc.).

2. Basic hand positions (first, second, third, etc.).

3. Changes of weapon position (used as parries, binds, presses, beats, and blade transfers).

4. Fundamental, basic thrusts and cuts (in thrusting weapons: direct thrust, disengagement, cut-over, counter-disengagement; in sabre: cut to head, cut to cheek, cut to flank, cut to chest, cut to forearm, and thrust).

These separate, basic movements (motor skills) unite into various combinations, thus creating more complicated actions adapted to the movements of the opponent, who must be outwitted. In other words, technique in fencing is only the beginning—in contradistinction to many sports with closed motor skills. The coach who only teaches movements (how to execute various strokes) commits a great error. The most important—and most difficult—job of a coach is to teach and perfect the pupil's ability to apply acquired actions in a bout with an actively counteracting opponent.

The efficacy of the application of fencing actions depends on psychomotor abilities (attention, perception, choice of action), technical-tactical capabilities, and tactical capabilities. Technical-tactical capabilities facilitate the execution of actions and their application in unforeseen conditions, relying on specific, learned sensory-motor responses. Tactical capabilities, on the other hand, make possible the application, in a bout, of chosen fencing actions in a foreseen, pre-programmed way. In competition, these two kinds of strictly interconnected capabilities—technical-tactical and tactical—constantly intertwine, providing efficacious application of actions.

It has to be strongly emphasized once more: in the efficacious application of technical-tactical and tactical capabilities in a fencing bout, an immense role is played by psychomotor abilities and coordination abilities (motor educability, motor control, and motor adaptability—with a particular aspect of the latter: lightning-fast motor improvisation).

"Lightning-fast motor improvisation" refers to situations when an athlete, in a competitive situation, uses a movement, or sequence of movements, in a form never before practiced, relying on basic well-acquired strokes, specific motor reactions, motor coordination, and technical-tactical abilities. (This phenomenon occurs not only in fencing, but also in tennis, soccer, and other combat sports and team games.) Hence there is an immense importance of exercises shaping motor coordination—in all of its levels and all sets of coordination abilities—and psychomotor capabilities.

Below is a series of examples of choosing exercises which teach and perfect the application of various actions in a bout—their choice, variable execution, and various technical-tactical and tactical abilities.[4] Here I give just a few examples of the various ways of choosing exercises in a lesson. Exercises, shaping various kinds of sensory-motor responses, operative tactical thinking, motor memory, various ways of taking decision in a bout, technical-tactical and tactical abilities, are described in more detail in many other works.[5]

One basic stroke, applied as different fencing actions.

The essence of these exercises is that one chosen, basic fencing stroke (e.g., direct thrust, disengagement-thrust, cut to head, parry, etc.) is applied in various situations in a bout as a chosen, concrete fencing action. Below are some examples.

1. *Direct thrust* in thrusting weapons is applied, successively or at random, as:

    - Attack (direct thrust, with a lunge or fleche, executed and applied as an offensive action in first intention);

    - Riposte (direct thrust, executed after a successful parry);

    - Counter-riposte (direct thrust after a parry of the opponent's riposte);

- Stop-thrust (direct thrust, as a counter-attack against the opponent's attack); remise (direct thrust, as continuation of one's own attack, either as a prolongation of attack or stop-hit against a riposte);

- Feint of direct thrust (direct thrust, as the beginning of a feint-attack);

- Feint of stop-thrust (finta in tempo) (direct thrust, as the first movement of a compound counter-attack: feint of stop-hit, derobe—executed against opponent's counter-time); etc.

2. *Cut to head,* in sabre, as:

   - Attack; riposte; counter-riposte; stop-cut; feint of attack; feint of counter-attack; counter-time (after parrying a counter-attack); remise; etc.

3. *Disengagement-thrust,* as:

   - Attack executed

     a. From a position of blade engagement (when the blades of the opponents are in contact with each other);

     b. From a position without engagement;

     c. On opponent's attempt to engage the blade;

   - Riposte by disengagement (when the opponent, after his attack is parried, takes a simple parry);

   - Counter-riposte by disengagement;

   - Derobe by disengagement (on opponent's attempt to beat or bind the blade);

- The final movement of compound attack;
- The final movement of compound counter-attack (for example: feint of derobe, derobe); etc.

4. *Riposte* as an offensive action after successful parry:

    - Riposte after parrying opponent's attack; or riposte after successfully parrying opponent's redouble (riposte by counter-time);
    - Counter-riposte (riposte after parrying opponent's riposte); a variety of counter-time (after successfully parrying opponent's counter-attack); etc.

5. *Lunge* (or fleche or other varieties of footwork) may be applied in many varieties (acceleration lunge, explosive lunge, waiting lunge, gliding lunge, etc.) and in many kinds of attacks, ripostes, or counter-attacks.

6. *Remise* is most often applied as a continuation of an attack (immediate prolongation of an attack in the same line) when, for example, the opponent's parry is not fully protective or the opponent ripostes with feints; it may be equally applied as remise of riposte, remise of counter-riposte, remise of stop-hit, or remise of counter-time.

Developing different varieties of sensory-motor responses as specific bases of technical-tactical capabilities.

In most textbooks, authors distinguish between simple and compound sensory-motor responses (sensory-motor reactions), among the latter of which they describe choice reaction and differential reaction. Personally, I distinguish seven varieties of sensory-motor responses: simple reaction, choice reaction, differential reaction, reaction to a moving object, switch-over reaction, reaction to a pre-signal, intuitive reaction (see Chapter 5).[6]

The Seven Varieties of Sensory-motor Response

1. *Simple reaction.* This sensory-motor response means reacting with a known response to a known, foreseen stimulus. In a laboratory, for example, one has to react by quickly pressing a button when a red light appears. In fencing, the pupil reacts with a foreseen action to a preannounced movement by the coach (the second method of conducting exercises) or, in a bout, when one reacts in a foreseen manner to a foreseen, expected movement by the opponent.

Exercises of simple reaction

On the coach's advance, the pupil executes direct attack with lunge (visual stimulus); on the coach's removal of blade (after blades were engaged), the pupil executes direct attack with lunge (visual-tactile stimulus)—the same exercise develops purely tactile response, when executed with eyes closed; on the coach's attempt to bind the pupil's blade, the pupil derobes; on the coach's direct attack, the pupil reacts with carte parry-riposte; etc. In all of these cases, of course, the student's actions and the coach's movements are previously announced.

2. *Choice reaction.* In a bout, the stimulus—the opponent's action—is unknown. Our choice of action, or of an action's final movement, depends on the opponent's unforeseen action (e.g., in attacks with unknown final or attacks with change of intention during their execution). This sensory-motor response—or, more precisely, the technical-tactical abilities based on this kind of reaction—is shaped applying different varieties of the third and fourth methods. Here are a few examples of exercises, shaping choice motor response (choice reaction):

Exercises of unforeseen defense

Master:	Executes, successively, various kinds of attacks.
Pupil:	Recognizes the threatened area of target and the kind, and manner of the attack, and defends himself by taking the appropriate parry or executing an appropriate counter-attack.

Attack with unknown final ("Open-eyes Attack"). This is a partly foreseen action. The pupil only foresees and plans the first movement of an attack and finishes it, recognizing the coach's movements. For example: if the coach does not react, the pupil finishes with a direct thrust or cut; if the "opponent" tries to defend himself with a parry, the pupil deceives it and hits the opening area of target; if the "opponent" applies counter-attack, the student finishes with an appropriate variety of counter-time.

A specific example in thrusting weapons (two options)

Pupil: Begins his attack with a step forwards and fourth binding.

Master (1) Does not react,

Pupil Finishes the attack with a direct thrust with opposition and lunge.

Or,

Master (2): Parries,

Pupil: Finishes with a disengagement-thrust with lunge. If the opponent derobes, the attacker executes counter-time by a second taking of the blade.

An example in sabre (two options)

Pupil: The sabreur begins his open-eyes attack by feint of cut to head and step or jump forwards.

Master (1): Does not react,

Pupil: Finishes the attack with a cut to head with lunge.

Or,

Master (2): Takes fifth parry,

Pupil: Finishes the attack with a cut to flank or chest with lunge. If the "opponent" (master) executes a stop-cut, the sabreur reacts with counter-time by the appropriate parry and riposte.

3. *Differential reaction*. This refers to situations when we have to recognize—and differentiate—movements which look very similar and yet are different, both in execution and intention.

- For example: the fencer must distinguish, differentiate, between a real straight attack—executed with the intention to hit—and a false attack—either meant as a preparatory action, trying to reconnoiter the opponent, or as a second intention attack with the desire to draw a parry-riposte in order to score a hit with counter-riposte. On the master's attack, If the fencer recognizes the attack as real, he takes the appropriate parry and riposte. If he recognizes the attack as a reconnoitering false attack, the fencer either does not react, or takes a small step back. If he recognizes it as a second intention false attack with the desire to score with counter-riposte, the pupil takes a parry and, with a very small delay, ripostes to the opening area of the attacker's target.

- Another example: in sabre, the coach executes attacks by cut to head, intermingling, in random order, correct, well-covered cuts with cuts which expose the forearm. Both movements are very similar, but the pupil must recognize and differentiate between correct cuts—against which he takes parry five—and incorrect cuts—to which he reacts with a stop-cut.

- Another example: in epee, the coach makes a very cautious, slightly short, direct attack as a reconnoitering action or a much faster and decisive similar attack with the intention to hit. The pupil must recognize the coach's intention and, in the first case, not react or, in the latter, step back or parry.

Thus the reactions to similar movements may have two varieties:

To each movement, the pupil reacts differently, or. he reacts with a parry or counter-attack in one case and does nothing in the other.

Differential reaction is very important in trying to recognize the difference between a simple attack and a feint, or between a preparatory action and a real action.

4. *Reaction to a moving object.* In tennis, volleyball, or basketball, a player notices the flight of a ball, defines its trajectory and speed—and reacts: catching or hitting the ball, in the proper moment, not too early and not too late. In fencing, it is similar—only the distance is shorter and the speed is faster. The fencer watches the movement of the opponent's weapon and tries to execute a parry at the best moment—not too early (for then the opponent can change the movement of his weapon) and not too late (for then the fencer will be hit). As the research of W. Keller and myself has demonstrated—much to the surprise of many fencers—reaction to a moving object in fencing is an excellent and most reliable sign of a fencer's abilities and form. Understanding the importance of this variety of sensory-motor response, we may appreciate the importance of change of rhythm—and especially of speeding up the final phase of a cut or thrust. We may say that change of rhythm is one of the most important factors in surprise ("timing," "scelta di tempo," "l'à propos").

In lessons, the master must try to develop this reaction and change of rhythm by specially devised exercises. For example: the coach executes many attacks from various distances and with various speeds, and the pupil tries to parry at the "right" moment—not too late, to avoid being hit, and not too early, to prevent the attacker from being able to change his movement. One should also do many exercises developing the ability to change rhythm. For example:

- A slow, careful parry with a lightning-fast riposte;
- Slow binding of the opponent's blade with an advance and then an extremely fast beat and direct thrust with lunge or fleche;
- Certain sets of movements, like parry-ripostes, executed variably as rather slow or really fasts movements;
- Various combinations of advance and lunge with change of speed and rhythm.

I have found—often take advantage of the fact—that exercises with bean bags or tennis balls are excellent for developing reaction to a moving object, in addition to various qualities of attention, perception, motor adaptability. Furthermore—and very important—they are also fun. Strangely enough, and much to the surprise of many fencing masters, skills shaped by exercises with bean bags or tennis balls, such as motor coordination and accuracy and speed of reaction to a moving object are easily transferred to fencing situations (unlike long-distance running or skipping rope). This touches the important issue of specificity of training and transfer of skills. Blind imitation of track and field exercises is not very advisable for a fencer and does not ensure a transfer of skill.

As I keep saying to my students, "Running around a soccer pitch does not ensure the improvement of soccer players, much like walking around a table does not improve the skill of billiard players."

5. *Switch-over reaction.* This kind of reaction means a change of preconceived movements and a chosen motor program in response to the unexpected movement of an opponent. It occurs, of course, when a fencer applies a foreseen action—either first or second intention—and the opponent reacts contrary to expectations. Below are some examples:

Exercise 1: Change of intention in a first intention action. In a lesson, the fencer executes, many times in succession, a feint-attack, hitting the coach in the uncovered, opening area of target after deceiving his parry or parries. His intention is to score a hit by this kind of attack and he concentrates on it and chooses the appropriate motor program. From time to time (but not too often) without any warning, the coach—instead of taking the expected parry—executes a stop-hit. In such a case, the pupil changes his preliminary motor program and executes counter-time, using parry, beat, or thrust with opposition.

Exercise 2: Change of intention in a second intention action. The pupil, an epeeist, practices foreseen, second intention counter-time. He begins his action with an advance and feint in low line, to which the coach reacts with a stop-hit over the arm. Then the pupil executes foreseen counter-time. From time to time, the coach does not execute stop-hit, then the pupil must finish the attack with direct thrust to thigh; or the coach parries eight and the pupil deceives his parry and finishes the attack in high line.

In shaping and perfecting the ability, based on switch-over motor response, to change decision while executing a foreseen action, it is very important for the coach to allow the pupil to hit many times with the original foreseen action—either first or second intention. Otherwise, if the coach introduces a surprise action (not the one the pupil expected) too early, the pupil will, unwittingly, perform the following executions as though they were open-eyes attacks—quite a different capability.

6. *Reaction to a pre-signal.* Very often, the competitor—in tennis, volleyball, fencing, etc.—before executing a chosen stroke, unwittingly betrays his intention by change of position, contraction of muscles, or some preliminary movement. In tennis, for example, the player very often does not react to the flight of the ball, but foresees its path by watching the preliminary movement of the opponent's swing. An experienced fencer sometimes starts to parry before his opponent actually begins his attack. The fencer reacts to a "pre-signal," which considerably shortens the time of motor response.

Example:

Maneuvering on the piste in bout-like conditions, the fencing master tries to surprise his pupil with a fast direct attack with lunge. The pupil watches his "opponent" very carefully and tries to notice a pre-signal to start his defense as soon as possible. Since betrayal of one's intentions favors the opponent's defense, the pupil should also practice concealing his intentions and executing his attacks without the slightest preliminary movement.

7. *Intuitive reaction.* This is a sensory-motor response based on "statistical intuition." The fencer takes the decision based on

not fully conscious mental processes, intuitively relying on the experience of hundreds of similar situations, both in training and competition. In a lesson, the coach may choose one of two chosen foreseen actions—for example, a direct attack (the variety of attack is defined) or a given feint-attack (also defined). The pupil, very concentrated, tries to penetrate the "opponent's" thoughts and, above all, to rely on his "statistical intuition" to predict which of the two possible attacks (or any other foreseen, preannounced actions) the coach will apply. If his intuition tells him that it will be a direct attack, the fencer must defend himself with a parry. If he foresees a feint-attack, then he does not move and the coach hits his guard position. Neither the coach nor pupil has the right to change his intention during the action, nor are they allowed to use "open-eyes" actions—this is the only way to assess the rightness of the intuitive prediction. The following concrete examples will make it easier to understand:

Example in Sabre:

The pupil, on-guard, holds his sabre in tierce position. The coach has the choice of either a direct attack—cut to head with lunge—or feint to head, cut to flank. If the pupil expects a direct attack to head, he defends himself with parry five; if he expects a compound attack—head-flank—he keeps his weapon unmoved in tierce position. After a certain number (e.g., ten) of trials, the roles reverse: when the pupil expects that the coach will parry, he executes compound attack—head-flank; if the pupil expects the coach to remain in tierce position, he executes direct attack to head.

Example in Foil:

The pupil starts his attack with beat and finishes with a direct thrust, when he does not expect the coach's parry, or by disengagement thrust, when he intuitively expects the coach's parry four. Again, after a certain number of trials, the roles change.

Example in Epee:

The pupil has to choose, intuitively, between: feint of direct thrust, disengagement, when he expects the coach to parry four; or counter-time by thrust in sixth position, when he expects the coach's stop-hit.

Contrary to what one might think, this is not a game of chance, coincidence, or good luck. I have conducted such, and similar, exercises many times with our leading fencers and it turns out that great competitors—like Franke, Parulski, Woyda and others—when in good form, are able to correctly guess eight or nine times out of ten, both when defending and attacking. Exercises of this kind were introduced years ago by the famous Hungarian fencing master, Laszlo Borszodyi, who called them a "lottery" without, however, trying to explain the phenomenon of statistical intuition. To honor the memory of the great master, I call such exercises "lottery à la Borszodyi."

Developing various technical and technical-tactical abilities, while perfecting one chosen action

The very essence of this way of choosing and conducting exercises is that we select one defined fencing action and practice it successively, in different manners and with shifting emphases, perfecting given technical or technical-tactical capabilities. Using the example of direct attack with lunge, we proceed in the following order:

1. *Correct execution of direct attack.* Here, the direct attack with lunge is executed on the spot, without maneuvering, with emphasis on correct execution of movement; the coach stays "like a rock" and allows himself to be hit (the first method of conducting exercises in a lesson). The aim of such practice is to teach and perfect proper form of movement—correct coordination between the movement of the hand and legs, the appropriate rhythm, accuracy of movement (the first level

of motor coordination—movement in space; directing the movement).

2. *Speed of execution.* This is the same as above, but the fencer tries, not only to execute the movement correctly, but also to execute it as fast as possible. Thus, we develop speed of execution (the second level of motor coordination—movement in space and time; the first method of conducting exercises).

3. Speed of response to a visual stimulus. On the coach's preannounced movement (e.g., advance) the pupil executes his attack, trying to start it as soon as possible (the execution of the action need not be very fast, just early). The fencer, in this way, improves the latent period of simple reaction—the time from the appearance of stimulus (coach's advance) to the beginning of the movement (motor, or executory, period of reaction). (The second method.)

4. *Speed of response to a tactile stimulus.* The fencer, with eyes shut, reacts—executes his attack—when the coach removes his blade from a position of engagement. (The second method.)

5. *Speed of response to a visual-tactile stimulus.* The pupil tries to see and feel the coach's engagement. He reacts with a direct attack on the absence of blade—when the coach detaches his blade from engagement. This is the fastest kind of response in fencing—particularly important in epee fencing. (The second method.)

6. *Speed of sensory-motor response (speed of reaction and speed of movement).* The competitor, on a pre-announced signal—visual or tactile—tries to begin his attack as soon as possible and execute it as fast as possible, thus perfecting speed of motor response (time of latent and executory periods of motor response). Of course, the preparatory period also improves—the high level of attention; preparing the motor program of an action;

trying to perceive the expected stimulus as soon as possible. (The second method.)

7. *The same chosen action, applied while maneuvering on the piste, in bout-like conditions.* The coach and pupil maneuver on the piste in conditions resembling a bout. The pupil tries to surprise his "opponent" with an unexpected, sudden direct attack with lunge. Here, the fencer perfects, not only the speed of latent period and the speed of movement, but also mobility, reconnoitering, predicting the opponent's movements, and—above all—sense of surprise ("timing," "l'à propos," "scelta di tempo"): the ability to perceive, in a fraction of a second, and take advantage of, a suitable situation to launch a foreseen attack (e.g., a careless advance, signs of lowering attention, etc.). (A sophisticated form of the second method, containing certain elements of the third method.)

8. *Shifting of attention.* The exercises are conducted as in the point above, but the coach, from time to time (though not too often)—in a surprising manner—tries to attack directly and hit his pupil. The fencer, concentrated mostly on preparing and applying his foreseen attack, has to shift his attention and change his intention in ion of the chosen action (direct attack), it also improves choice reaction. (The third method.)

Developing a chosen technical-tactical ability by means of various actions (one capability – different actions).

The essence of this way of choosing and conducting exercises and selecting the appropriate methods, is that the fencer mainly learns and perfects a chosen technical-tactical capability using various, sometimes very different, actions. Here are some examples:

1. *Assessment of distance and choice of appropriate footwork.*

   a. The coach does not move (he stays "like a rock") and the pupil executes successive thrusts, each time changing the distance—first very near, hitting with a bent arm, then slightly further, hitting with fully extended arm, then with an advance, then with short lunge, then with a full lunge, then with a very long lunge, then with advance-lunge, etc.—being sure to not execute the movements rhythmically (constant, stable rhythm leads to a lowering of attention).

b. The coach keeps the pupil's blade engaged in a certain position (e.g., four or six). From time to time, though not rhythmically, the coach detaches his blade from the pupil's weapon, at the same time changing the distance, moving backward or forward. The pupil reacts with a direct thrust, his footwork depending on the distance—in place, with a step forwards, short lunge, full lunge, etc. Here, apart from assessment of distance, the pupil develops his simple reaction to a visual-tactile stimulus.

c. The fencer begins his attack with a step forward. The coach either stays still or moves forward or backward. The pupil, accordingly, finishes his attack with a lunge of appropriate length.

d. The fencer begins his attack by binding the coach's blade with an advance. The coach does not move, or steps forwards, or jumps backwards. The pupil, assessing the distance, finishes his attack by direct thrust with opposition and lunge of appropriate length.

e. The master attacks and pupil defends himself with a parry. After the pupil's parry, the coach leans slightly forwards, remains in the lunge, returns to on-guard position, or very quickly jumps backwards. Depending on what the coach does, the pupil, appropriately: ripostes with a bent arm, ripostes with full extension of arm, ripostes with advance, or ripostes with lunge or fleche.

f. The coach tries to bind the pupil's blade with a step forwards; the pupil derobes on the spot. The coach tries to engage the pupil's blade without moving forwards or backwards; the pupil attacks by disengagement with lunge. The coach tries to engage the pupil's blade and then immediately steps back and reacts with a parry to the pupil's feint; the pupil executes feint of disengagement with advance and disengagement with lunge (deceiving the coach's parry). Here, apart from assessment of distance, the pupil learns to choose the right action.

2. *Control of speed and rhythm of movement.* As everybody knows, speed is a very important factor in a fencing bout, but it is much more complicated then speed in other sports, where it means only the velocity of one movement or displacement (running, ski-running, swimming, cycling, etc.). Speed in fencing is not rhythmic. It has different directions. It is connected with a constant change of the situation, reaction to the opponent's movements; involving coordination of arm and leg movements, with general motor coordination and a feeling of surprise ("timing," "l'à propos," "scelta di tempo"). Change of rhythm—especially speeding up the final movement of an attack—is a very important factor in misleading the opponent, taking him by surprise, and scoring a hit. There are some world class fencers whose movements are generally rather slow, but who can change rhythm and react very quickly (latent period of reaction is very short, final period of reaction is not so short). One of the biggest mistakes a coach can make in an individual lesson is to conduct exercises by executing all movements rhythmically. As with many of the other frequently met bad habits and

thoughtless ways of conducting exercises by coaches, this never ceases to amaze me.

Examples of Exercises

Following are examples of exercises, developing and perfecting control of speed, acceleration, adaptation of speed to the opponent's movement and the tactical situation, change of rhythm, etc.:

- The pupil practices various actions—offensive and defensive—each time with a different speed and a different rhythm, paying specially attention to the final acceleration of an attack or riposte.

- The pupil practices varieties of attacks with different speeds and different coordination between the arm and legs: fast direct thrust with a short, explosive lunge (one outburst of speed); attack with acceleration lunge, with very fast increase of speed at the end; open-eyes attack with waiting lunge, beginning with slow, rather wide movements and ending with a sudden, lightning-fast acceleration; attack with a sharp, fast beginning and a slightly slower ending as an unforeseen action.

- The pupil begins with a slow binding of the blade with advance and then finishes with a very fast beat and thrust with lunge.

- The pupil slowly makes a feint of a parry and then a very fast ultimate parry (e.g., when the "opponent" begins an open-eyes attack with a feint to head, the pupil takes a slow parry five and when the "opponent" finishes the attack to flank, the pupil takes a very fast parry two and ripostes.)

- The pupil intermingles: attack with advance, then lunge (rhythm: one-two, three); attack with advance-lunge (rhythm: one, two, three); attack with pattinando (rhythm: oooone, two-three); attack with balestra-lunge (rhythm: one-two).

- The pupil executes a compound attack with many feints and different rhythms of both the arm and leg movements.

- The pupil executes a false attack very slowly and then a real attack very quickly.

- The pupil makes a rather slow preparation, then a very fast real action (e.g., slow false attack with a short lunge and then a very fast jump forward— fleche).

- The pupil executes attacks with different varieties of fleche.

These are only a few examples of how to develop chosen technical-tactical abilities by means of various exercises and various actions. Similar exercises might be chosen and applied to teach and perfect the ability:

- to define the threatened line during the opponent's attack, riposte or counter-attack;

- to change decision while executing a foreseen action;

- to differentiate between false and real actions; the ability to differentiate between simple and compound actions;

- to stop or prolong an encounter, when necessary;

- to direct the thrust or cut into the opening area of the opponent's target;

- to choose the appropriate parry;

- to choose between parry and counter-attack; etc.

Various ways to choose and execute a fencing action

1. *Foreseen, first intention actions.* All actions—mainly attacks—that are foreseen (with a ready motor program in the brain) and executed according to a preliminary program.

2. *Foreseen, second intention actions.* Here, the first movement does not intend to hit the opponent. Its object is to draw a certain action from the opponent (e.g., parry-riposte or counter-attack). The first movement is not intended to hit, but to provoke the opponent's predicted action, for example: a counter-attack—against which, one applies counter-time; parry-riposte—or a parry-riposte--against which, one applies parry, counter-riposte. The fact that we expect, or even provoke, a certain action—by using feints or false attacks—facilitates fast, accurate and—above all—early application of a foreseen movement.

   - *Exercises:* second-intention counter-time, second-intention counter-riposte, second-intention remise, second-intention redouble, etc.

3. *Unforeseen actions.* Here belong—above all—unforeseen actions of defense: defensive actions (parries, evasions and retreats) and offensive-defensive actions (different varieties of counter-attack). As unforeseen actions, counter-time and renewed offensive actions may be used—and also practiced.

Examples of exercises:

- Coach and pupil manaeuver on the piste. The coaches uses different varieties of unannounced simple actions; the pupil chooses and executes the correct response.

- The coach executes an attack with bent arm and hesitation; the pupil chooses and executes the correct counter-attack.

- The coach executes simple and compound attacks at random; the pupil chooses appropriately whether to parry or stop-hit.

- The pupil executes a pre-announced action; the master then executes an unexpected and unannounced attack. The pupil must defend himself.

4. *Actions with unknown final* ("open-eyes"). Open-eyes actions are usually attacks. The pupil begins his attack with a feint, gaining distance, not yet knowing how he will finish (only his first movement is foreseen and pre-programmed). The final movement is chosen only after recognition of the opponent's response. (The third and fourth methods.)

Examples:

- A foilist begins his attack by binding the opponent's blade in four with an advance. If his "opponent" (coach) does not react, he finishes his attack by direct thrust with opposition and lunge; if the opponent tries to parry, the fencer finishes by disengagement; if the opponent derobes the first attempt to bind, the pupil finishes with a subsequent taking of the blade.

- Another example: A sabreur begins his open-eyes attack with feint to chest and advance. If the coach takes parry four, the pupil deceives it and cuts to flank; if the opponent does not react, the fencer cuts to chest; if the opponent counter-attacks, the fencer applies the appropriate counter-time.

5. *Change of intention during the execution of an action.* A fencer executes a foreseen action (e.g., attack of first or second intention) but his opponent does not react as

predicted, so the attacker must change his intention and movements (switch-over reaction). For example:

- An epeeist wants to score a hit by feint in low line and disengagement hit in high line. If, however, the opponent counter-attacks—instead of the anticipated parry eight—the attacker must change his intention and score a hit by counter-time: opposition thrust in six.

- A sabreur wants to execute a compound attack—feint to head, cut to flank. His opponent does not react to the feint, so he must change his preliminary program and finish his attack with a cut to head.

These tactical situations are discussed in detail in Chapter 2. Understanding and knowing well the essence and classification of fencing actions will make choosing the appropriate exercises easier for the coach. Although some pupils may show predilection for one way of choosing actions in a bout—some like first intention foreseen actions, others like second intention foreseen actions, while still others prefer partly foreseen actions, etc.—the coach should teach and perfect all varieties but, most frequently, those varieties which correspond to the pupil's personality, temperament and tactical preferences.

Fencing on one's own initiative and as a response to the opponent's initiative (pupil's initiative/coach's initiative). This way of choosing exercises in a lesson is of great importance. In competition, the fencer must be able to act on his own initiative—trying to catch his opponent by surprise—as well as effectively respond to the opponent's initiative (very important here is lightning-fast assessment of the situation and choice of the appropriate action). It seems so clear and obvious but, as I often say, the most difficult thing is to notice the obvious.

In practice, it often happens that a coach chooses exercises in a very one-sided way. Very often coaches choose and conduct exercises that are almost exclusively on their own initiative; in this way, the pupil may learn how to react to certain situations but does not learn how to impose and show his own initiative. Conversely, some coaches choose exercises based only on the pupil's initiative; the pupil then does not learn how to react to his opponent's initiative.

1. *Actions on the pupil's initiative.* This includes all actions in which the pupil actively maneuvers on the piste, trying to impose his initiative, creating situations suitable for the application of offensive actions. Also included are those actions which draw certain predicted movements from the opponent, in order to counteract them with a foreseen action—for example: an active fencer, "carelessly" closing the distance, provokes the opponent's attack and, ready for it, easily parries and ripostes. Mobility, initiative, attention and perception and all kinds of preparatory actions play a vital role.

2. *Actions on the opponent's initiative.* The pupil carefully watches—and appropriately reacts to—the opponent's (coach's) movements—both displacements on the strip and movements of the weapon. Frequently, the pupil applies foreseen and unforeseen actions of defense—defensive and counter-offensive actions. He also applies offensive actions as a response to the opponent's movements (too wide a movement of the weapon, signs of lowering of attention, rhythmic repetition of certain movements, careless closing of distance, etc.).

Different varieties of a given action.

There are many varieties of certain actions. For example, there are simple attacks and compound attacks. A simple attack, executed with one movement, may be: direct; with disengagement; with counter-disengagement; with cut-over (coupé). Among compound attacks, we distinguish: attacks with action on the blade (in my view; see Chapter 2); feint attacks; feint attacks preceded by action on the blade. We also distinguish many different varieties of riposte, counter-riposte, counter-attack, and counter-time (again, see Chapter 2). Here, as an example, are different varieties of counter-time:

- Counter-time by parry-riposte (against stop-hit),

- Counter-time by successive parries (against compound counter-attack),
- Counter-time by thrust with opposition,
- Counter-time by stop-hit against a stop-hit,
- Counter-time by a second taking of the blade (against derobement),
- Counter-time by successive parries or actions on the blade (against feint-derobe, derobe).

Different ways of applying a chosen variety of action.

Apart from various ways of executing a given action (different varieties of attacks, parries, ripostes, counter-attacks, and counter-time) extremely important is, not only the chosen variety of a given action, but the way we choose its application (psychological basis of decision). We may choose a given action as foreseen first intention, foreseen second intention, unforeseen, partly foreseen open-eyes, and partly foreseen change of intention during the execution of an action.

Let us consider, for example, one variety of counter-time (counter-time by thrust in line of six) against one variety of counter-attack (stop-hit over the pupil's arm). On the pupil's advance with the point threatening the coach's low line, the coach executes counter-attack by stop-hit over the pupil's arm. The pupil executes counter-time by thrust in sixth position. The identical variety of counter-time may be the result of three different ways of making the decision:

1. *Counter-time as a foreseen second intention action.* The pupil advances with a feint of thrust in the low line, provoking the coach's stop-hit from above. Expecting and provoking the movement, the pupil easily defeats it by applying a foreseen opposition thrust with lunge. In such drills, everything is foreseen and the coach always reacts with a stop-hit to the pupil's feint.

2. *Counter-time as change of intention during an action.* The pupil practices and repeats many times, compound at-

tack with advance-lunge: feint of thrust in low line (the coach takes parry eight), disengagement with which he deceives the parry and finishes the attack with a thrust in high line to arm or trunk. This feint attack is repeated many times, but the coach, from time to time (but not too often), instead of taking the expected parry eight, applies stop-hit. As a reaction to the stop-hit, the pupil must change his primary intention and motor program, and apply an unexpected counter-time by thrust in opposition in six. It ought to be stressed here that the coach should not apply the stop-hit too early or too often in practice because, if he does so, the pupil subconsciously will change his action into an open-eyes attack, which is quite different.

3. *Counter-time as one possible final of an open-eyes attack.* The pupil begins his attack with unknown destination ("open-eyes"), feinting in the low line with an advance, closely watching his opponent. If the coach does not react, the fencer finishes his attack by thrust to thigh with lunge; if the fencing master takes parry eight or parry two, the pupil deceives the parry and hits the forearm from above by disengagement thrust with lunge; if, however, the coach, against the pupil's feint, reacts with a stop-hit, the pupil executes counter-time by thrust with opposition in six with lunge.

The exercises above demonstrate that the same movement, or rather the same sequence of movements, executed in very much the same technical manner can be tactically applied in completely different ways.

Exercises mainly developing tactical capabilities.

1. *Developing different tactical capabilities.*

   - Assessing the opponent's capabilities, style of fencing, and intentions.

   - Concealing one's own intentions and misleading the opponent.

- Directing the opponent's movements: drawing and taking advantage of certain actions.

- Preparing (preparatory actions) one's own real actions—maneuvering on the strip, gaining distance, imposing one's own initiative, distracting the opponent's attention, etc.

2. *Choice of tactics against various tactical types.*

- Choice of actions, fencing against an opponent with a markedly bent arm, who relies, in defense, mostly on parries.

- Choice of appropriate actions and tactics, fencing against an opponent who relies mainly on counter-attacks.

- Choice of tactics against an opponent of the "fly-fisherman" type, who relies mainly, when attacking and riposting, on flicks.

- Choice of tactics against a "crawling worm" type, who fences hunched over and close to the ground.

- Application of various actions, and different ways of choosing them, against a left-handed opponent (this requires that the coach be able to effectively wield a weapon with his left hand).

- Choice of tactics and actions against a concrete, known competitor.

Exercises developing tactical abilities, preparatory actions, and the ability to cope with a certain type of opponent—or a specific, chosen opponent—are very difficult. So I will give a few additional remarks on the subject.

A very important and obvious duty of a coach is to give some lessons—or conduct certain exercises in a lesson—left-handed. The pupil learns how to execute various actions against a left-handed opponent. This is very important in competition because the fencer who practices against a left-handed coach is much more confident against a left-handed opponent. It is also very important for the coach who gives many individual lessons during the day, because giving lessons left-handed: assures rest to the right hand; promotes transfer of skills from the left side to the right, and prevents scoliosis.

Very important, and quite difficult, is the coach's ability to play the role of a concrete, chosen opponent. As I mention in another chapter, our leading sabreur, Pawlowski, had difficulties against the left-handed Hungarian, Horwath. I studied Horwath's tactics in competition and on film and conducted exercises with Pawlowski, playing the role of Horwath. These exercises brought Pawlowski very good results in international competitions.

Another example: The 1964 Tokyo Olympic champion, Grigory Kriss, had very serious difficulties fencing against my pupil, Bogdan Gonsior. So, Kriss' coach, Koltchinski, specially prepared him. To compensate for not having a very long reach (he was not very tall and Gonsior was very tall with long arms and legs), Koltchinski conducted lessons with a special, very long, epee. The results (unfortunately for me and my pupil) were very successful in the decisive bout to reach the final four in the Tokyo Olympic Games. Kriss—for the first time in his life—beat Gonsior, 10-3 and went on to win the gold medal.

To teach certain preparatory actions—for example, foreseeing the opponent's reactions—the coach can "unwittingly" betray his intentions as a reaction to the pupil's preparatory false attack. Then, if the coach betrays his intention of stop-hitting, the pupil applies counter-time. If the coach "accidentally" shows his intention to parry, the pupil applies a feint attack.

It is very important to conceal one's own intentions and not to betray oneself with certain "pre-signals." So, the coach tells the pupil to apply a given variety of attack (e.g., direct cut to head, in sabre or direct thrust to trunk, in thrusting weapons). If the pupil attacks correctly, without any preliminary movements, the coach does not react and is hit; if, however, the pupil gives any preliminary signal, the coach takes a parry.

Apart from specially chosen exercises, a very good way to teach preparatory actions and tactical abilities is a training bout with the coach.

CONCLUSIONS

"The more important a given task is in achieving victory, the more attention we should pay to it in training."
--Zoltan Schenker Ozoray

The most important task and feature of the entire process of training (see motto) is the efficacious transfer of abilities, sensory-motor skills, and technical-tactical and tactical capabilities from practice to training bouts and then from training bouts to competition—one could say that this is the essence of the training process in fencing. In certain sports, like gymnastics or figure skating, one learns various motor skills and then applies them in competition according to a preconceived program without an opponent and without any change in the external situations. Of course, even in such "simple" sports, there is the pressure of rivalry, arousal, and competitive anxiety; yet, it is much easier to demonstrate one's skills in competition. Usually, in these "easy" sports, an athlete finds less difficulty in displaying his skills in competition. In fencing and other combat sports, as well as in team games, it is much more difficult and complicated because the athlete has to: perceive and assess the situation, which is constantly changing; choose the right action and apply it correctly and efficiently in various ways, depending on distance and the opponent's movements or actions. So, in fencing, we must assume that skills and capabilities are fully acquired by the athlete only when he can apply them successfully and assuredly in competition. As I have stressed many times, fencing coaches who do not understand this obvious truth teach fencers motor skills as though they were closed, as in gymnastics.

While conducting various exercises—including those in an individual lesson—the fencing master must always keep in mind the following:

1. Most exercises in a lesson ought to consist of actions that the fencer directly transfers and applies in a

bout—thus, those actions which constitute a fencer's "fighting repertoire."

2. Some of the exercises in a lesson, however, do not constitute the actions which a fencer directly transfers and applies in a bout. These exercises ought todevelop certain reactions and capabilities which facilitate the application of various actions and tactical capabilities in competition. These are the exercises which—although not directly applicable in competition—shape, develop, and perfect accuracy and speed of perception, various qualities of attention, choice of action, motor coordination, speed of reaction and movement, feeling of surprise, control of rhythm of one's own movement, etc.

3. "Mechanical," thoughtless repetition of the same movements is... a waste of time and gives a fencer nothing useful. Even worse—and unfortunately quite common—are stylized, exaggerated, stupid, senseless, unrealistic movements applied by a coach, which not only do not teach anything useful, but—contrary to the coach's intention—teach bad movements and wrong reactions. I have mentioned these bad habits before but, to remind and explain what I mean, I will give one more example of an exaggerated, artificial and silly procedure: a coach, giving a sabre lesson, raises his hand very high and demands a parry from his pupil—it is obvious that the proper action against such a movement ought to be stop-hit (see the previous chapter).

4. An old Russian proverb says, "All birds can flap their wings, but not all of them can fly." Let us teach and conduct exercises in such a way that our pupils are not only able to flap their wings (execution of certain fencing actions in predicted and unchanging situations), but are also able to fly—and not only fly, but fly fast, high, and in different manners (efficacious application of learned skills in a bout).

5. Of course, we must remember that a coach not only teaches fencing, but educates his pupils, not only physically, but mentally, socially, and morally. We must also remember that the entire process of training ought to be based on a model of competition, taking into account a pupil's individual traits (the principle of individualization; team cohesion; the leading role and example of the coach). This is expressed very aptly and coherently by an Italian saying, "Maestro di scherma—maestro di vita." ("Master of fencing—master of life.")

. References

1. Czajkowski, Z. "*Lekcja indywidualna w szermierce*" (part I and II), *Sport Wyczynowy* No. 7-8/2000, 9-10/2000.
2. Czajkowski, Z. "Celem ćwiczeń nie jest „dawanie w kość", ale podnoszenie umiejętności ucznia."*Sport Wyczynowy* No. 11-12/1997.
3. Czajkowski, Z. *Trening szermierza*, vol. I and II, AWF, Katowice 1988.
4. Czajkowski, Z. "Wiedza, umiejętności, osobowość i praca trenera." *Człowiek i Ruch – Human Movement*, No. 2/2000.

   Saytchook, L.V. *Fiechtovaniye – posobiye dla trienierov*, Fizkultura i Sport, Moskva 1964.

   Sabock, R.J. *The Coach*, Human Kinetics Publishers, Champaign 1985,
5. Czajkowski, Z. *Trening szermierza*, AWF, Katowice 1984,

   ____________. *Nauczanie techniki sportowej*, second edition, RCMSKFiS, Warszawa, in press.

   Bogen, R.M. *Obootcheniye dvigatielnym dyeystviyam*, Fizkultura i Sport, Moskva 1985.
6. Czajkowski, Z. "Teoria i metodyka współczesnej szermierki," *Sport i Turystyka*, Warszawa 1968.

   Wojciechowski, Z. *Theory Methods and Exercises in Fencing*, Amateur Fencing Association,

   Bulotchko, K.T. *Fechtovaniye*, Fizkultura i Sport, Moskva 1967,

   Arkadyev, V.A., Hozikov, J. *Fechtovaniye*, Sovyetskaya Rossiya, Moskva 1962,

   Vass, I. *Parbajtorvivas*, Sport, Budapest 1965.
7. Czajkowski, Z. "Nawyki czuciowo-ruchowe w działalności sportowej." ZSKF Makroregion Śląski, Katowice 1995,

   ____________. "Wpływ motywacji na opanowanie nawyków czuciowo-ruchowych i skuteczne ich stosowanie w zawodach." *Sport Wyczynowy* No. 3-4/2004.

   __________. "Szermiercza praca nóg – przykład ćwiczeń wielozadaniowych." *Sport Wyczynowy* No. 5-6/2004.

16. Just Before a Competition

"The hardest thing to do is to begin."
--Wendy Cochrane Czajkowska

PRE-COMPETITION STATES

"I do not know if I was what you call afraid; but my heart beat like a bird's both quick and little; and there was a dimness came before my eyes which I continually rubbed away, and which continually returned."
--Robert Louis Stevenson, Kidnapped

All athletes, immediately prior to competition, experience certain emotional states—known under the name of pre-competition states. Certain forms of pre-competition states are an important factor in accelerating the process of functional adaptation of the organism to any effort.

Normally—although by no means always—pre-competition states manifest themselves by increased functions of all of the systems and organs that will eventually be engaged in performing the intended tasks connected with participation in competition. Here I am referring to the physiological mechanism of pre-competition states, but, as we will see later on, the psychological mechanism is of equal importance.

Pre-competition states are based on previous conditioning. A man reacts not only to concrete external stimuli, but also to signals symbolizing these stimuli in the form of words or thoughts. Not only such primary stimuli as the sight of the salle and opponents, but even the mere thought of an impending competition, may cause excitation in cortical canters. The impulses from these canters flow to the various organs which will take part in the intended activities.

Pre-competition states become more intense and pronounced just before the competition, when a whole series of strong stimuli is acting: the sight of the salle and pistes; the scoreboards; meeting other fencers and watching their warm-up; hearing the clash of the blades; noticing other coaches, officials, and judges; etc. Also, thoughts and emotions connected with competitions play a considerable part. A very sensitive fencer, having read thus far, may already feel a slightly increased pulse rate!

Just before the competition, the excitation of certain cortical centers—and a high level of arousal of the cortex as a whole—influences the sympatho-adrenergic system—responsible for the functional state of various organs and systems and of the entire organism. The excitation of this system causes many phenomena, among them: acceleration of breathing, acceleration of pulse, increased arterial blood pressure, increased trophic influence on muscle tissue, increased secretion of certain hormones, a higher level of sugar in the blood, etc. All these changes tune the system in to a higher functional level, increasing its arousal and capacity for effort.

The deep biological significance (preparation of the organism for increased activity) is only one important aspect of pre-competition states. The other aspect—very important for all athletes, but especially for fencers—is the psychological one.

Pre-competition states are only useful when they do not transgress certain optimal limits. In this respect, they resemble the relationship between motivation and performance: too little motivation produces poor performance, the right amount of motivation gives an optimal performance, and too much motivation again results in poor performance (see Chapter 6). If you really, desperately want to do something, you become frozen with stage fright and can do nothing. This is sometimes the explanation of unexpected and disastrous failures of top athletes in major events.

Pre-competition states can take several forms. In many cases, the emotional states manifest themselves by an optimal degree of arousal and optimal adaptibility of nervous processes, preparing the organism for effort and facilitating: perception, decision making, and the subsequent execution of actions. However, in certain circumstances, and with certain fencers, the arousal is too much or too little. This depends, to a large degree, on the temperament—on the type of nervous system, which is inborn—and on an acquired ability to control and direct one's thoughts, emotions, and pre-competition states.

If the arousal is too intense, excessive excitatory processes occur in the systems and organs which are to be engaged in the intended work. Such signs may appear as: muscular tremor, restlessness, disorder of the digestive system, etc.

Conversely, excessive inhibitory processes may cause drowsiness, yawning, lack of desire to fight, etc.

Although pre-competition states show numerous varieties of forms and nuances, it is customary to distinguish the following three main, and most typical, forms (connected with the level of arousal and type of achievement motivation—prevalence of motive of success or motive of avoiding failure, etc.):

1. Pre-competition fighting readiness,

2. Pre-competition fever,

3. Pre-competition apathy.

The most desirable of these is, of course, the state of fighting readiness (optimal level of arousal, self-confidence, strong motive of success). Externally, this state manifests itself by increased pulse and breathing, slight perspiration, slightly increased micturition, and almost imperceptible tremor. The fencer subjectively feels a desire to fight, he gets slightly impatient waiting for the beginning of fights, he imagines various actions on the strip, he thinks up various strokes against his potential opponents, he believes in his victory. Generally, he is in a bold and optimistic mood; he is active, concentrated, and ready to fence. From the psychological point of view, the state of fighting readiness may be characterized as follows:

- Increased concentration on impending bouts,

- A high level of concentration of attention (intensity, range, selectivity and divisibility),

- Increased acuity and efficacy of perception,

- High level and speed of taking decisions, analytical and operative thinking,

- Pleasant emotions.

The state of pre-competition fever is characterized by a high level of arousal, nervousness, very marked perspiration, general tremor and tremor of the extremities, restlessness, over-excitement, and palpitation of the heart. A fencer in a state of pre-competition fever cannot concentrate his thoughts, is very restless, sometimes very talkative, has no faith in himself, overestimates the strength of his opponent, and may even show signs of panic: a high level of a motive of avoiding failure—fear of defeat. The salient features of pre-competition fever, from the psychological point of view, are:

- A high level of arousal, strong nervousness—which sometimes disorganizes the controlled activity and behavior of a fencer,

- Lack of emotional stability—very quick changes of mood, oscillating between extreme optimism and equally extreme pessimism,

- Impairment of perception, scattering of attention, and inability to concentrate,

- Weakening of memory—a fencer frequently forgets important elements which he knew well before,

- Impairment of sensory-motor skills, bad perception, bad orientation, and bad execution of actions,

- Marked predominance of excitory processes.

The third main form of pre-competition states—pre-competition apathy—is perhaps the least desirable of these states. The fencer is sleepy and apathetic. In this state there is a marked prevalence of inhibitory processes. The competitor's reactions and movements are slow and lazy; he cannot force himself to execute anything with energy and speed. The weakening of excitatory processes and the increase of inhibitory processes, in the central cortex is very often due to excessive fatigue or over-training, and takes the form of protective inhibition. It may also be due to certain traits of a weak inhibitory temperament (the melancholic as described by Hippocrates). Sometimes the protective inhibition is caused by complicated, conditioned cortical processes connected with the conscious realization, to an excessive degree, of the negative aspects of the approaching tasks in competition (inadequacy of one's own preparedness; very strong, experienced, and well-trained opponents; high stake of the competition; lack of support of one's coach; poor previous system of training; etc.). The characteristic traits of pre-competition apathy are:

- Low level of arousal, high level of a motive of avoiding failure, and lack of self-confidence;
- A marked decrease of excitability, lowering of all psychological processes—reaching sometimes a state of sleepiness;
- Over-estimation of the difficulties, and a lack of desire to participate in the competition;
- Lassitude, and unpleasant and negative emotional states.

Marked states of impairment are not always seen in such an obvious and clear-cut form as those described above. There are many intermediate forms. To give an example, we may distinguish a state of insufficient arousal (too little activation), which is one of the complex stages between pre-competition apathy and fighting readiness. Although this state is rather positive as far as mood and general feeling is concerned (there is neither fear nor apathy), a fencer in such a state, shows a certain turgidity and lack of freshness. He demonstrates a friendly attitude towards his team-mates and opponents alike, which—if carried too far—takes the edge off his fighting attitude in a bout. A fencer in a state of insufficient arousal is unable to show his best, or display his potential abilities, in a bout. Such a situation may arise with an inexperienced fencer who sets too low a task for himself before a competition (e.g., to reach direct elimination—quite satisfied with that achievement, he fences much worse in the first stage of direct elimination than in the pools). Even quite experienced fencers, especially if insufficiently trained, may set too low a standard for themselves and, unable to direct their own emotional state, enter the competition with insufficient arousal. Here a word of warning is necessary, as such a state, if frequently repeated, becomes habitual, and it is very difficult to break with such a habit.

Not only are there many intermediate forms of pre-competition states, but a single competitor, before different competitions, may experience different pre-competition states. Also, a fencer may not only behave differently at different competitions, but he may even pass through various forms of pre-competition states at the same competition. For example, a fencer enters the salle very optimistic and self-possessed, getting ready to fence and full of good spirits. In fact, he is in a state of fighting readiness. But then he sees very powerful opponents making very impressive warm-up exercises, overhears some comments about their strength, and gradually becomes slightly nervous. Then, due to bad organization and lack of punctuality (only too-well known to most fencers!) there is some confusion with the pool and the beginning of the competition is delayed. Our fencer gets more and more nervous, reaching the state of pre-competition fever. If the directoire technique still works badly, and there are some protests about the distribution of the pools, the waiting becomes unbearably long for our fencer—who, to begin with, was very optimistic and combat ready; then too nervous and excited; now, as a result of protective inhibition, becomes apathetic.

Negative emotional states and undesirable forms of pre-competition states are more frequently met with among inexperienced fencers. One way of combating these states is frequent participation in competitions, preceded by a thorough, systematic, and rational training, including the appropriate psychological preparation.

The result of a competition may depend, to a large extent on the form and character of the pre-competition state. Therefore, it is important for both the pupil and the coach to understand the physiological and psychological background of these states, and to be able to control and modify them in the required direction.

A very efficient way of influencing the course and character of pre-competition states is warming up: well-chosen and -conducted warm-up exercises just before the competition. The right attitude of the fencing master, who, by his approach and advice, influences the pupil in the right direction, is also extremely important; as is conscious effort on the part of the pupil himself (see the following chapter).

It has been mentioned before that a fencer, in the course of one long tournament, may undergo various forms of pre-competition states: both beneficial and negative. This is why a fencer, both in the process of training before the competition, and just before a competition, should consciously try to prepare himself psychologically, trying to avoid the bad forms of pre-competition states and foster the good one.

Pre-competition apathy (and competition anxiety), which has been mentioned as particularly bad for the competitor, may occur, not only just before the competition (the primary occurrence), but may be—and often is—the result of very intense thought about the competition, resulting in over-excitation many days before the competition. The fencer himself realizes that this is the bad influence of obsessive thinking and various fears (fear of opponents, fear of bad results, fear of judges), yet cannot rid himself of such thoughts and emotions. This produces a nervous tiredness and then, as a result of protective inhibition, a state of pre-competition apathy occurs. This is a particularly dangerous kind of pre-competition apathy and is difficult to combat.

Pre-competition apathy that appears just before competitions is much easier to deal with. In such cases, a very energetic warm-up—with emphasis on speed—very often eliminates protective inhibition and helps to introduce the optimal state of excitation.

To psychologically prepare a pupil before competitions, one may use various methods, taking into consideration the fencer's level, temperament, and whole personality. It is very important to adapt and diversify the methods of education and psychological preparation when dealing with extreme types of extroverts and introverts.

Here are some of the methods that may be used some time before the competition to ensure the best pre-competition state and optimal level of arousal and motivation just before an important tournament:

1. A fencer sets himself the goal of winning the competition and very calmly and decidedly tries to convince himself, and everybody else, that he is going to do this. He keeps saying, "I'll be first!," "I

can, and will, win this tournament!," "I must display all my possibilities and win a gold metal," etc.

This, of course, is good for very experienced and top fencers with really good chances of winning competitions. However, such a system of auto-suggestion has a certain flaw in it. If things do not go as well as expected in the competition, he may break down and fence well below his real abilities, ceasing to struggle at all, losing even the chance of a good place.

2. Another type of fencer approaches a competition with the attitude, "I am not very well prepared for this competition—lack of training, touch of lumbago, heavy professional work—so I cannot be expected to do very well, and neither the tournament, nor the results I may have, is terribly important anyway." This attitude forms a kind of emotional protection against possible bad results. If the fencer does really badly in the competition, he is not unduly worried, and his coach should not be unduly disappointed. If he does well, it is a nice surprise for everybody and bolsters up his spirits.

This method produces a slightly apathetic attitude towards results and may lead to the mentality of a second rate, mediocre fencer. The fencer who chooses this method of psychological preparation should, while trying to convince everybody else that he is not well-prepared and that the competition is not all that important, strive, none the less, to gain the best possible results.

3. The best form of preparation for competition—at least for certain fencers—is for the fencer to detach himself, as far as possible, from the competition and opponents. In such a case, the fencer is determined to fully exploit the abilities and skills he has gained during training. He wants to show all he is able to do: his full technical, tactical, and physical preparedness. Such competitors compete and fight with full determination in all circumstances, trying to achieve the best possible result. This is a good kind of psychological preparation for competition for fencers with inborn and cultivated psychological endurance, whose plans are far-reaching and ambitious, and who treat each separate competition as a step towards reaching an eventual goal to be attained in perhaps a few years time. This method has also certain dangers: prolonged and deep auto-suggestion, practiced for a long time

and long before the competition, may lead sometimes to over-excitation.

These are only a few examples of psychological preparation before competition. Every fencer, after attempting to analyze his own personality and temperament, should work out his own personal approach to this problem.

As regards the pre-competition states which occur immediately before competition, the best way to deal with them is: a) conscious self-control and the directing of one's own emotions and thoughts; b) the friendly, influential advice of the fencing master; c) a complete warm-up.

A few years ago, under the auspices of the Polish Olympic Committee, Dr. Wiktoria Nawrocka conducted extensive research on the psychological aspects of high competitive sport, using questionnaires, tests, experiments, and observations. Among other things, she examined pre-competition states in 800 leading Polish athletes, representing twenty-seven branches of sport, including fencing.

According to the intensity, signs, and symptoms of pre-competition states, she classified all the athletes examined into five groups:

1. 15.4% of athletes examined showed a state of mild arousal, equivalent to the state of fighting readiness—an optimal level of arousal, self confidence, a desire to compete, and a strong motive of success.

2. 25.4% of athletes showed signs and symptoms of medium arousal.

3. 22.7% of athletes showed signs and symptoms of great excitement—equivalent to pre-competition fever.

4. 11.5% of athletes examined displayed mild apathy.

5. 3.2% showed a marked degree of apathy—equivalent to pre-competition apathy.

6. 11.7% of athletes examined showed no marked symptoms of pre-competition states.

The pre-competition reactions demonstrated under groups 2, 3, 4, and 5, have—partly or totally—a negative character and may badly influence the athlete's performance.

Pre-competition states appeared: a) just before a competition in 38% of athletes; b) a few hours prior to competition in 32.1% of athletes; c) a few days before a competition in 26%; d) a few weeks before a competition in 2.6% of athletes.

One may expect that, with the development of an athlete's career, the strength of pre-competition states should decrease, but actual examination revealed that only 61.2% showed a lowering of the intensity of emotions before competition. In 29.8% of athletes, the intensity of pre-competition states stayed at the same level. In 8.2% of cases, the strength of pre-competition states markedly increased with the passage of years, which shows that pre-competition states have a traumatic influence on the nervous system. It is highly characteristic that this group contains mostly athletes who showed either pre-competition fever or pre-competition apathy.

A few years ago, at a Conference of Polish Fencing Masters devoted to the subject of fencers' psychological endurance, we all came to the conclusion that an important component of—and at the same time an index to—a fencer's psychological endurance, is his pre-competition state.

In order to help the competitor, the fencing master must identify the type of his pupil's pre-competition state. Looking for the following points will help in his assessment:

1. Contacts with other people—both complete isolation and excessive desire for contact, are signs of insufficient psychological preparedness.

2. Emotional and motor mobility—here we may notice either excessive restlessness mobility and emotional tension, or low mobility, apathy and inertia. There are, of course, many intermediate forms.

3. Objective signs (physical, visible, signs), due to the function of the vegetative system (e.g. pallor, perspiration, tremor, etc.).

Apart from the already-mentioned influence of the coach, the pupil's self-control, and specially chosen warm-up exercises, one may also recommend such activities for the fencer to combat and regulate the negative signs of pre-competition states, as: checking his equipment, fulfilling certain small tasks just before a competition, helping to a less experienced team-mate, carrying on conversations on subjects not connected with competition, etc.

The question of pre-competition states is not confined to the half hour just before the competition starts, but should be taken into consideration during the whole course of training.

A very important factor in regulating pre-competition states and emotions during competitions is a profound analysis, made by the coach and pupil, of previous defeats in competitions. As is well known, a defeat, especially if subjectively felt as unjust, increases the emotional intensity in pre-competition states prior to the next competition.

WARMING UP

"A pre-competition warm-up lesson is either moral support for the competitor or a means for the fencing master to show off."
--Vitali Andreyevich Arkadyev

A warm-up is a set of energy fitness and fencing exercises intended to prepare the fencer properly for the main part of the lesson, or to take part in competition. This sub-chapter deals purely with preparation for taking part in competition.

For the efficient work of muscles and the full utilization of their functional possibilities, a certain degree of arousal of the central nervous system is essential. Among other things, this is one of the reasons why warm-up exercises are obligatory before a competition.

Jogging, running, and general gymnastic and limbering exercises increase the excitability of the sensory area of the cerebral cortex. Such introductory exercises also increase the excitability of the autonomic nervous system. A certain role is played here by emotions and the interaction of various receptors of the pulmonary and cardiovascular systems.

A warm-up before a competition, influences the function of internal organs, stimulates the activity of the pulmonary system (influences the depth and frequency of breathing, thus improving pulmonary gaseous exchange), and also stimulates the circulatory system: increase of heart rate, increase of cardiac output, increase of body temperature, rise of blood pressure, increase of the amount of blood in circulation, and increase in the amount of active capillaries in muscles.

Apart from the stimulation of various organs and systems and the adaptation of the whole organism to effort, the warm-up also fulfils a more specific purpose: ensuring conditions for the best execution of fencing actions, increasing concentration and divisibility of attention, "sharpening the reflexes," and activating the fencer's fighting spirit.

The exercises used when warming up should be the most appropriate and adequate for fencing, and should attune the fencer, in a comparatively short period of time, to the optimal state of preparedness for taking part in competition. Furthermore, the warm-up should ensure that the optimal state can be maintained over quite a long period of time.

Since athletic training is a specific form of the adaptation of the organism to increased, special demands, warming up is one of the essential factors in speeding up the process of adaptation.

Many observations and much experience have shown that a properly conducted warm-up acts—both physiologically and psychologically—as a factor regulating pre-competition states. In the case of excessive arousal—pre-competition fever—the impulses from the acting muscles to cortical centers may diminish unduly high excitation; and vice-versa: in states of excessive inhibition—pre-competition apathy—muscular activity may exert a mild excitatory influence.

The process of warming up may be divided into two parts: general and specific (fencing). The purpose of the general part of warming up is to increase the general functional level of the organism and its capacity for effort. The aim of the fencing-specific part of warming up is to establish the optimal relations between the kind of movement used in fencing and the functions of the central nervous system.

Warming up before a competition may be carried out with or without the fencing master.

When carried out without the fencing master, it consists of:

1. General warm-up exercises.

2. Fencing exercises with a team-mate; at first simple, and then more complicated movements with increased speed.

3. Free play, beginning with quite slow, very loose play, and ending with a fight at full speed and with full concentration.

A warm-up conducted with the fencing master consists of:

1. General exercises carried out by the competitor himself.

2. A short individual warm-up lesson with the fencing master (by "warm-up" lesson, I mean the type of individual lesson with the purpose of preparing a fencer for a competition and not, as understood by some coaches, the first, introductory, part of any individual lesson).

3. Loose play and bouts with team-mates.

Experiments have shown that after a very short warm-up consisting of one minute of running, the optimal level of arousal obtained lasts for 1.5 to 2 minutes . After a longer interval, the benefit of warming up subsides. It has also been proven experimentally that, in sports where speed is a very important factor, warm-up exercises should be carried out just before the start of competition. Before a 100-meter run, an athlete carries out a very thorough warm-up only once. In jumping, throwing, etc.—apart from the preliminary, thorough warm-up—an athlete makes a very short, additional warm-up before each jump or throw. A fencing competition consists of many bouts, and this is why, along with the main warm-up, short sessions of warming up should be held before each round.

In the direct elimination rounds, it is often necessary to perform additional, short warm-ups before each bout—especially if the intervals between them are prolonged. Such a warm-up may consist of a few limbering and flexibility exercises, and a few fast movements of weapons, accompanied by a lunge or fleche. At later stages of a competition, when fencers are already tired, it is often advisable to do small, additional warm-ups consisting of only non-fencing exercises or fencing exercises executed with the left arm.

The duration, intensity, and type of the main warm-up executed before the competition, depend on the character of the tournament, amount and strength of opponents, and the strength of the fencer concerned. A very experienced, top-class fencer who expects to reach the final may make a slightly shorter and less intense warm-up before the preliminary pool, where he meets weaker opponents; here the pool itself serves as a very specific fighting form of warming up. A less experienced and less well-trained fencer, in order to do well in the preliminary pool, and gain as much experience as possible, should perform a very thorough warm-up.

Before a team match, with only three bouts for each member of the team, warming up should be long and very thorough.

The increased body-temperature induced by warming up should be kept up by putting on warm-ups or a sweat suit between bouts.

Here is some practical advice about the intensity and length of a warm-up before a competition.

- The main, thorough warm-up should be finished about ten to twenty minutes before the beginning of the competition.

- A thorough warm-up before competition should contain various exercises and last about twenty-five to thirty minutes—ten minutes devoted to running, jogging, sprinting, stretching, and other general exercises; and fifteen to twenty minutes devoted to fencing exercises and loose play.

- The warm-up, including a short lesson with the fencing master, may consist of ten minutes general exercises, a ten to fifteen minute warm-up lesson with the coach, and ten minutes of loose play.

- Loose play before a competition should begin with mild, slow movements with emphasis on correct execution of strokes and regulation of distance, followed by gradual introduction of speed, timing, and acuity of perception and concentrated attention.

- As even an experienced fencer may feel a certain tension during the first bout of competition, it is good to start this bout without any undue hurry and risk, and only after having overcome this nervous tension, get into full stride.

- Between the successive rounds of competition, short warm-ups—a few minutes only—are recommended.

- If there is a long interval before the semi-final or final—(a lunch interval, etc.)—the warm-up ought to be as thorough and intense as before the competition.

- If the competition lasts for several days, one should save nervous energy, In fencing, muscular tiredness subsides relatively quickly, but the mental, emotional, and perceptual aspects of tiredness last for a longer time. Therefore, in such long and exhausting competitions, one should do more general exercises and less loose play when warming up.

Three aspects of warming up should be particularly stressed:

1. A properly conducted warm-up should not only increase the functional possibilities of the organism and its physiological preparedness for a fight, but should also ensure the equally important psychological preparedness of the athlete: acuity of perception, constant concentration, speed of orientation and reaction, divisibility of attention, and general state of fighting readiness. It is obvious (though very often overlooked) that

a fencing master supervising his pupils' warm-up cannot be satisfied with the mere speed and correctness of execution of fencing strokes, but must pay careful attention to the signs of psychological preparedness.

2. By means of properly chosen exercises for warming up, one may regulate and influence the pre-competition state of fencers. If the fencer is too excited and has difficulties in controlling his nervous tension, the warm-up lesson should contain exercises with emphasis on relatively slow, precise movements; complicated actions; changes of rhythm; adapting the pupil's movements to the fencing master's actions; and the lesson should be conducted in a calm and controlled manner. An apathetic and inhibited fencer should be stimulated by means of very fast and energetic exercises, using maximum speed and fast responses to the fencing master's actions. The whole lesson ought to be conducted in a very energetic, mobile, and fast manner.

3. Once more, I would like to point out the principle of specificity. Some fencers, when warming up—like in regular training—one-sidedly, and greatly, overestimate the value of "general," all-round, physical fitness, running around the salle twenty times, with surprising enthusiasm. I have to repeat once more: each extreme may, and often does, lead to the absurd. Running around a pitch does not improve the skills of soccer players, just like walking around a table does not improve the skills of billiard players.

Lastly, in carrying out warm-up exercises, the fencing master, according to the tactical type of his pupil, ought to put emphasis on either first and second intention foreseen actions, or on unforeseen (improvised) actions, or on partly foreseen actions (actions with unknown ending and actions with change of intention during their execution).

Well-chosen and rationally conducted warm-up exercises form a very important step towards success in competitions.[1]

References

1. Czajkowski, Z. "Wiedza, umiejętności i praca trenera," *Człowiek i Ruch – Human Movement,* No. 2/2000; "Knowledge, Skills, Personality and Work of a Coach," *The Swordsman,* Spring 2001.

17. At the Competition

"As far as our knowledge goes, at least, we may say that our success in manipulating people lags far behind our success in manipulating circumstances."
--H.J. Eysenck

This chapter is not meant for a fencing master who limits the scope of his activity to quietly giving lessons in a corner of the salle, but for those coaches who understand that their task is much wider and more versatile, including, among other things, their active presence at competitions.

One of the first and basic duties of the fencing master at a competition is to make sure his pupils are properly warmed-up—done either on their own or by getting lessons from their coach. The significance of warming up cannot be over-estimated. It not only ensures the technical preparedness of the competitor, but has also an immense psychological and physiological influence. By his attitude and choice of exercises, the fencing master may influence and direct the pre-competition state of his pupils (for example, pep up an inhibited fencer or cool down an overly-nervous fencer).

Warming up competitors is, of course, only the beginning of a fencing master's duties during a competition. He must direct his pupils or team during the various stages of the tournament, discreetly take care of them, be ready with advice and help, calm them down or bolster up their spirits as the need arises. He must very carefully watch the course of the competition, observe his pupil's—and the opponent's—bouts, and try to make highly detailed observations of the style of fencing, technique, and tactics of the leading fencers. The conclusions which he reaches from these observations should be shared later with his pupils to form a foundation for further work on their fitness, technique, tactics, and psychological preparation.

A good coach very carefully watches his pupils in action—trying to assess to what degree they can use strokes and actions which they learned during training, in real fighting conditions. He must assess their good points and weaknesses.

With an eye to future training—and knowing that a fencer's progress depends mainly on developing his strong points combined with the elimination of the most important faults—the fencing master must notice the most significant mistakes made by his pupils at a competition (see Chapter 10).

Mistakes committed by fencers in the course of a bout fall into several categories, the most important being:

1. Faulty perception (defective, inadequate perception of the tactical setting of the bout; slow reaction—for example: late recognition of an attack, resulting in a late parry),

2. Faulty execution (too slow, too fast, or wrong execution of a stroke, although the choice of action is correct—for example: riposte with hesitation; betraying one's intentions; inaccurate movements of an attack),

3. Faulty thinking (application of a wrong action, wrong choice of stroke, wrong decision—for example: stop-hit against a fast simple attack; choice of wrong parry).

To recapitulate and simplify: a fencer's mistakes and errors may be due to: a) wrong perception and reaction, b) bad technique, and c) incorrect tactics (of course, there may be two or three kinds of mistakes at the same time). Taking this into account, the fencing master must pay special attention to the errors and mistakes made by his pupils in competitions, and then, after analysing them with his pupils, try to rectify them by carefully chosen exercises.

While trying to help his pupils as much as possible, the fencing master must not, under any circumstances, go too far in this respect. Such practices as: fussiness over tiny details, carrying fencing bags for the pupils, bombarding pupils with an avalanche of advice and instructions, distracting pupils by constant questioning, interference with officials and referees, etc., are not only tactless and irritating, but also kill pupils' initiative and do not encourage them to think for themselves.

Also, contrary to what some coaches seem to think, shouting, "You must win!" "Come on!" "Keep it up!" etc., just when the fencer on the strip has to concentrate to the maximum, do not help at all but, on the contrary, irritates him and dissipates his attention.

A fencing master, as is natural enough, vividly identifies with his pupils when they fence—especially in tense matches. Just the same, however exciting and dramatic the events on the strip, he must preserve calmness and self control. A nervous coach, especially one who loses his temper, complaining about bad presiding or shouting loudly about scandalous mistakes by the judges, does not help his team at all, but, on the contrary—by intensifying the atmosphere of nervousness (in some teams, bordering on hysteria)—makes it more difficult to keep the situation under control and considerably lowers the chance of eventual victory.

Another serious mistake made frequently by inexperienced fencing masters acting as team coaches, is to offer remarks, usually critical ones, just after a competitor has lost a bout. This is very wrong indeed, as a fencer who has just lost a bout is irritated enough with himself, very often angry at the director, and his self-esteem has suffered. In such a situation, the critical remarks of the coach bring him no advantage, but irritate him even more. It is much better to wait a few minutes until he has calmed down a little bit and then, in a calm and friendly manner, offer some constructive advice stressing the point that the next bout is now more important. Equally irritating and unbearable is the type of coach who, trying to attract the attention of officials and fencers, does not stop giving loud and ostentatious advice, running to the piste with towels, spare blades, etc., and generally trying to impress everyone and make himself the center of attention.

The importance of the fencing master's advice, encouragement, and friendly support for his pupil cannot be over-estimated. One of the aims of his attitude is to install optimism and self-confidence. Now comes the point when the pupil is about to fence a very powerful opponent, obviously much more experienced and skillful than himself. What is the fencing master to say when the pupil asks, "Do you think I am going to win?" Some people maintain that the answer should always be positive. I am of a different opinion. To assure an obviously weaker fencer that he is going to win would not be quite honest, would be detrimental to the pupil's morale in case of defeat (which is quite likely to happen), and an obvious admission to not understanding fencing profoundly. To my mind, the answer should be, more or less, like this: "Look, you have been fencing for only three years and your opponent is much more experienced and has already won many tournaments. To beat him will obviously be very difficult. You must try to put up a good fight and try to learn from it and enjoy it as much as possible. Remember also that, by fencing with determination, self-control, and courage, choosing the right strokes and fast, simple actions, you may even beat him. Such things do happen sometimes but don't worry if he beats you." I think that such advice is honest, takes off unnecessary strain and helps the pupil to fence in a relaxed manner.

As regards advice and tactical instruction during a competition, the fencing master is usually—but only in a sense—in a better position than the competitor on the strip. The coach sees the bout from the side; he is calmer (or should be!); he is able to assess certain tactical situations better, more precisely, and more comprehensively; he also has the advantage of greater experience and knowledge of fencing. This last remark, of course, only concerns fencing masters who constantly watch competitions. Obviously, a fencing master who teaches only fencing technique, in the formal and narrow sense of the word, knows much less about tactics than his own pupils who take part in many fencing tournaments.

However, the value of the fencing master's tactical instruction and advice given between bouts, is reduced by the mere fact that his remarks are based on observations made as an onlooker, without actually facing the opponent, weapon in hand. This is why the fencing master is in a better position than the fencer on the strip in one sense only, as an onlooker's observations have their good and bad points.

Taking into consideration a certain one-sidedness of the fencing master's observations, his tactical instruction and advice during a competition ought to be of a general nature. Bearing in mind the coach's general advice, the competitor must fence and—feeling the rhythm of the opponent's movements, coming face to face with his actions, and feeling the blade with his own weapon—choose his own tactics and selects his own concrete actions.

To give an example: before a bout, the coach draws his pupil's attention to the fact that the opponent he is about to fence, when surprised by an attack, usually takes a very efficient parry but hesitates with the riposte or executes a compound riposte. Against such a hesitant or compound riposte, one may remise or redouble. This is the coach's general advice. Now the pupil, having this in mind, makes additional reconnaissance on the strip, chooses the kind of false attack necessary to provoke the opponent's parry and compound riposte. He selects, himself, the moment to execute his false attack and variety of renewed offensive action to nullify the opponent's compound riposte.

The competitor must always remember that the fencing master's advice should not be taken blindly, but should be verified on the strip in confrontation with the tactical circumstances and the opponent's actions.

It is of the utmost importance that the coach, when giving tactical instruction and advice during a competition, should take into consideration the amount of experience, technique, and possibilities of a given fencer.

It cannot be too strongly emphasized that the fencing master's advice on tactics and the choice of stroke should never be such as to cause the given pupil difficulty in trying to put it into practice. If this should happen, such advice does more harm than good, because:

1. The pupil trying, on the fencing master's advice, to use a stroke which he has not sufficiently mastered, will execute it badly and, perhaps, out of time; and will more than likely get hit.

2. An action, recommended by the fencing master, but too difficult for that particular pupil to execute, will lower the fencer's self-confidence and lead to tension, apprehension, and hesitation in his actions.

3. Such a situation is sure to lower the pupil's concentration—a new worry is added; he cannot, and is afraid to, comply with the coach's instructions, and the thought of it may become obsessive.

The most difficult and critical situations for a fencer in a competition are when he experiences moments of impending danger. I mean such situations as: the score is 4-4; barrage; the winning of a medal or qualification for the final depends on a given bout; the result of the bout determines the result of a team match; etc. In such a situation, it is especially important that:

1. The coach's conduct must not make the competitor nervous and should not irritate the director (this might be compared to the basic medical principle, *primum non nocere:* first, do no harm).

2. The coach's conduct and attitude should have a favorable influence upon the self-control and emotional state of the competitor.

3. In critical situations, it is much more important to influence the pupil in the right directions—calming him down, encouraging him, etc.—than to offer concrete technical and tactical advice.

During the 1996 European Championships in Limoges, my pupil, Magda Jeziorowska—after having won many difficult bouts with many strong and experienced opponents—met five-time World Champion Gianna Hablützel-Buerki of Switzerland in the last bout for the gold medal and European title in women's epee. Magda was very nervous and, after the first period, Buerki led 6 – 1!

During the interlude before the second period, I came to Madga. She was very anxious and worried, and kept asking nervously, "What should I do, Professor? What should I do?"

I was also very excited, but managed to appear cool and composed, and told her very calmly, "Magda, I am not going to give you any advice about what action to use—you'll see it clearly yourself when you calm down. Please, calm down. Suppress your arousal and anxiety. You have nothing to lose. The worse that can happen is that you'll get a silver medal, which is a success. If you manage to suppress your anxiety, you might win."

The next period finished 7-7. In the final period, Magda won with comparative ease, gaining the gold medal.

This is such an important aspect of a coach's behavior during competition that I will give another example from real life. Here is a short excerpt from the memoirs of Wojciech Zablocki, the eminent sabreur, four-time team sabre gold medal winner in World Championships, winner of many medals in World Championships and Olympic Games:

> Preparation for the Olympics in Rome lasted a very, very long time and we were all very nervous just before and during the

> competition. In individual sabre, in the semi-final, I began to fence very badly—reacting very late—and lost my bouts, one after another. Before the end of the semi-final, I was sure that it was the end of my career. I had given up completely when Czajkowski came to me and said very calmly, "If you don't win the last two bouts it might not be very good"—it was already very bad. "Drink black coffee and run and jump in the corridor, even if you don't feel like it." I did what he said—although I was not quite convinced—only to calm my conscience.
>
> But I won the next two bouts and, to make the final, I met the well-known Italian fencer, Ferrari in barrage. I won 5-4 and, for the second time in my life, reached the Olympic final.[1]

As I have mentioned, a cascade of advice and encouragement, and taking too much care of an athlete during competition are decidedly not to be recommended.

Some very well-known and great fencing coaches, like Bela Bay of Hungary or Vitali Arkadyev of the Soviet Union, left their pupils on their own (without any advice, encouragement, etc.) during competitions.

When one of Arkadyev's favorite pupils, Tatyana Lubetskaya, lost an important bout with a less-known fencer and came to her master complaining that he did not help her at all, he answered calmly, "I give you all I can before and after competition. It's up to you to show your best in a bout."

She interrupted him. "But I lost!"

Arkadyev's counter-riposte was, "So what? You'll lose another time and another time, and then, perhaps, you'll learn."

Sometimes, however, concrete technical and tactical advice may be necessary and useful.

- One more thing ought to be stressed: when giving advice, trying to encourage a competitor and help him reach the optimal levels of motivation and arousal, one should address extreme extroverts and extreme introverts differently. Words directed to an extreme introvert ought to be very mild, gentle, calm, and persuasive; when one addresses an extreme extrovert, one should be rather sharp, brisk, and commanding.

Simply put, the main tasks of the fencing master at a competition are as follows:

1. Conducting or supervising warming up.
2. Taking care of—and positively influencing—the attitude and behavior of the competitors.
3. Organization and management of the team, including transport, food, rest, etc.
4. Discreetly and tactfully giving advice and help.
5. Careful and meticulous observation of the competition.
6. Preparing a report of important competitions, and —together with his pupils—makinga detailed analysis: the results, style of fencing, and tactics of his own pupils and the main opponents; new tactical elements; psychological endurance; recommendations for further training; etc.

(After the 1953 World Championships in Brussels, when—after many years of much less success—the young Polish sabre team won the bronze medal in a very flamboyant manner, the president of the Polish Fencing Union, Otto Finski, organised a special conference for coaches and competitors, discussing: preparation and participation in the World Championships; the style, technique, and tactics of the Hungarians, Italians, and other teams; our positive and negative points; conclusions; tasks for future training; etc.

Over the next few years, the young sabre team won the gold medal in World Championships four times and the silver medal at the Olympic Games twice.)

Taking advantage in practice of observations made at competitions.

A discussion on the approach and activities of a fencing master during competition would be incomplete if I did not mention two important points—one is the question of personal responsibility for the team, and the other is the fencing master's own experience as a competitor.

The direction of the team during a competition must be in the hands of one person, only. It should be self-evident that only a fencing master with great experience—who understands and feels the atmosphere of a competition, who was a competitor himself—may be a good and efficient team captain and be able to direct his competitors, giving them good, rational, and practical advice. The immediate vicinity of the strip is hardly the place for round-table, committee meeting discussions. The fencing coach/team captain must very tactfully, but firmly, ensure conditions which allow the team to sit together and concentrate before and between bouts. This very often means the need to edge out well-meaning people who disturb by their comments and advice—and this may turn out to be the least of the coach's troubles during the competition. It is incomprehensible and astonishing how many people fail to understand that a fencing master acting as a team captain has generally enough knowledge of fencing and the necessary competition experience to be able to give his fencers the needed advice and instruction. The cascade of, often contradictory, comments and advice from others is often confusing and certainly does not help a fencer on the strip.

Competitive experience on the part of the fencing master, though always extremely useful, is of special importance during competitions, particularly when there is a question of giving practical advice. For this reason, it is advisable for the coach to take part in as many competitions as possible and, if for some reason competitive experience is impossible, at least take part in loose play.

A fencing master who participates in tournaments can usually give much more to his pupils than a coach without competitive experience. The efficiency of a fencing master is not assessed by his own results in competition, but by those of his pupils. It is generally accepted that a good coach need not necessarily be a very good competitor, and vice versa: a top competitor may not always become a very good fencing master. The rare gift of harmoniously united competitive achievements and educational, coaching qualities is, of course, most precious and desirable. A study of the history of fencing shows that, among the best fencing masters—among masters who introduced many new elements into the development of fencing and who formed great champions and great masters of the younger generation—many were, themselves, good competitors and powerful opponents in a bout.

As Roger Crosnier writes in his *Fencing with the Foil*:

> "Young masters must remember that experience in competitive fencing is a very valuable asset, as it is not only their duty to teach technique, but also to initiate their pupils into match fighting and explain the difficulties which they may encounter. This is only possible if they themselves have experienced the nervous tension and atmosphere of competitions. Having added such knowledge to their teaching technique, they will be able to give the maximum of help to their pupils."[2]

References

1. Zabłocki W. *Z szablą przez olympiady. Poczet polskich olimpijczyków.* Warsaw, 1984. KAW.
2. Crosnier R. *Fencing with the Foil.* London, 1951. Faber and Faber.

Professor Zbigniew Czajkowski
A Maker of Champions in Three Weapons

19958365R00201

Made in the USA
Lexington, KY
17 January 2013